Julian of Norwich: "In God's Sight"

Julian of Norwich: "In God's Sight"

Her Theology in Context

Philip Sheldrake

WILEY Blackwell

This edition first published 2019
© 2019 John Wiley & Sons Ltd

The right of Philip Sheldrake to be identified as the author of this work has been asserted in accordance with law.

Registered Offices
John Wiley & Sons, Inc., 111 River Street, Hoboken, NJ 07030, USA
John Wiley & Sons Ltd, The Atrium, Southern Gate, Chichester, West Sussex, PO19 8SQ, UK

Editorial Office
The Atrium, Southern Gate, Chichester, West Sussex, PO19 8SQ, UK

For details of our global editorial offices, customer services, and more information about Wiley products visit us at www.wiley.com.

Wiley also publishes its books in a variety of electronic formats and by print-on-demand. Some content that appears in standard print versions of this book may not be available in other formats.

Library of Congress Cataloging-in-Publication Data
Names: Sheldrake, Philip, author.
Title: Julian of Norwich : in God's sight : her theology in context / Philip Sheldrake.
Description: First edition. | Hoboken, NJ : John Wiley & Sons, 2018. | Includes
    bibliographical references and index. |
Identifiers: LCCN 2018024557 (print) | LCCN 2018031021 (ebook) | ISBN 9781119099673
    (Adobe PDF) | ISBN 9781119099666 (ePub) | ISBN 9781119099642 (hardcover) | ISBN
    9781119099659 (pbk.)
Subjects: LCSH: Julian, of Norwich, 1343- | Devotional literature, English (Middle)–
    History and criticism. | Mysticism–England–History–Middle Ages, 600-1500.
Classification: LCC BV4832.3.J863 (ebook) | LCC BV4832.3.J863 S54 2018 (print) | DDC
    230/.2092–dc23
LC record available at https://lccn.loc.gov/2018024557

Cover image: © The Walters Art Museum
Cover design by Wiley

Set in 10/12pt Warnock by SPi Global, Pondicherry, India
Printed in Singapore by C.O.S. Printers Pte Ltd

10 9 8 7 6 5 4 3 2 1

To Susie

Contents

Preface

Julian of Norwich, the late medieval English woman mystical writer, is one of the most popular and influential spiritual teachers of our times in the English-speaking world. She has the capacity to inspire a wide range of people, whether they identify themselves as religious or not. Her message that the meaning of everything is "love" and also that, beyond our ability to understand, ultimately "all shall be well" speaks powerfully and paradoxically to our fragile human condition and to our often divided, dysfunctional, and violent world. Nevertheless, in this contextual-theological study of Julian, I hope to demonstrate that this message of love is not comforting in a simplistic way but is profoundly challenging both theologically and spiritually.

Julian's writings and teachings have had a significant influence on my own historical and theological studies of Christian spirituality over the last 30 years. I was first introduced to Julian in the early 1980s when I worked with the late James Walsh SJ as his assistant editor of *The Way* journal of Christian spirituality and its associated specialist supplements. In the 1970s James Walsh had been co-editor with Edmund Colledge of a major scholarly edition of Julian's texts as well as a modern translation in the on-going Paulist Press series "Classics of Western Spirituality." I am very grateful to James Walsh for his original inspiration and enthusiasm. In more recent years I was also in conversation with the late Grace Jantzen and with Joan Nuth, both of whom wrote insightful studies of Julian's theology.

Since the late 1980s I have used Julian of Norwich's texts in graduate courses at Heythrop College, University of London, at Sarum College (linked to the University of Wales), and in a range of MA and doctoral programs in the USA, most recently at Oblate School of Theology in San Antonio, Texas. Further insights have come from the lively exchanges with students that took place in seminars associated with these programs.

In recent years I have also led visits to Norwich focused on Julian for ordinands and staff at Westcott House in Cambridge, UK. In this context

I am particularly grateful to Robert Fruehwirth, the former Director of the Julian Centre, to Christopher Wood, Rector of St Julian's Church to which Julian's anchorhold was originally attached, and to Peter Doll, the Canon Librarian at Norwich Cathedral. Peter Doll and Christopher Wood have also been helpful about contemporary perceptions in the city of Norwich and the nearby University of East Anglia about Julian's life and context.

Finally, at various times while preparing this book I have been privileged to consult a number of scholars with an interest in Julian of Norwich. In particular, I would like to thank Bernard McGinn at the University of Chicago, Benedicta Ward at the University of Oxford, Rowan Williams at the University of Cambridge, Nicholas Watson at Harvard University, and Steven Chase at Oblate School of Theology and editor of *Spiritus: A Journal of Christian Spirituality*. All of these have been generous with their comments and advice. However, I take sole responsibility for final decisions while writing this book and for my overall interpretations of Julian.

It is important to underline that this book focuses specifically on the rich and complex theology of Julian of Norwich. Consequently, it makes extensive use of what is commonly known as her Long Text. This is the most theologically substantial of her writings. As we shall see, there are three surviving full manuscripts of this text and there have been extensive debates, often focused on linguistic questions, about which of them should be given priority. As a historian and theologian rather than a scholar of medieval English I am aware of these debates and make note of them in the Appendix to this book. However, I have tried not to become too focused on them in my analysis of Julian's theology. I have therefore made prudential decisions in the light of mainly theological and contextual considerations about which scholarly edition and which modern translation to use for quotations.

Unless stated otherwise, all the quotations I cite in this book are from the Long Text. For Middle English quotations I have mainly chosen to use the hybrid scholarly edition by Nicholas Watson and Jacqueline Jenkins. For a modern translation I have used the still popular edition co-edited by James Walsh and Edmund Colledge in the on-going "Classics of Western Spirituality" series.

I am very grateful to Westcott House in the Cambridge Theological Federation for providing a friendly context within which I have been able to research and write this book. I am also grateful to Oblate School of Theology in San Antonio for the opportunity to work with MA and doctoral students with an interest in Julian. The book is also part of the research portfolio associated with my role as a Senior Research Associate of the Von Hügel Institute at St Edmund's College, University of Cambridge.

Finally, as always, I dedicate this book to Susie whose own thoughtful interest in spirituality as well as her partnership, love, and conversation have been such a great support throughout this project. In addition, Susie has played a significant role in the design of the cover. The use of the color azure blue echoes Julian's parable of a Lord and a Servant and, in medieval times, symbolized the qualities of nobility, faithfulness and what is truly spiritual. The image of a young woman swinging on the letter Q is taken from the Claricia Psalter (Walters Ms. W.26) in the Walters Art Museum, Baltimore MD. Q is the first letter of the Latin word "Quid". In its interrogative form this suggests "Which?" or "What?" which reflects Julian's persistent curiosity and questioning in her writings.

Cambridge & San Antonio 2018   *Philip Sheldrake*

Introduction

> And all shall be well and
> All manner of thing shall be well
> By the purification of the motive
> In the ground of our beseeching...
>
> ...And all shall be well and
> All manner of thing shall be well
> When the tongues of flame are in-folded
> Into the crowned knot of fire
> And the fire and the rose are one
>   (*From T.S. Eliot's poem*
>   *"Little Gidding"* in The Four Quartets)

Many people first come to hear of Julian of Norwich via the paraphrase of her words as they appear in T.S. Eliot's poem, "Little Gidding," quoted above. The lines, with their imagery of fire, also echo the incendiary bombing in 1942 of St Julian's Church, Norwich (to which Julian's anchorhold had been attached). This was the year before Eliot's poem was published. In the midst of the Second World War, just as much as during the plague-ridden and turbulent late fourteenth and early fifteenth centuries, the notion that God's message to humanity through Julian was that "all shall be well" resonated powerfully.

Julian of Norwich, the late fourteenth-century and early fifteenth-century English woman anchoress, with her mystical writings has become one of the most popular and influential spiritual figures of our times. Why is this so? Interestingly, Julian's writings seem to have a capacity to address quite different audiences. Apart from scholars who are interested either in her literary importance as the first-known woman writing in the English vernacular or in her substantial and challenging theological thought, Julian and her teachings also engage a wide range of people who are seeking significant guidance for their own spiritual journey.[1] Perhaps

Julian of Norwich: "In God's Sight" – Her Theology in Context, First Edition. Philip Sheldrake.
© 2019 John Wiley & Sons Ltd. Published 2019 by John Wiley & Sons Ltd.

more surprising, others see in Julian an iconic figure in relation to contemporary counter-cultural standpoints such as feminism and lesbian theory.

As we shall see, the problem is that we actually know remarkably little for certain about Julian's identity and life. Attempts to reconstruct Julian's personal profile are really only a matter of guesswork. As a result, there is the gentrified Lady Julian but there is also the illiterate Julian (the "simple creature, unletterde" in her own words) who must have dictated her texts rather than written them herself. There is the educated daughter of the gentry or of the wealthy Norwich mercantile class but there is also the incomer from the North of England as is perhaps evidenced by Northern dialect words used in surviving manuscripts. There is the widow with the experience of childbirth and of raising children but there is also the former nun. There is the well-read scholar of theology but there also the more modest thinker whose knowledge of the tradition was selective and probably based solely on conversations with someone who was more theologically educated. There is the feminist icon who, for example, writes about God our mother and, more recently, there is also the suggestion of a lesbian Julian who "lived with" someone called Lucy.[2] This wide spectrum of possible life narratives underlines how important it is to take care to distinguish between what Julian was, or may have been, in herself and what twenty-first century readers seek to draw from her and her writings which in some way addresses their preoccupations and sensibilities.[3]

Contemporary commentators highlight specific aspects of Julian's writings that appear to commend her to present-day readers. For example, she is a medieval woman who succeeds in producing significant theology at a time when this was officially and largely a male preserve. Then her teachings focus on a God whose meaning is love and only love. Julian also uses feminine, specifically motherly, imagery for God and employs this in constructive ways. In the midst of a violent, confusing, and often painful period of history, Julian offers a consistent vision of optimism and hope. Finally, her spiritual teachings are explicitly democratic and are aimed at a broad audience of readers ("mine evenchristen," or "my fellow Christians") rather than merely at some spiritual elite. This emphasis on Julian as wisdom figure and spiritual teacher is reflected in a wide range of spiritual and devotional literature.[4] Julian of Norwich has also inspired what are known as "The Julian Meetings" or Julian Groups who foster the practice of contemplative prayer as well as an American Episcopalian religious order of men and women, the Order of St Julian.[5] Having said this, in the midst of all Julian's contemporary popularity it is important not to over-simplify Julian or to reduce her teachings to what is immediately attractive in spiritual terms precisely because her thinking is theologically complex and also profoundly challenging.

In this book I will seek to offer a contextually related study of the theology that Julian expresses in her writings. I say "writings" in the plural because Julian wrote two distinct but closely related versions of the *Revelations of Divine Love* (sometimes known as *Showings* or, in her own words, *A Revelation of Love*). As we shall see in Chapter 1, there is the earlier more personal Short Text that directly expresses her visionary experiences and a later, much longer and theologically more complex Long Text. This later extensive work, the fruit of at least 20 years' further intense reflection, is a rich and original work of theological-spiritual teaching. For this reason the study that follows gives most attention to the Long Text while noting aspects of the Short Text where these are particularly interesting or relevant.

In brief, what was Julian? For many contemporary readers, Julian is essentially a visionary mystic whose writings continue to be both beautiful and inspirational. There is a great deal of contemporary fascination with mystics and the notions of mystical experience or mystical consciousness. I will return to the question of mysticism briefly in a moment. However, it is important to be clear at the outset that while Julian's texts were provoked by her initial visionary experience, the Long Text in particular is not essentially a devotional work but is a work of "theology in context" in a variety of senses.

In Chapter 1 I will discuss what little we can reasonably surmise about Julian's likely identity and will also seek to place her and her writings in historical, cultural and spiritual contexts. The aim will also be to draw out the likely connections between these contexts and her teachings. However, at the outset it must be constantly underlined that we know relatively little about Julian herself or about the progress of her life from her writings, from surviving wills or from the account of a visit to her by another of the so-called fourteenth-century English mystics, Margery Kempe.

As already noted, Julian's writings, particularly the Long Text, have achieved immense popularity and spiritual influence since the early twentieth century. Alongside Julian's popular public, scholars universally acknowledge that Julian's texts are neither solely a record of her mystical visionary experiences nor essentially devotional. Rather, particularly in her Long Text, she offers theologically substantial, innovative, and important teaching. If we describe Julian's writing as theological, a central question concerns the precise genre of theology that we are dealing with. Judgments about this vary. However, it is now widely agreed that the attempts made by the scholars Edmund Colledge and James Walsh, in their important 1978 two-volume critical edition, to make Julian a detailed expert in relation to the Bible and with an extensive background in the longer theological tradition were misplaced. As someone who was first introduced to Julian of Norwich's writings by the late James Walsh in the early 1980s, I feel sure that this judgment reflects the particular sensitivities of the editors' own religious and intellectual context. It seems likely that they felt it was important at the time to defend the surprising notion that a medieval woman could be considered to be a theologian at all, let alone one comparable to medieval male thinkers.

As I will describe in detail in Chapter 2, I believe that it is useful to think of Julian's theology in three important ways. First, it is what scholars now refer to as "vernacular theology" that is symptomatic of an emerging "age of the vernacular." This notion has a number of dimensions which will be explained further but a significant aspect is that her theology addresses a broadly based audience of "mine evenchristen" (that is, "my fellow Christians") rather than merely a readership of monastics, clergy, or scholars. Julian's writing is also mystical theology in the classical sense. Finally, in describing Julian's theological style we need to give prominence to Julian's own stated purpose in relation to her transformative theological message. In summary, this purpose is to address the urgent needs of her audience at a time of great political and economic uncertainty, war, plague, social disturbance, and major divisions in the Christian community. In this "age of anxiety," Julian's theological method should also be considered as a form of practical-pastoral theology, responding to her cultural, social, and religious contexts.

In terms of previous theological studies of Julian, the majority are at least 15 years old. Brant Pelphrey's *Love was His Meaning: The Theology and Mysticism of Julian of Norwich* (1982) is no longer available. Grace Jantzen, the author of a particularly well-known and respected historical-theological study, *Julian of Norwich* (first published 1987), died prematurely in 2006. The 2000 edition of her book with its revised Introduction is still in print. However, while still an important contribution to our understanding of Julian, Jantzen's book inevitably does not take into account some more recent developments in Julian scholarship. Another respected theological study of Julian by Joan Nuth, *Wisdom's Daughter: The Theology of Julian of Norwich* (1991), is now out of print. I am reliably informed that it is unlikely to be revised or reprinted. The volume by Frederick Christian Bauerschmidt, *Julian of Norwich and the Mystical Body Politic of Christ* (1999), offers an interesting but rather particular interpretative stance in relation to political theology. Another book with a specific hermeneutic is Kerrie Hide's *Gifted Origins to Graced Fulfilment: The Soteriology of Julian of Norwich* (2001). As the title suggests, this is essentially a study of Julian's theology of salvation combining a close reading of Julian's text, spiritual sensitivity, and dialogue with contemporary issues. Two other admirable scholarly volumes, Denise Nowakowski Baker's *Julian of Norwich's Showings: From Vision to*

Book (1994) and Christopher Abbot's *Julian of Norwich: Autobiography to Theology* (1999), are fundamentally historical and textual studies more than comprehensive theological essays. The recent extensive book on Julian of Norwich by Veronica Mary Rolf, *Julian's Gospel: Illuminating the Life and Revelation of Julian of Norwich* (2013), is a passionate and compelling personal dialogue with Julian and her text. However, it is not an academic theological study. It is particularly useful in its broad account of Julian's historical, social, and religious contexts. However, it is open to criticism that its reconstruction of Julian's own identity and life is far too detailed, is based on creative imagination and prior assumptions, and goes well beyond the available evidence.[6]

The most recent book-length, and explicitly theological, study in relation to Julian is *Julian of Norwich, Theologian* (2011) by Denys Turner of Yale University. However, several features stand out. First, there is no in-depth survey of Julian's historical, social, or religious contexts. Second, the book does not offer an extensive textual analysis. Third, rather than being a comprehensive study of all the elements of Julian's theology, Turner focuses on his own philosophical-theological questions and reflections that were provoked by studying Julian's writings. In particular, Turner addresses the theodicy question and the theme of sin and salvation. While this study is interesting and rich, Turner's approach underlines an important distinction that needs to be made between theological reflections *provoked* by Julian and a scholarly contextual study of Julian's own theology in all its breadth.[7]

The present book seeks to take the second approach. It is intended to be a contextually grounded and text-related study of the key elements of Julian's own theology rather than a series of my own theological-spiritual reflections. Consequently, it seeks to highlight how and why Julian's understanding and teaching, even what she believes is provoked by her visionary insights, in some way reflects the world she inhabits and the needs of her contemporary fellow Christians and fellow citizens. The book will also seek to base itself as far as possible on a faithful reading of Julian's texts, especially the Long Text, as well as on her own declared theological-spiritual purpose in relation to her intended audience.

However, any process of textual interpretation is unavoidably complex. A historical text such as Julian's is necessarily in dialogue with the very different horizons of the contemporary reader. With a theological or spiritual text like Julian's, from a context other than our own, we are inevitably conscious of different perspectives. An important question concerns our motive for reading such a text and what we seek to gain from it. It is one thing to seek an accurate technical understanding of the text, held at a distance. However, if we also seek to engage with the theology or spiritual wisdom at a deeper level we cannot avoid the question of how far to respect a text's own values and assumptions in relation to our contemporary context. This is not a straight-forward matter. Recent developments in interpretation theory (hermeneutics) promote an approach where the wisdom embodied in a text moves beyond the author's original framework of meaning to be creatively re-read in the light of the new context in which a text finds itself. Thus, without ignoring the original context of Julian's text, or her motives in writing it, we may unlock ever-richer meanings that the author never considered. The pursuit of meaning undoubtedly demands that we understand the technicalities of a text. However, conversely, a real conversation with a classic text expands our vision rather than merely extends our pool of data. We may interrogate the text but our questions and assumptions are, in turn, reshaped by the text itself. This process is what is sometimes referred to as the "hermeneutical circle."[8]

Julian as a Mystic

Julian of Norwich is conventionally described as a mystic. In many people's minds this is associated with the fact that, according to her own testimony, she experienced a series of visions while seriously ill and apparently dying, aged 30 and a half, in May 1373. Through these visionary experiences of Christ's passion and suffering, Julian believed that she had received sixteen "showings" or revelations from God which underpinned her later theological reflection, writings, and teaching.

The nature of mysticism, and the purpose of "mystical experiences" when they occur, is much debated. In popular writing, the word "mysticism" is often used to refer to esoteric insights or wisdom derived from some kind of direct and intense personal experience of God or the Absolute, however this is understood. However, the coherence and legitimacy of the terms "mysticism" and "mystic" have been frequently questioned in Christian and wider academic circles. This is precisely because they appear to bypass more rational approaches to religious language and religious knowledge in favor of a more experiential, interior, and non-rational approach to spiritual wisdom. The terms also seem to promote subjectivity over established religious authority.[9] One of the most original and influential twentieth-century thinkers and writers about mysticism was the French interdisciplinary scholar and Jesuit priest, Michel de Certeau (1925–1986). He can be more or less credited with establishing that, as a distinct category related to religious experience, the concept of "mysticism" (*la mystique* in de Certeau's words) originated in early seventeenth-century France. Of course, as a historian, de Certeau was well aware that the remote origins of the concept lay much earlier in the thirteenth and fourteenth centuries, especially with the Rhineland mystics and the Flemish Beguines. However, the key point in its formalization as a framework of interiority distinct from doctrine or wider Church life was much later. Indeed, as de Certeau underlines, "mysticism" or "the mystical tradition" is an artificial construct that retrospectively recruits earlier spiritual writings into a framework of what he refers to as "experiential knowledge."[10]

Is there a distinction to be made between "a visionary" and "a mystic"? In his theological reflections on Julian's thought, Denys Turner questions both the legitimacy of applying William James' experientialist notions of "a mystic" to Julian and other representations of her as "a visionary" in contrast to being a mystic.[11] However, the Julian scholar Grace Jantzen, in a further book on gender and Christian mysticism, noted the importance of the "rootedness in experience" of medieval women who produced what are known as mystical writings. Such experience was often visionary. The point is that such visionary experience becomes the basis for the women's authority as spiritual teachers. This made them different from many theological writers and even from many male mystics of Julian's time. Unlike women, the men had often benefited from conventional theological education and had theological status.[12]

Jantzen asks why women of Julian's time should have had more visionary experiences than men and valued these more highly. She judges that this cannot be reduced to stereotypical differences of temperament between women and men. The more likely explanation is differing perceptions of authority. Insofar as women had internalized the notion that conventional systems of religious "authority" were a male clerical preserve, they had to refer to some other form of validation. What better basis for authority was there than a direct vision of God? Jantzen points out that in Julian of Norwich, as in Hildegard of Bingen, "visions" were not merely heightened experiences or the medium for private enlightenment. Their value was that they paved the way for teaching. In Julian's case, her visions offered her another way of seeing reality, which she understood as a gift from God. This other way of seeing might be a comfort to her fellow Christians who were struggling with despair at the horrors of their surrounding world as well with their own sense of failure and guilt. Visions therefore became the medium of a deeper spiritual understanding of who God is and how God works in the world and therefore of the ultimate hope of a positive destiny for all humanity.

Julian's Writings: The Authentic Julian?

From the Long Text, chapter 37, it is clear that Julian intended her writings to be accessible to a general public. She insists on the importance of reaching a wide audience. Her visions, and the teachings that arise from them, are for the good of all her fellow Christians without exception. "I was lerned to take it to all him evenchristen, alle in generale and nothing in specialle." However, Julian's actual readership for some 200 years after her lifetime (which probably ended sometime in the second decade of the fifteenth century) is something of a mystery.

As I will mention in more detail in Chapter 1, Julian's Short Text survives in only one fifteenth-century manuscript belonging originally to the Carthusian monks of Sheen near London which also contains parts of other mystical writings. Nothing is recorded until 1910 when it reappeared in the sale of Lord Amherst's library to the British Museum (now the British Library). It was first made available to a wider readership in the following year via a modernization by Dundas Harford. The more theological Long Text survives in variations of its complete form in three manuscripts, known as Paris, Sloane 1, and Sloane 2, which is essentially a copy of Sloane 1. There is also a selection of excerpts from the Long Text within a late fifteenth-century anthology in the archives of the Roman Catholic Westminster Cathedral in London. It is difficult to establish with total precision what Julian originally wrote in her Long Text. First of all, there is a long interval between her lifetime and the probable dates of all three surviving manuscripts of the complete text. In addition, the three manuscripts differ from each other to some degree and so some judgment about their relative authority is important for our understanding of Julian's theology.

There are three available scholarly editions that contain both of Julian's Middle English texts: the Short Text and the Long Text. The first, dating back to 1978, was edited by the late Edmund Colledge and the late James Walsh and is entitled *A Book of Showings to the Anchoress Julian of Norwich*.[13] Colledge and Walsh also produced one of the most widely used modern English translations of Julian's writings, again containing both Short and Long Texts. This is the 1978 volume, *Julian of Norwich – Showings*, in the extensive and continuing Paulist Press series, "The Classics of Western Spirituality." This was based on their scholarly Middle English edition. However, in reference to this translation of the Long Text, it is important to note an unfortunate misprint. In Chapter 5, in the sentences about Julian being shown something small, no bigger than a hazelnut, the answer to Julian's question "What can this be?" is omitted. It should go on to say "And I was given this general answer: it is everything which is made."[14] Both the Colledge and Walsh scholarly edition and their modern translation are based essentially on the Paris manuscript because they see it as more complete and more sophisticated. However, they adopt a few alternative readings from Sloane when they judge these to be superior.

The second available scholarly edition appeared in 2006, produced by Nicholas Watson and Jacqueline Jenkins, and is entitled *The Writings of Julian of Norwich*. Overall, in recent years this has become the preferred edition among many scholars and students.[15] In their introduction Watson and Jenkins offer a compelling argument, supported by evidence from the single fifteenth-century Short Text manuscript (Amherst) that the Paris manuscript preserves Julian's literary style plus passages that Sloane omits or abbreviates. However, their editorial decision is to provide a synthetic or hybrid edition of the Long Text while using Paris as the base manuscript.[16]

Finally, the third and most recent scholarly edition of Julian's writings, produced by Barry Windeatt, appeared towards the end of 2016.[17] Windeatt seeks to present a text that he believes is as close to Julian's Middle English as possible. He therefore uses Sloane as the base manuscript because he judges that it is linguistically conservative while adding in material from Paris to cover the various omissions in Sloane.[18] In 2015 Windeatt also produced a modern translation of both of Julian's texts, with a significant Introduction, in the "Oxford World Classics" series.[19]

Another well-known modern English translation of Julian is the current Penguin Classics volume, *Julian of Norwich: Revelations of Divine Love*, translated by Elizabeth Spearing.[20] Her translation of the Long Text is based on the 1976 edition of the Middle English text (revised 1993) by Marion Glasscoe and this is derived from the manuscript known as Sloane 1.[21] As Glasscoe mentions in her Notes, the Paris manuscript contains various passages that do not appear in Sloane. Thus, for example, on this basis the modern translation by Colledge and Walsh contains the striking section in Chapter 6 about how God's goodness is shown in even "our humblest needs," illustrated delicately and briefly by reference to the process of defecation! Spearing's Penguin Classics translation, based solely on Sloane, omits this section.

As already noted, the so-called Short Text survives in only one manuscript which is therefore the basis for all three of the scholarly editions as well as the modern translations by Colledge and Walsh, Spearing, and Windeatt.

Interestingly, while comparisons between the Short and Long Texts are regularly made, the differences between the historic manuscripts and the impact of these on what appears or does not appear in the widely read modern translations are rarely mentioned. The various theories about why the surviving Long Text manuscripts differ and about which may be closer to Julian's original text are complicated. The different theories and the arguments in favor of each of them are outlined in the Appendix at the end of this book.

In the context of this book, I have chosen to follow the recent scholarly editions of Watson and Jenkins and also Windeatt although I have also consulted the older two-volume edition of Colledge and Walsh. Quotations in modern English are mainly from the translation by Colledge and Walsh in the series "Classics of Western Spirituality" with some reference to Windeatt's translation when I have some questions about the translation of Colledge and Walsh.

About the Book

The approach I have taken in this book is informed by my mixed academic background in history and historical theory, in theology and Christian spirituality, including the study of Christian mysticism, and in philosophy, including interpretation theory.

Chapter 1 on Julian's context explores in some detail what we know about Julian and her texts. This embraces the main features of her overall fourteenth-century and early fifteenth-century context as well as the nature of Julian's specific social, political, and religious milieux and how these seem to impact on her work and together provide an important interpretative key. We will explore briefly how Julian's gender is a key consideration. I ask why it is notable that this is a vernacular Middle English work rather than one written in Latin. Indeed, the so-called Short Text is the first text of any kind in English that we know for certain to have been written by a woman. Julian was a contemporary of the first major English writers Geoffrey Chaucer and William Langland in what was a developing "age of the vernacular."

Chapter 2 then examines why Julian can be described as a theologian alongside being understood as a visionary mystic. It also offers an overview interpretation of the nature of Julian's theology, its genre, purpose, and audience, including a brief analysis of interpretations offered in previous studies of Julian. The chapter underlines the difference between exploring theological themes provoked by Julian's writings and seeking to present a study of Julian's own theology. The central theological themes addressed by Julian are then outlined. At the heart of Julian of Norwich's teaching is an unequivocal sense of divine love based on what she understood to be God's own self-revelation. This message of love, and this alone, is "oure lords mening." Julian clearly believed that this was both a vital and a challenging message for her fellow Christians. The remainder of Julian's sophisticated theological insights and her urgent pastoral message, as expressed in her later and longer text, are built essentially on this foundation. The final chapter 86 of the Long Text underlines that Julian's book, while begun by God's gift, is "not yet completed." This highlights the reality that Julian's theological journey is necessarily incomplete. Authentic theological reflection, not least Julian's, takes us to the frontiers of the knowable and into the realm of the unknowable ("a marvellous great mystery hidden in God" as Julian notes in her chapter 27).

Chapter 3 examines the central importance in the Long Text of the parable of a Lord and a Servant (chapter 51). I begin the theological study with this parable because in important ways I believe that it is a vital key to understanding the whole dynamic of Julian's theology as well as its central themes. Even though the parable seems to have formed part of the original "revelations," it was not included in the earlier Short Text. This is because, as Julian herself affirms, it took extensive reflection over many years as well as further divine revelation before the meaning of the parable became clear to her. The parable is presented as God's answer to Julian's various anxieties and questions about her experience of daily sinfulness yet her deep sense of God's lack of blame. How are the two realities of human sinfulness and God's lack of blame compatible? In many respects this chapter and its narrative are pivotal to Julian's theological and spiritual quest. In my judgment, the focus is not so much on the classic philosophical theodicy question as on a radical realignment of Julian's understanding of human identity, sin, and the nature of God as our lover rather than as our wrathful judge. In Julian's own words, she affirms that "I saw no wrath in God" (chapter 46). The parable, with Julian's explanation, provides the foundation of the themes explored in the following four chapters: on the nature of God and God's action, on creation and human identity (Julian's theological anthropology), on sin and salvation, and on prayer as a journey of desire.

In addition, Chapter 3 also briefly explores an important insight in Julian's theology regarding "ways of seeing" and the radical difference between how and what we natively "see" from a human standpoint and what God "sees" and then shows in part to Julian. This difference is graphically illustrated in the parable. These "ways of seeing" relate closely to the notion of time and place – God's and our own. In the light of Julian's sense that God's meaning is only love, I suggest that the theme of "seeing" – not only *what* is seen but also how it is seen – is an important thread running throughout Julian's theological reflections in the Long Text. "Seeing" does not imply merely visual experience but also embraces epistemological issues – that is, what we understand and know and how we come to know truly. Thus, Julian's repeated phrase "in my sight" means "as I understand it." This contrasts with "in God's sight." The contrast between two ways of seeing is between Julian's (and, by implication, every human being's) natural and limited way of understanding human existence and God's all-embracing (and, by implication, the only true) way of seeing reality. Julian indicates that she was briefly, and necessarily partially, led to see reality from God's viewpoint. This "seeing with interior eyes" is typical of what is known as mystical theology: borne not of rational analysis but of interior intimacy with God. A number of difficult questions emerge alongside the encouraging and life-giving vision that God reveals to Julian. For example, what is she to make of the fact that "I saw not sin" (chapter 27)? Such issues not only stretch Julian's understanding and sense of meaning but also raise questions about how she is to relate these mystical insights to the teachings of "Holy Church" about guilt, punishment, and human destiny.

Chapter 4 examines Julian's imaging of God and of God's "meaning." This not only explores her famous theme of God as Mother but, more broadly, examines the riches of her Trinitarian theology which derived from her original vision of the Passion of Jesus Christ. Julian's image of God as Mother is arguably one of the best-known themes that contemporary readers highlight in her writings. However, despite some people's misconceptions, I note that Julian is by no means unique among medieval spiritual writers, whether women or men, in using motherhood imagery for Jesus. However, Julian is distinctive both in the way she deploys the image of Jesus as Mother and in her unequivocal sense that this image expresses something essential about the nature of God as such. What is seen in the suffering figure of the crucified Jesus can be said of God-as-Trinity. Equally, there is considerably more to Julian's "revisionist" portrayal of the nature of God, her Christology, and her Trinitarian theology – as well as her understanding of God's relationship to humankind – than simply feminine imagery.

In the light of her theology of God, Chapter 5 examines Julian's theological evaluation of the material order as created, loved, and sustained by God as well as her highly positive (yet partly apophatic) theological anthropology – her understanding and evaluation of human identity. In the light of Julian's changed understanding of the interrelationship between God-as-Trinity, God's Incarnation in the person of Jesus and Jesus' suffering and death on the cross, her evaluation of creation and her theology of human nature undergo a significant change. For Julian, echoing the theological anthropology of Augustine (whether consciously or not), there are two dimensions to human existence (or "the soul"). These are termed "substance" and "sensuality." Importantly, this is not a dualistic distinction between soul and body or between spiritual and material aspects of human existence. "Substance" stands for that dimension of human identity that is forever united to God whereas "sensuality" stands for the contingent, changeable, incomplete (and potentially sinful) dimension of "the self."

This theme leads naturally to Chapter 6 which considers in more detail Julian's soteriology and eschatology, especially her paradoxical approach to sin. The theme of sin and salvation is strongly present in Julian along with the theme of God's mercy. When Julian was briefly brought to see reality through God's eyes she is led to exclaim, "I saw not sin" (chapter 27). Through this, Julian came to realise that "sin has no share of being" – that is, it has no ontological reality. Rather, it is a negation of reality, an "absence". This has led some commentators to speculate that Julian, despite her instinctive doctrinal caution, is really a universalist. Ultimately, everyone will be saved. Perhaps Julian implies that the "great deed" that she is told God will perform on the last day, linked to God's persistent affirmation that "all will be well and all manner of thing will be well," may be the ultimate redemption of everything, even of hell. However, another alternative is that just as "sin has no share of being" neither has hell, the traditional consequence of unrepented sin. In the end, all that "exists" (and will exist eternally) is so only in the embrace of God's love. On this reading, an alternative logic in Julian's eschatology may be "non-being" – that is, nothingness or annihilation. If we accept that Julian's theology was firmly "in context," her context implied limitations. Julian could not easily go against what she had inherited and what she understood as the teaching of "Holy Church." In that sense, it seems unlikely that Julian was a universalist in a straight-forward way even if, at some level, she may have worried that this was somehow implied by what she had been shown. Finally, important dimensions of Julian's soteriology are a rich theology of hope and a sense of God's mercy.

Finally, Chapter 7 discusses Julian's understanding of prayer and of the spiritual journey: a journey of longing and desire that reflects God's own eternal longing. Because prayer-as-relationship is central to Julian's teaching, and because within this she explicitly links the nature of human longing to God's eternal longing, the chapter is an appropriate conclusion to a study of Julian's theology. It has been regularly noted that Julian says nothing directly about methods of prayer or about other spiritual practices. Nor does Julian refer to the classical stages of prayer or of spiritual development such as the *triplex via* or "three ways." That said, it is arguable that, aside from her visionary experiences, Julian may have been influenced by the meditative tradition of visualization or imaginative participation in Christ's Passion, as portrayed in scripture. This would have been accessible to Julian via Aelred of Rievaulx's *Rule of Life for a Recluse*, in Part 1 of Walter Hilton's *Scale of Perfection*, also written for an anchoress, and in the famous Franciscan-influenced *Meditationes vitae Christi* which was available in an English translation towards the end of the fourteenth century. Prior to her visions, Julian desires and prays for three things: recollection of the Passion, bodily sickness (which troubles psychologically attuned modern readers), and the three spiritual "wounds" of contrition, loving compassion, and longing for God. This three-fold desire implies transformation at depth and throws a new light on a spirituality of self-emptying or *kenosis*. Four other elements of Julian's approach to prayer stand out. First, Julian is sensitive to, and realistic about, dryness in prayer (chapter 41). Second, Julian uses spoken words, particularly regular "ejaculations." Thus, she exclaims, "Blessed be God" or "Blessed may you be!" Third, Julian regularly mentions "beseeching" which is related to longing and desire. Our longing arises from God's longing within us. "I am the ground of your beseeching" (Long Text, chapter 41). Finally, there is "beholding" (for example, chapter 43). This is not passive and relates both to loving contemplation of God our Maker and to an abundance of charity for others. God also "beholds" us and sees us without blame.

The Conclusion to the book, on Julian's practical-pastoral purpose, seeks to draw together a coherent picture of Julian's overall theological perspective. In the light of Julian's declared pastoral purpose in writing her book, as well as her democratic and inclusive sense of audience ("mine evenchristen" – fellow Christians – chapter 8), the Conclusion will ask what she sought to offer to all her fellow Christians by way of practical-pastoral lessons about the Christian life. Julian herself persistently sought to grasp what was God's "meaning" and the meaning of her visions. In the end she is led to see that love, and only love, is God's meaning. Thus, it may be surmised that her purpose was to give birth to a renewed understanding of, first, the nature of God and God's action in the world and, second, of human existence and the hope for the positive consummation of all things in God's final "great deed" beyond historical time. As the last chapter 86 of the Long Text clearly states, "it seems to me that it [this book] is not yet completed." Here, Julian indicates an intentional incompleteness to her spiritual-theological narrative. This leads to further references to Julian's eschatology.

> For truly I saw and understode in oure lords mening that he shewde it for he will have it knowen more than it is. In which knowing he wille geve us grace to love him and cleve to him. For he beholde his hevenly tresure with so grete love on erth that he will give us more light and solace in hevenly joye, in drawing of oure hartes fro sorrow and darknesse which we are in.
>
> What, woldest thou wit thy lordes mening in this thing? Wit it wele, love was his mening. Who shewed it the? Love. What shewid he the? Love. Wherfore shewed he it the? For love. Hold the therin, thou shalt wit more in the same. But thou shalt never wit therin other withouten ende.
>
> *(Watson and Jenkins, eds., chapter 86)*

For truly I saw and understood in our Lord's meaning that he revealed it because he wants to have it better known than it is. In which knowledge he wants to give us grace to love him and to cleave to him, for he beholds his heavenly treasure with so great love on earth that he will give us more light and solace in heavenly joy, by drawing our hearts from the sorrow and the darkness which we are in.

What, do you wish to know your Lord's meaning in this thing? Know it well, love was his meaning. Who reveals it to you? Love. What did he reveal to you? Love. Why does he reveal it to you? For love. Remain in this, and you will know more of the same. But you will never know different, without end.

(Translation from Colledge and Walsh, Showings*).*

Notes

1 Interestingly, in the mid-twentieth century Julian was also rediscovered by literary figures such as T.S. Eliot and the English intelligentsia. See, for example, Barbara Newman, "Eliot's Affirmative Way: Julian of Norwich, Charles Williams and Little Gidding," in *Modern Philology* volume 108, number 3, February 2011, pp 427–461.

2 For feminist readings of Julian, see, for example, Grace Jantzen, *Power, Gender and Christian Mysticism*, Cambridge: Cambridge University Press, 1995, especially pp 146–156, 165–168, 176–184, 238–241 and 301–304. Also Joan M. Nuth, *Wisdom's Daughter: The Theology of Julian of Norwich*, New York: Crossroad, 1991, Introduction pp 1–4. The notion of a lesbian Julian is mentioned by Sarah Salih in her essay "Julian's Afterlives," pp 208–218, in Liz Herbert McAvoy, ed., *A Companion to Julian of Norwich*, Cambridge: D.S. Brewer, 2008. Salih refers to a novel by Jack Pantaleo, *Mother Julian and the Gentle Vampire*, in which the anchoress Julian is "oned" with her maid-companion Lucy.

3 On the wide range of recent examples of different "receptions" of Julian's writings, see Sarah Salih & Denise Nowakowski Baker, eds., *Julian of Norwich's Legacy: Medieval Mysticism and Post-Medieval Reception*, New York: Palgrave Macmillan, 2009.

4 Examples include Gloria Durka, *Praying with Julian of Norwich*, Winona, MN: St Mary's Press, 1989; Jean Furness, *Love is His Meaning: Meditations on Julian of Norwich*, Essex: McCrimmons, 1993; Monica Furlong, ed., *The Wisdom of Julian of Norwich*, Grand Rapids, MI: W.B. Eerdmanns, 1996; Robert Llewelyn, *Circles of Silence: Explorations in Prayer with Julian of Norwich*, London: Darton, Longman & Todd, 2002.

5 The founder of the order, Fr John-Julian, has written an extensive book, *The Complete Julian of Norwich*, Brewster, MA: Paraclete Press, 2009.

6 See Brant Pelphrey, *Love was His Meaning: The Theology and Mysticism of Julian of Norwich*, Salzburg: Institute für Anglistik und Amerikanistik, 1982; Grace Jantzen, *Julian of Norwich*, 2nd edition, London: SPCK 2000; Joan M. Nuth, *Wisdom's Daughter: The Theology of Julian of Norwich*, New York: Crossroad, 1991; Frederick Christian Bauerschmidt, *Julian of Norwich and the Mystical Body Politic of Christ*, Notre Dame: University of Notre Dame Press, 1999; Kerrie Hide, *The Soteriology of Julian of Norwich*, Collegeville, MN: The Liturgical Press, 2001; Denise Nowakowski Baker, *Julian of Norwich's Showings: From Vision to Book*, Princeton, NJ: Princeton University Press, 1994; Christopher Abbott, *Julian of Norwich: Autobiography and Theology*, Cambridge: D.S. Brewer, 1999; Veronica Mary Rolf, *Julian's Gospel: Illuminating the Life and Revelations of Julian of Norwich*, Maryknoll, NY: Orbis Books, 2013.

7 Denys Turner, *Julian of Norwich, Theologian*, New Haven, CT: Yale University Press, 2011.

8 For an overview of hermeneutical theory and issues of interpretation in reference to classic spiritual and theological texts, see Philip Sheldrake, *Explorations in Spirituality: History, Theology and Social Practice*, Mahwah, NJ: Paulist Press, 2010, Chapter 2 "Interpreting Texts and Traditions: Understanding and Appropriation." Some critical issues in interpreting mysticism, including feminist and postmodern perspectives, are also discussed in Chapter 6 "Mysticism and Social Practice: The Mystical and Michel de Certeau."

9 Much of this reflects the still influential thinking of the American philosopher and psychologist of religion, William James, expressed particularly in his famous 1902 Gifford lectures. See his *The Varieties of Religious Experience* which is available in various modern editions. For an extensive and useful analysis of different approaches to the nature of mysticism from theological, philosophical, and psychological perspectives see the appendix to the first volume of Bernard McGinn's on-going history of Christian mysticism, *The Foundations of Mysticism: Origins to the Fifth Century*, London: SCM Press, 1992, "Appendix: Theoretical Foundations. The Modern Study of Mysticism."

10 See Michel de Certeau, English translation, *The Mystic Fable*, volume 1, Chicago, IL: University of Chicago Press, 1992; and volume 2, 2015. Also his essay "Mystic Speech," in his book *Heterologies: Discourse on the Other*, Minneapolis, MN: University of Minnesota Press, 1995.

11 See Turner, *Julian of Norwich, Theologian*, pp 27–31.

12 See Grace Jantzen, *Power, Gender and Christian Mysticism*, Cambridge: Cambridge University Press, 1995, especially Chapter 5 "Cry out and write: mysticism and the struggle for authority," pp 157–192.

13 See Edmund Colledge & James Walsh, eds., *A Book of Showings to the Anchoress Julian of Norwich*, Toronto: Pontifical Institute of Mediaeval Studies, 1978.

14 See Edmund Colledge & James Walsh, eds., *Julian of Norwich – Showings*, Mahwah NJ: Paulist Press, 1978.

15 Nicholas Watson & Jacqueline Jenkins, eds., *The Writings of Julian of Norwich*, University Park PA: The Pennsylvania State University Press, 2006.

16 See Watson & Jenkins, eds., *The Writings of Julian of Norwich*, Introduction, Part Three, On Editing Julian's Writings, pp 24–43.

17 Barry Windeatt, ed., *Julian of Norwich: Revelations of Divine Love*, Oxford: Oxford University Press, 2016.

18 See Windeatt, ed., *Julian of Norwich: Revelations of Divine Love*, "Textual Introduction," pp liii–lxviii.

19 See Barry Windeatt, ed., *Julian of Norwich: Revelations of Divine Love*, Oxford World's Classics, Oxford: Oxford University Press, 2015.

20 See Elizabeth Spearing, ed., *Julian of Norwich: Revelations of Divine Love*, London: Penguin Books, 1998.

21 See Marion Glasscoe, ed., *A Revelation of Love*, Exeter: University of Exeter Press, 1993. This edition is aimed primarily at an English literature audience. The "negotiation" between a religious-theological perspective and a literary one is well illustrated by the series of publications of conferences organised by Glasscoe and E.A. Jones. There are seven volumes in the series: *The Medieval Mystical Tradition in England*, Exeter: University of Exeter Press, 1980 & 1982; subsequently, Cambridge: D.S. Brewer, between 1984 and 2004.

Chapter 1

Julian in Context

The contemporary rediscovery of the fourteenth-century anchoress, Julian of Norwich, as an important mystical writer, theological thinker, and spiritual teacher has inevitably led to a great deal of speculation about her origins and life. Whatever the long-term value of Julian's teachings, no mystical or theological writing exists on some ideal plane removed from the historical circumstances in which it arose.[1]

Julian's possible background and her historical context affect our contemporary interpretation of what she wrote. Without some awareness of her context, it is all too easy to make Julian an honorary member of our own times or to pick and choose the aspects of her writings that appeal to us or to make overall judgments about her without seeking to honor what she herself intended to communicate in her writings.

Who was Julian?

Who Julian was, her social background, her education, her life experience prior to becoming an anchoress, when she became an anchoress – even where she was born – are all matters of speculation. The name "Julian" by which she is known is also likely to have been an adopted one. It was quite common for medieval anchorites and anchoresses to assume the name of the church to which their anchorhold (or cell) was physically attached. In the case of Julian of Norwich, her anchorhold was next to the parish church of St Julian Timberhill in Norwich which survives in reconstructed form to this day. The church has been known by that name since the tenth century but it is not absolutely clear to which St Julian it is dedicated. There are several saints of that name. One suggestion is St Julian the Hospitaller because he was the patron saint of ferrymen and the local ferry ran across the River Wensum very close to the church.

However, another suggestion is that the title of St Julian's Church somehow touched Julian of Norwich's own personal and painful

Julian of Norwich: "In God's Sight" – Her Theology in Context, First Edition. Philip Sheldrake.
© 2019 John Wiley & Sons Ltd. Published 2019 by John Wiley & Sons Ltd.

experience. A growing consensus, not least in Julian's own city of Norwich and in the parish of St Julian, is that the underlying echoes in the Long Text may point to a woman who was a widow and had lost a child at a young age. The text has the flavor of someone who suffered the darkness of such a loss. For example, chapter 61 briefly and poignantly notes that an "earthly mother may suffer her child to perish." If so, it is speculated that a likely date was the plague of 1362 because that particular outbreak did not simply lead to the death of twenty per cent of the city's population but, unusually, the majority of deaths were of children. In this environment, devotion to St Julian of Le Mans would have attracted people, perhaps Julian of Norwich among them, because the saint was famous for miracles of curing children and even of raising them from the dead. St Julian's Church was the responsibility of the nuns of Carrow Priory (popularly referred to as Carrow Abbey). Interestingly, the manuscript of the Carrow Abbey Psalter still survives in the Walters Art Museum in Baltimore, MD. In it the usual liturgical calendar is supplemented by a special feast day dedicated to St Julian of Le Mans. Whether the parish church was technically dedicated to this St Julian or not, it would seem that St Julian of Le Mans was well known to the people of Norwich.[2]

Having said this, all attempts at reconstructing Julian of Norwich's life must be treated with caution. The only evidence we have about her identity consists of what is present in her two texts, a mention of bequests made to her in several surviving wills, and the record of a visit to her (probably around 1413) by another of the late medieval English mystics, Margery Kempe. This is described in Margery's dictated autobiographical work, *The Book of Margery Kempe.*

Julian says very little about her own life and circumstances in the texts that she herself wrote, apart from the bare details of her original visionary experiences and references to further interior enlightenment some years later. In the second chapter of what is typically known as her Long Text, or *A Revelation of Love*, Julian writes of a "revelation" made to her in "the year of our Lord one thousand, three hundred and seventy-three [1373] on the thirteenth day of May."[3] As the third chapter makes clear, this occurred when she was "thirty and a half years old" during a "bodily sickness in which I lay for three days and three nights." On that basis we can presume she was born around 1342 or 1343. The only other biographical details offered in Julian's texts occur in a short, probably scribal, preface to her so-called Short Text, or "A Vision Showed to a Devout Woman," in its one surviving manuscript. This records that "her name is Julian, who is a recluse at Norwich and still alive, anno domini 1413." There are oblique hints about two other dates within the Long Text and these will be referred to in my discussion of the relationship between this text and the Short Text.

As we have seen, there have been speculations that Julian was born and grew up in the North of England rather than in Norwich and that she must have arrived there later. As we saw briefly in the Introduction, these speculations arise from some supposed evidence of Northern dialect in Julian's two texts although as we saw this is highly ambiguous. In terms of my own interpretation, while necessarily remaining tentative, I can see no overwhelming reason to move away from the conventional assumption that, whatever the history of her texts, Julian herself was indeed a "woman of Norwich" (or somewhere nearby), from an affluent background. This view is explicitly reinforced by Nicholas Watson and Jacqueline Jenkins in their relatively recent scholarly edition of Julian's writings.[4] Barry Windeatt's most recent edition does not seem to contradict this.

Evidence from Wills

The Jesuit scholar Norman Tanner can be credited with a systematic search for references to Julian in various bequests in surviving late medieval wills.[5] These are also laid out in Appendix B of the scholarly edition of Julian by Watson and Jenkins.[6] Four wills survive that bequeath money to Julian, one in Anglo-Norman and three in Latin. The Anglo-Norman will is by Isabel Ufford, Countess of Suffolk and the daughter of the Earl of Warwick. This was "proved" (that is, established as authentic) in 1416. Twenty shillings were left to "Julian, recluse at Norwich." Of the Latin wills, the earliest bequest – and, indeed, the earliest evidence of Julian's status as an anchoress – dates from 1393 or 1394. This is the will of Roger Reed, the Rector of St Michael's Church, Coslany, in Norwich. Although the will was damaged by fire in recent years, we know from a prior reference in the scholarly edition of Colledge and Walsh (pp 33–34) that it left two shillings to "Julian anchorite." A further will of the chantry priest Thomas Emund, dated 1404, left "twelve pence to Julian, anchoress at the church of St Julian in Norwich" and also "eight pence to Sarah, living with her." It is not clear whether Sarah was also an anchoress or was Julian's maid. This is the only direct reference to Julian by name that links her to an anchorhold at St Julian's Church. Finally, the will of John Plumpton of the city of Norwich in November 1415 states "Item: I bequeath forty pence to the anchoress in the Church of St Julian's, Conesford, in Norwich and twelve pence to her maid. Item: I bequeath her former maid, Alice, twelve pence." Assuming that "the anchoress" is Julian, and even if she did not live beyond 1415, it means that Julian reached the age of at least 74.

It is worth noting the motivation for such bequests. The contemporary concerns with death, God's judgment, and the possibility of eternal punishment explains a great deal about why people left bequests to people like Julian. It was seen as vitally important to have spiritual people to pray for benefactors and especially for their speedy release from purgatory and for their eternal well-being. In that sense, an anchoress such as Julian of Norwich became a kind of servant or employee of the benefactor but one who looked after the spiritual rather than material needs of the employer.

Apart from offering a sense of Julian's own life, the tradition of bequests to men and women anchorites in Norwich raises some further questions. Bequests in the mid-thirteenth century suggest that there were anchorites in the city at that point. However, there seems to be a gap between 1312 and the presence of Julian towards the end of the fourteenth century. Apart from the instability of the times there is no obvious explanation for this. However, what it does suggest is that Julian does not seem to have been the product of a continuous stream of recluses in the city. This makes her stand out even more. However, during her life as an anchoress the numbers of recluses in the city increased to around ten. This does not prove that Julian gathered a circle or school of solitaries around her but it seems likely that she was responsible for the increase by way of inspiration.

The Visit of Margery Kempe

The only other external evidence for the life and work of Julian lies in the text of another late medieval English woman visionary, Margery Kempe (*c.*1373 to later than 1438), daughter of John Brunham, a wealthy merchant, Mayor of Bishop's Lynn (now King's Lynn) in Norfolk, and Member of Parliament. Married at the age of 20 to John Kempe and mother of some fourteen children over 20 years, Margery had visionary experiences and eventually went through a profound spiritual conversion. This led her to reach an agreement with her husband to lead a life of celibacy and then to go on an extensive series of pilgrimages before returning to Lynn. It seems she first began to dictate her spiritual autobiography in the early 1430s and it was eventually completed in 1438. The complete manuscript of her work was only rediscovered in 1934.[7]

The relevance of Margery Kempe to the study of Julian of Norwich lies in her description of a visit and extensive conversation with Julian (*c.*1413) at a relatively early stage in her spiritual journey. In Book 1, chapter 18 of her autobiography (the second of two chapters about a visit to Norwich), she notes that after a visit to a Carmelite friar in Norwich, William Southfield, she was "commanded by our Lord" to "go to an anchoress in the same city who was called Dame Julian." The main focus of their conversation seems to have been Margery Kempe's desire to test out whether her visions and revelations and resulting spiritual sentiments were authentic or whether she was being deceived. She notes that Julian "was expert in such things and could give good advice." After listening to Margery Kempe, Julian's response was to thank God and to advise her to be obedient to God's will and to fulfil whatever God "put into her soul" if it was not obviously contrary to "worship of God" and was to the "profit of her fellow Christians." Once again, Julian seems to have a strong sense of the pastoral purpose of all authentic spiritual experiences. Kempe cites Julian as saying:

> The Holy Ghost never urges a thing against charity, and if he did he would be contrary to his own self, for he is all charity. Also he moves a soul to all chasteness, for chaste livers are called the temple of the Holy Ghost and the Holy Ghost makes a soul stable and steadfast in the right faith and the right belief.

The conversation between them "for many days that they were together" was essentially a lesson in "testing the spirits," or discernment, to see whether one's spiritual experiences or desires are of God or not. Special revelations, once tested, must be trusted. It would seem from this evidence that Julian was seen as an authority on the Christian tradition of discernment. More broadly, Margery Kempe's account also provides evidence that Julian received visitors who came to talk about their spiritual journeys. Interestingly, although Margery Kempe had a liking for devotional texts in English, she makes no mention of Julian's writings as opposed to her spiritual reputation. Yet by 1413 Julian would have long since completed her Short Text and very likely also the Long Text. There do seem to be a few interesting similarities between Margery Kempe and Julian's texts. For example the image of the soul as the seat of God echoes the Long Text, chapter 68. The concern for the faith of Holy Church echoes the Long Text, chapter 9. There is also the use of such terms as "fellow Christians" or "evenchristen."

Margery Kempe's account of her meeting with Julian also has Julian refer to a number of biblical texts as well as to St Jerome and St Bernard on the gift of tears. This brings us briefly to the debates about Julian's previous background and education. As already noted, the first evidence we have for Julian as an anchoress is in a will dated 1393 or 1394. This is roughly the same time when contemporary scholars suggest that Julian began to write the Long Text. Without suggesting that Julian's motive for entering the anchorhold was to become a theological-spiritual writer, it is nevertheless the case that the solitary life would have offered her the space to think about and to meditate upon her experiences and then to gather together her insights in a focused way. The more contentious, and ultimately insoluble, question is what kind of education Julian had, and what life she led, before entering the anchorhold and what connection this had to her initial visionary experience.

Julian's Education and Previous Life

Julian claims to be "simple" and "unlettered" – or, as in the Sloane manuscripts, "a simple creature that cowde no letter." However, the internal evidence of her writings suggests otherwise and that Julian was a person of profound intellect. For example, her Long Text is meticulously organized and manifests literary skills that rank her as a pioneer of English prose, quite apart from the substantial theology. This would make her own self-judgment perhaps an exercise in humility, or self-protection against any accusation of female impropriety in claiming theological-teaching authority, or a way of underlining that what was of value was God-given rather than the product of her own capacities, or a combination of all of these.

Over 50 years ago, the Dominican writer Conrad Pepler suggested that Julian was familiar with Thomas Aquinas.[8] In their 1978 scholarly edition of Julian's texts, Edmund Colledge and James Walsh, as we shall see in the next chapter, promoted Julian as someone with an extensive knowledge of theological sources who could therefore be seen as on a par with medieval male theologians. First of all, they offer a massive list of scriptural citations or scriptural echoes and more generally evidence of Julian's own translations from the Latin Vulgate which suggests that she had a good grounding in Latin. They also suggest that Julian was aware of classical rhetoric. Beyond that they suggest that she had read widely in the spiritual classics, both in the vernacular and in Latin. Finally, they argue that Julian shows a good knowledge of the theology of Augustine and Gregory the Great and seems to have been influenced by The Golden Epistle of the Cistercian William of St Thierry and more generally by Cistercian monastic writings.[9] More recent scholars, including me, while acknowledging Julian's scriptural and theological capacities, mainly consider Colledge's and Walsh's extensive list of works that she had read to be over-exaggerated. I have already suggested that they felt the need to justify the notion that a medieval woman could be considered to be a serious theologian.

To summarize, in my judgment, Julian was certainly literate, able to read and write in Middle English, and maybe with some capacity to read Latin. Before considering how she accessed whatever theological texts she did read, the more immediate question is how she was educated and where.

Some commentators conclude that Julian was a member of the lesser gentry or even of the aristocracy. This would have made for easier access to education and have provided Julian with the means to support herself financially as an anchoress. Specifically, one local Norwich historian in the 1950s detected from available records that there was a prominent woman named "Julian" whose dates seem consistent with what we know or can surmise about Julian of Norwich. This is someone called Lady Julian Erpingham, sister of Sir Thomas Erpingham who, among other things, fought at Agincourt and was a close friend of Henry V. The Erpinghams were a notably devout family with close connections to the Dominicans, St Julian's Church, and Carrow Priory. Lady Julian married Roger Hauteyn who was killed in 1373 (the year of the "showings"), leaving her childless. It would seem likely that she moved back to her family home close to St Julian's Church. If she was indeed our "Julian of Norwich" this may be where she had her near-fatal illness surrounded by her family. However, according to further researches by Fr John-Julian, a recent writer on Julian of Norwich, it seems that Julian Erpingham subsequently remarried someone called Sir John Phelip and had three children, the last of whom was born in 1389 when her second husband also died. In my view, these details make Lady Erpingham's identification with Julian of Norwich less likely. However, Fr John-Julian also points out that in the late Middle Ages the children of the gentry were often sent away to be raised and educated elsewhere. On this basis, Julian would have been free to become an anchoress around 1393. However, an additional problem with this theory is that if Julian of Norwich is to be identified with Lady Erpingham she would have died in 1414. Unfortunately, this does not fit with the evidence provided by the surviving wills, already mentioned, one of which is dated 1416. In addition, Norman Tanner suggests that Julian was probably still alive in 1429 because bequests to an anchoress of St Julian's Church, admittedly unnamed, continue to that date.[10] However, there are also problems with Tanner's suggestion because if Julian was still living in 1429 she would then have been 86 years of age – remarkable at that time.

Even if, for practical reasons, we reject the identification of Julian of Norwich with Lady Julian Erpingham, some other scholars who speculate about her social background favor the gentry or a lower aristocratic milieu. For example, Alexandra Barratt draws attention to Julian's prominent preoccupation with the themes of lordship and service.[11] Other writers note that East Anglia in Julian's time was a populous and prosperous region that was home to numerous gentry families.[12] The term "gentry" meant people who owned land, controlled villages, or held public office such as being a Justice of the Peace or a Member of Parliament. This is not necessarily the same as ennobled or aristocratic. Such people were preoccupied with courtesy and gentility. However, even if Julian was previously married and was a mother, the traditional gentry "consort" category and preoccupations do not appear to fit. There is no strong indication in her writings of the normal concerns of a consort.[13] Another author suggests that the inclusion and naming of Julian's maids in two of the surviving wills is unusual. It may imply that these maids gained a degree of status by association with a gentrified Julian. The same author notes that an anchoress was de facto the head of a small household. Interestingly, Julian's theodicy revolves around the rhetorical example of a servant (chapter 51) where the servant's eagerness to fulfil the lord's desire is both his undoing and yet the making of him. This, it is suggested, fits with the nature of late medieval social relations where "service" was no longer considered demeaning but was part of a "nexus of obligation, honour, service, love and reward."[14]

Julian's literacy, whether as a child of Norfolk gentry or a child of the wealthy Norwich merchant class, could have come from being one of the girls educated by the nuns of Carrow Priory. While one or two commentators seem to believe that Carrow did not educate ordinary children but only aspiring nuns, Norman Tanner in his scholarly study of religion in late medieval Norwich is fairly clear that the convent did take in girls as boarders to be educated.[15]

The more contentious issue concerns how and where Julian acquired her theology. The short answer is that we do not know. It was unusual, but not unprecedented, for a medieval woman to compose theology. Some commentators have assumed that this necessarily points to Julian having been a nun, presumably of Carrow, before she entered the anchorhold. In this context, Julian's three wishes and God thanking her "for your service and your labour in your youth" (chapter 14) have been interpreted as a reference to her earlier life as a nun. The problem with this is that it involves a prior assumption that in Julian's time only nuns would be seen as involved in spiritual service and labor. However, this is highly questionable. By the fourteenth century the growing availability and valuation of lay spiritual resources and new spiritual movements, plus a sense that lay Christians could lead an intentional spiritual life through the medium of pious confraternities, undermines any assumption that Julian's three spiritual desires, as well as God's "thanks" for her spiritual work, necessarily points to a prior monastic lifestyle. To return to the question of Julian's theological education, it would also be naïve to assume that being a nun at Carrow guaranteed access to theological books or to theological training. Many medieval nuns were not theologically well-educated and their grasp of Latin was largely by rote through the regular recitation of the monastic Offices.

As is typical among medieval women mystical writers, Julian does not cite any sources other than the Bible. This has led to all kinds of speculation. It is true that she seems to know the Bible well but the generous list of biblical parallels in Part Two of the scholarly edition of Colledge and Walsh (pp 779–788) is judged by contemporary scholars to be far too extensive. Equally, College and Walsh over-estimate a belief in Julian's theological sources, whether patristic or medieval. Modern commentators judge that most of Julian's apparently direct sources are more likely to be general parallels to themes found throughout the mystical tradition rather than anything more explicit.

Rather than assume that, as a putative nun, Julian had access to library resources at Carrow, it is more likely that her theological knowledge, manifested in the Long Text, came via priest advisors while she was an anchoress. This, of course, assumes that she did not complete her Long Text – indeed, perhaps did not even begin writing it – until she had entered the anchorhold. Such advisors, or theological conversation partners, may have helped obtain books from the important religious libraries in the city. The library of the Benedictine community at the cathedral was one of the best theological collections in the country and this, along with the library of the Augustinian friary close to Julian's anchorhold at St Julian's Church, became well-known centers of learning in the late Middle Ages.

So, had Julian been a nun before she entered the anchorhold? The short answer is that we cannot possibly know. The supposed evidence is circumstantial and based on certain assumptions. What do the various commentators suggest? Colledge and Walsh in their 1970s scholarly edition of Julian's writings believe she was a nun. Perhaps more surprisingly, the more recent scholarly edition by Watson and Jenkins also suggest that there is "a strong possibility" that she was a nun of Carrow. Joan Nuth in *Wisdom's Daughter*, her study of Julian's theology, also suggests that Julian was probably a nun but in her later volume on the English mystics, *God's Lovers in an Age of Anxiety: The English Mystics*, she is less sure. In her respected study of Julian, Grace Jantzen is inconclusive: saying "yes" to connections to Carrow but admitting that there is "no evidence" that she was a nun. She rightly notes that Julian's writings do not have a nun-like feel, target all her "fellow Christians" rather than a narrow monastic audience, and make no overt reference to monastic spirituality or to the monastic approach to biblical meditative exegesis known as *lectio divina*. Insofar as there are echoes of *lectio*, these are just as likely to have originated in the late medieval "laicization" of the tradition in devotional practices and meditation manuals.

The most compelling presentation of an alternative view that Julian of Norwich had been married and widowed and also had had a child or children is paradoxically from Sister Benedicta Ward, a member of a women's monastic community, who is also an Oxford University medieval scholar and Church historian.[16] As we have already seen, this viewpoint also corresponds to the contemporary local consensus in the city of Norwich. Although some of the assumptions in Sister Benedicta's 1988 essay have necessarily been overtaken by more recent scholarship, this does not detract from her other insights. Benedicta Ward rightly questions assumptions that educated and deeply spiritual writers were naturally nurtured in the monastic tradition. She also notes that there had always been a tradition of non-monastics becoming solitaries. For example, the famous early thirteenth-century *Ancrene Wisse* text was aimed at three lay women. Benedicta Ward points out that the scribal note at the beginning of the Short Text simply refers to a "devout woman" who is a recluse at Norwich in 1413. This, the relevant wills, and the testimony of Margery Kempe make no reference to Julian being, or having been, a nun. There is no reference to Julian in the surviving records of Carrow Priory and, like Grace Jantzen, Benedicta Ward correctly notes that there is absolutely no reference in Julian to monastic formation or practices. Julian's writings do not bear the mark of "the cloister." Rather, her desire for three gifts (Short Text, chapter i) are fully in line with the devout aspirations of lay people in her times. The descriptions of Julian's initial illness fit better with a household of family and friends where she was visited by "the parson, my curate" with "a little boy" and a cross (Short Text, chapter ii). So Benedicta Ward suggests that Julian was a young widow living in her own household with servants and her mother. The Long Text, chapters 60 and 61 appear more natural and coherent if we relate them to the actual experience of motherhood – suckling a child at the breast, guarding a child tenderly yet, when it is older, permitting it to be punished for its faults and also allowing it to fall "for its own benefit" – that is, to learn from the experience of getting hurt. Finally, Benedicta Ward hazards a guess that the powerful and poignant image in Long Text, chapter 64, of "a body lying on the earth...without shape and form," compared to a "pit of stinking mud," that produces a "most beautiful creature, a little child" who then glides up to heaven, may echo her own experience of a child who had died. However, it must be noted that this is only a guess and it may be argued that this imagery of death was conventional at the time.[17]

In passing, it is notable that there is no evidence of any posthumous cult of Julian of Norwich despite the reputation for both holiness and spiritual wisdom that she must have enjoyed judging by the bequests made to her and the references to her in Margery Kempe's spiritual autobiography.

Julian's Texts

The precise dates when the two versions of Julian's writings, the Short Text and the Long Text, were written is not made explicitly clear by her. As a consequence this remains a matter of scholarly debate. However, Julian does note that she did not immediately understand the parable of a Lord and a Servant which is the heart of chapter 51 of the Long Text and which was part of her original visionary experience. It is probably for this reason that the parable does not appear at all in the Short Text. Equally probably, Julian's reflections on Jesus as Mother and, more broadly, on God as Mother depend in some way on her eventual understanding of this parable and therefore also do not appear in the Short Text. Chapter 51 itself notes that it was "twenty years after the time of the revelation except for three months" that she received a further "inward instruction" which helped to clarify matters regarding the parable. That would date the new insight to around 1393, presumably after the Short Text had been written. Also, in the final chapter 86 of the Long Text, Julian refers to her continuous desire after her initial visionary revelations "to know in what was our Lord's meaning." She notes that she received a further spiritual revelation that answered her questioning "fifteen years after and more" – that is, around 1388. There have been speculations that the Short Text may have been a later abridged version of the Long Text but this viewpoint is not the scholarly consensus. Whatever the dating of the two texts, it seems more likely that the Short Text precedes the Long Text.[18]

Based on this internal evidence, it also seems likely that Julian did not begin the Long Text until at least 1388 and perhaps later. It has been noted that chapter 1, which summarizes the sixteen showings or revelations, makes no mention of the parable of a Lord and a Servant. This suggests that the writing of the Long Text may have been an extended process with a first draft being written somewhere between 1388 and 1393 with further revision taking place after that date in the light of the further "inward instruction."

Fundamentally, the move from an earlier Short Text to a later Long Text represents a shift from a more experience-based narrative by Julian as participant to a teaching-centered presentation by Julian as interpreter, informed by extensive reflection and also, apparently, by further divine revelation. Equally, in this regard it has been noted that the language of the Long Text is much more plural than the Short Text; it uses "we" rather than the more subjective "I." The Short Text is basically a scene-by-scene account of her visionary experience in twenty-five chapters and roughly eleven thousand words. In contrast, the eighty six chapters of the Long Text, which at around sixty-three thousand words is roughly six times longer, offers a revisionist teaching aimed at a wide readership about the "meaning" of God, the nature of creation, human identity and destiny, and their interrelationship. Nicholas Watson, one of the editors of a relatively recent scholarly edition of Julian's writings, argues in an earlier article that the Short Text was not simply written from notes fairly soon after the visions; that is, shortly after 1373. In the form in which we have it, Watson suggests that it may not have been finished until up to 15 years later; that is, in the mid to late 1380s. He argues, therefore, that the Long Text may not have been started until the 1390s and could well have gone through several revisions until Julian's death in the second decade of the fifteenth century.[19]

Julian's World: Society and Country

The fourteenth century and early fifteenth century, both specifically in England and in wider Europe, have been described as an "age of adversity": one of the bleakest periods in medieval history characterized by the diversity and magnitude of human suffering.[20]

In fourteenth-century England, government suffered from two ineffectual monarchs, Edward II (1307–1327) and Richard II (1377–1399). They were separated by the longer reign of a much stronger king, Edward III (1327–1377). However, his attention was deflected from domestic concerns by his preoccupation with war – with Scotland and with France. In the latter case, this developed into what became known as the Hundred Years' War (1337–1453). War no longer pretended to operate according to chivalrous ideals but was ruthless, brutal, and destructive. This not only led to an increased death toll among the men of England (resulting in many widows) but also to marauding mercenaries wandering the English countryside, plundering and making travel dangerous for ordinary people.

The various wars had a serious knock-on effect at home. There was heavy taxation to fund the wars which impacted on the local clergy and on the poor. As a result government and knights were seen as responsible for a massive waste of resources. In particular, the notorious third poll tax of 1381 provoked the outbreak of what became known as the Peasants' Revolt. This began in South-east England and sought the reduction of taxation and the end to serfdom. Eventually a group from Kent led by Wat Tyler and inspired by the sermons of a priest, John Ball, marched on London. Because there were so few royal troops available, they were joined by local city folk and pillaged and burnt property associated with government. The young king, Richard II, was initially forced to give in to many demands but eventually Wat Tyler was killed, the rebels dispersed, and the concessions rescinded. In East Anglia, to which the rebellion had spread, the Bishop of Norwich Hugh Despenser defeated the rebels. Eventually troubles in the North and West Country were also confronted and order restored.

As if war, government incompetence, and social injustice were not enough, the fourteenth century also saw serious famine throughout Europe. This was followed by plague, known as the Black Death, which hit England in 1348 and again in 1361–1362, 1368–1369, and during the 1370s: all during Julian of Norwich's lifetime. Indeed, as we have seen, the speculation about Julian as widow points either to the wars or to the plague as the likely cause of the possible loss of a husband and children.

Julian's World: Religion and Church

The plagues and famines led to some superstitious reactions. The devil was seen to be at work, as is hinted in Julian's texts (for example, Short Text, chapter xxi or Long Text, chapter 13). Or, in the face of the loss of half the population of Europe in the Black Death, the Jews (collectively blamed for the death of Jesus) were treated as scapegoats and accused of deliberately spreading the disease by, for example, poisoning water wells. Of course, the city of Norwich was already associated with the supposed twelfth-century martyrdom of William of Norwich, a 12-year-old boy, who was killed and was believed to have been murdered by Jews. He subsequently became the object of a religious cult. The situation of Jews in Norwich had particular complications in that they were French-speaking. They were therefore closely associated in people's minds with the relatively recently established, and resented, Norman ruling class. The boy William's family were Anglo-Saxon.

More generally, the plague was seen as God's punishment for sin, for example in Langland's *Piers Plowman*. This fitted into a widespread emphasis in fourteenth-century religion on eternal punishment, fear of which was fuelled by much of the preaching to which lay people were exposed. Catechesis was predominantly about sin and salvation and the bishops were rigorous in their promotion of individual confession to a priest. Not surprisingly, fear of God's wrath was a determining feature in many people's relationship with the divine. The notion of love and mercy (except in the narrow sense of forgiveness of sin if people repented) was in short supply. Apart from other considerations, this is what makes Julian's theology and spiritual message so radical.

On a broader front, the Western Church was in chaos during Julian's lifetime. Between 1309 and 1377 the Frenchman Pope Clement V and then a succession of seven Popes left Rome and lived in Avignon in

France. This so-called "Babylonian Captivity" was also associated with scandalous luxury and the marketing of Church jobs. In 1377, the last of the Avignon popes, Gregory XI, returned to Rome, supposedly inspired by the words of the woman mystic, Catherine of Siena. He died the following year and an Italian reformer, Urban VI, was elected to succeed him. This provoked a revolt among the Cardinals who elected another Frenchman who returned to Avignon. This led to the so-called Great Schism which split the Western Church and lasted until 1418 when it was ended by the Council of Constance.

England seems not to have been strongly influenced by the Continental heretical religious movements such as the so-called heresy of the Free Spirit. However, in the later fourteenth century John Wycliffe, priest, Oxford theologian, and in 1361 Master of Balliol College, indirectly inspired a religious rebellion in England known as Lollardy. Slowly he became disenchanted with the state of the Church and eventually advocated its complete overhaul, structurally and doctrinally. He opposed hierarchical styles of authority, clerical models of priesthood, and certain popular devotions associated with indulgences and money, such as veneration of images. He promoted the vernacular bible, came to see scripture as the sole authority in doctrine and morals, and eventually adopted the doctrine of predestination, promoted a reformed sacramental theology as well as a reformed liturgy, attacked monasticism, and eventually advocated the end of the papacy. However, even though condemned and forced to leave Oxford, he paradoxically retained the parish living of Lutterworth in Lincolnshire where he lived until his death in 1384. His followers, known as Lollards, were not academics but proceeded by way of popular preaching and the promotion of the English bible. They became associated with social reform and the priest, John Ball, who inspired the 1381 Peasants Revolt preached Lollardy even though Wycliffe himself opposed the rebellion. Lollardy survived into the fifteenth century when it eventually became an underground movement which arguably blended into English Protestantism at the time of the Reformation.

The Bishop of Norwich from 1370 until 1406, and thus during Julian's adulthood, was Henry Despenser. He became a leading figure in the persecution of the Lollards and in advocating the death penalty for convicted heretics. This was enforced after the accession of Henry IV in 1399. The so-called "Lollard Pit" in Norwich, where Lollards were burnt at the stake, was very close to Julian's anchorhold. While Julian's texts were written before executions began she would surely have been well aware of the developing Lollard controversy while writing the Long Text. This may partly explain Julian's concern to indicate that she believed "as Holy Church teaches."

On a more upbeat note, the period of Julian's lifetime was also one of the increasing "laicization" of spirituality and access by lay people to spiritual texts, the bible, and other religious material. As we shall see in Chapter 2, Julian's writings can be characterized as "vernacular theology." In broad terms, as noted in the Introduction, this is symptomatic of a growing "age of the vernacular" in which Julian sits alongside the literary giants Geoffrey Chaucer and William Langland. The concept of the "age of the vernacular" has several dimensions. At its most basic, it implied the gradual shift from writing literature in Latin or Norman-French to writing in English. Since the Norman Conquest of England in the eleventh century, "English" in its original Anglo-Saxon and then Middle English forms had ceased to be an acceptable literary language and became effectively the spoken language of the common people. The move back to literary English also implied social and cultural changes whereby a descendent of the language of the defeated Anglo-Saxons gradually became the language of the crown and the administration. Finally, the "age of the vernacular" also implied a growing democratization of ideas and the availability of, for example, religious literature to an increasingly educated and literate laity.

Middle English was known for its alternate spellings and pronunciation depending on the dialect used in different parts of the country. Because English was formed of many languages, standardization has been an on-going issue. Modern English came into being as standardized Middle English – that is, the preferred dialect of the crown, the court, and the civil administration. The key dialect was from East Midlands which eventually spread to London. This contained Danish forms not often used in the North or the South of the country because the Danes settled heavily in the Midlands. Examples are the work of Geoffrey Chaucer, John Wycliffe's translation of the New Testament, and William Caxton, the first printer. French ceased to be the official legal language of England in 1362. A few decades later, King Henry IV (1399–1413) did not speak in Norman-French.

However, from roughly 1200 onwards there was a growing use of various vernacular languages across Europe and not merely in England. This speaks of other developments in Church and wider society. These include the growing accessibility of written material to lay people, the increasing role of women as writers and the expansion of the notion of "theology" beyond formally structured expositions of abstract ideas to embrace personal experience, for example via visionary literature or poetry. There was also the availability of manuals of instruction (or catechisms) in English aimed at enhancing lay people's grasp of the Christian faith. One example is the text known as the *Lay Folks Catechism*, sponsored by Archbishop Thoresby of York in the middle of the fourteenth century.

This became a religious best-seller during the latter part of the century and on into the fifteenth century.

Julian's Norwich

Throughout the late Middle Ages, Norwich was one of the half dozen leading English cities. There are suggestions that its population may have been as large as twenty five thousand in the 1330s but that it was reduced to about eight thousand after the Black Death.[21] By about 1500 Norwich was the second city after London, with around ten thousand inhabitants. The city was also the regional capital of one of the most prosperous, and also artistically sophisticated, parts of England. The port of Norwich was connected by the River Wensum to the sea and there were vibrant trade links between the city and both the Low Countries and the Rhineland. It is notable that the port of Norwich expanded during the Hundred Years' War because the South coast ports were more exposed. Thus Norwich became one of the main gateways to England, served by roads and water-ways to London and to the North of England. There was a significant expansion of the wool and the cloth trade during this period with Norwich as a major export center. Interestingly, Julian of Norwich seems particularly aware of the textures of cloth and of colours which she describes with precision. It has even been suggested that Julian's image "I saw God in a pointe" (chapter 11) may refer to needle-point (or lace-point), with "a pointe" representing a stitch.[22] This is highly speculative, as is the reaction of some people that Julian's family may have been involved in the cloth trade or that it reflects the fact that stitching or lace-making were common activities of anchoresses.

Apart from regular trading connections between the port of Norwich, Flanders, and the Netherlands, there was increasing immigration into Norwich by Flemish cloth workers and merchants. It seems that a small community of Flemish and Dutch merchants with families may have lived in Norwich during Julian's time. References to a Netherlandish community in the city and in wider Norfolk in the late Middle Ages also appear in the records of Norwich, Lynn, Great Yarmouth, and in the Norfolk Records Office. For example, a certain John Asger, "once a merchant of Bruges" according to the memorial in St Lawrence's Church Norwich, was sheriff in 1416 and became Mayor of Norwich in 1426. His son, also called John, apparently born in the Netherlands, seems to have owned the tenement in which one of the quasi-Beguine groups in Norwich lived from the early 1430s. It seems that both father and son died in 1436. Another Asger (or Asgar) called Robert seems to have been city treasurer in 1415–1416. Asgars appear in documents as late as 1475.

This may indicate that generations of the same Flemish family not only resided in the city but also held civic office.

These North Sea connections link with questions about the possible influences of Flemish and Rhineland spirituality. Opinions about this differ. In general terms, the Church was institutionally strong and varied in late medieval Norwich. There were some fifty parishes, a large cathedral run by a community of Benedictine monks, a Benedictine convent at Carrow just outside the city, several colleges of secular clergy living together, several hospitals run by brethren who led a conventual life, four friaries representing the major Orders (Franciscan, Augustinian, Dominican, and Carmelite), and possibly one or two other smaller mendicant groups, plus a significant number of anchorites and anchoresses at different points. Interestingly, the Benedictine-run cathedral had one of the best libraries in England and was reported to be a center of lively theological debate. Additionally, the house of Augustinian (or Austin) Friars across the lane from Julian's anchorhold also had a significant library and was a *studium* or house of studies for the order. There is some evidence that outsiders such as Julian could borrow books from such libraries.[23]

From the 1430s there were also up to three small groups of women who resembled Continental Beguines. This would seem to postdate Julian. However, more recently it has been suggested that a group of such women lived in a house in the churchyard of St Peter Hungate at a time before Julian disappears from the records. The medieval building survives as a restaurant, "The Briton's Arms," on Elm Hill. It is possible that these groups were sponsored by the local Flemish and Dutch merchant community. Norwich seems to have been the only English city where such groups existed. What is not so clear is whether, and to what degree, the spirituality associated with Flanders and the Netherlands played a role in late medieval Norwich. More generally, there was a widespread development of lay spirituality as well as new spiritual movements in the late medieval Church. These particularly flourished in cities like Norwich. Thus, apart from the clerical, monastic, mendicant, and quasi-Beguine groups, Norwich boasted a number of lay confraternities and spiritually imbued craft guilds as well as a range of other activities that offered a significant spiritual ethos to the newly wealthy and educated city laity. In that sense the lay Christians of late medieval Norwich had a wide range of spiritual and religious resources.[24]

As an appendix to the growing importance during the late Middle Ages of Norwich as a port and international trading center, it is interesting to note the power of Julian's imagery of the sea in chapter 10. This chapter is what is described as the second showing or revelation in which Julian is taught about God's desire that we should see the divine presence, albeit partially, in this life. However, on the face of it, it seems to be a rather strange move from the opening of the chapter where Julian contemplates Jesus on the cross, his face covered in blood, to having her understanding "let down into the bottom of the sea." Apparently this experience happened once. Beyond the question of what this taught Julian about God, it is interesting to ask what ordinary experiences it may reflect. It may refer to Julian's experience of living in Norwich where the River Wensum, which is relatively close to St Julian's Church, was periodically beset by storms from the North Sea when waves flooded the marshes and houses close to the river. Julian may also have heard about the dangers of the North Sea from stories told by fishermen in the port. Such an awareness may connect to Julian's imagery of herring scales in reference to the drops of blood on Jesus' face in chapter 7. Herrings were one of the basic foods in medieval Norwich. In their notes on this chapter Watkins and Jenkins suggest that the image of the sea may instead echo Julian's awareness of Psalm 139, verses 9–10: "If I take the wings of the morning and settle at the farthest limits of the sea, even there your hand shall lead me and your right hand shall hold me fast" (NRSV Bible).

The Position of Women

The overall social position of women in England at the time of Julian of Norwich can only be described in terms of patriarchy.[25] That said, the status and role of women obviously varied according to certain factors including where they lived, whether they were unmarried, married, or widowed, and what social class they belonged to. It is also the case that the position of women inevitably altered in the aftermath of the Black Death, which left many of them as widows and also reduced the male workforce. Wealthy widows were sometimes able to live as powerful members of their communities. Equally, others in cities such as Norwich were able to work in a limited range of occupations including lace-making and even ale brewing.

Women were often seen as inherently weak and defective. What power they had, not least sexual power, was seen as negative and a source of danger: particularly to men. This is reflected in some of the spiritual and anchoritic literature available to Julian. Thus the *Ancrene Wisse* or *Ancrene Riwle* in its second part, "The Outer Senses," in reference to the story of Dinah, daughter of Jacob, in the Book of Genesis, chapter 34, comments "The Holy Spirit caused all such things to be written in the book to warn women of their foolish eyes." Equally, women must not show themselves to men because it brings out the "animal" in them! Yet, later on in the same section the *Ancrene Wisse* also offers an image of

God's positive response, even obedience, to a woman. God becomes human because of what Mary says to the Archangel Gabriel. John the Baptist exults in his mother's womb when Mary greets her cousin Elizabeth. Jesus turns water into wine at the wedding feast of Cana when his mother Mary presses him to do this. And in the Gospel of Luke, chapter 2, the child Jesus once found by his mother in the Temple becomes obedient to his mother once again.[26]

Within Julian's own writings there is a fascinating contrast between the Short Text and the Long Text. In the Short Text, Julian seems uncomfortably aware of a woman's presumption in writing, especially in ways that were meant to teach other Christians. However, she is persuaded that her visions are not for her personal benefit and that therefore she must record them. This does not sit easily with her and she appears to worry that it may not sit easily with her readers. There is a very interesting contrast within the Short Text, chapter vi. "But God forbid that you should say or assume that I am a teacher, for that is not and never was my intention; for I am a woman, ignorant, weak and frail." While Julian may not have been aware of the theological writings of Jean Gerson, Chancellor of the University of Paris from 1395, his negative attitude to the idea of women teaching would have been symptomatic of Julian's time. Gerson remarks that "the female sex is forbidden by apostolic authority to teach in public, that is either by word or by writing.... All women's teaching, particularly formal teaching by word and by writing, is to be held suspect unless it is diligently examined, and much more fully than men's."[27] However, Julian then goes on to say that she cannot be silent, or be silenced. "But because I am a woman, ought I therefore to believe that I should not tell you of the goodness of God, when I saw at that same time that it is his will that it be known?" Fundamentally the Short Text self-justifies with several "buts." In contrast, in the equivalent passage in the Long Text, chapter 9, Julian drops her apologies for being such a daring woman, asserts her orthodoxy, and substitutes a profound reflection on the value of such special revelations, even to a woman. "I am not good because of the revelations, but only if I love God better..." "But in everything I believe as Holy Church preaches and teaches." "And to this end and with this intention I contemplated the revelation with all diligence, for throughout this blessed revelation I contemplated it as God intended." Scholarly feminist readings of Julian suggest that she refused to be silenced in the face of contemporary suspicions and that, particularly by the time of the Long Text, she had found her own confident voice. Importantly, Julian does not restrict her message to her fellow women but addresses her teaching to all her fellow Christians, men and women.[28]

Spirituality in England

While Julian was a product of her particular time and place, she was also the inheritor of the long-standing tradition of spirituality in England. Importantly, while there were some specific native characteristics, the overall approach to spirituality in England was not totally insular but was connected to broader spiritual streams from continental Europe. Apart from Benedictine and Franciscan spiritual writings, mentioned below, in particular we may note the Augustinian spiritual ethos as developed by the French Victorines, Hugh of St Victor and Richard of St Victor. Their spiritual writings also made accessible the mystical theology of the anonymous sixth-century writer known as Pseudo-Dionysius who certainly influenced the anonymous author of *The Cloud of Unknowing* in the 1380s. What is less clear is to what degree the important thirteenth-century Rhineland mystical tradition, associated especially with the Dominicans Meister Eckhart, Johannes Tauler, and Henry Suso, had an impact in England.

It is reasonable to suggest that the intensely visual character of Julian's "showings" is likely to have been influenced in part by certain external spiritual stimuli and was not simply a matter of unprovoked visionary experiences. This has two important elements. The first strong possibility is that Julian was exposed to the tradition of late medieval paintings and sculptures of Jesus' Passion and cross. In particular, some commentators draw specific connections with the notable school of East Anglian art which was at its height during the fourteenth century. From the surviving art of Julian's period we can see that the artists of the East Anglian School excelled in portraying Christ's Passion with both significant physical detail and also emotional pathos. Indeed there is an explicit reference in Julian's Short Text, chapter i, to "paintings of the Crucifixion, which are made by God's grace, according to Holy Church's teaching, to resemble Christ's Passion, so far as human understanding can attain." The second likely influence was the tradition of meditative visualization in relation to scripture and in particular to contemplation of Jesus' humanity. This was present in Cistercian writers, not least the twelfth-century Englishman Aelred of Rievaulx in his *Rule of Life for a Recluse* (of which, more in a moment), as well as in the Franciscan meditative tradition, not least the anonymous spiritual text, *Meditationes Vitae Christi*, once thought to be written by Bonaventure and dating from the mid-fourteenth century. This work was particularly influential in introducing scriptural meditation to educated lay people. It also became available in an English translation around the end of the fourteenth century or beginning of the fifteenth century as *The Mirror of the Blessed Life of Jesus Christ* by the Carthusian monk Nicholas Love at Mount Grace Priory, Yorkshire.[29]

Another possible influence on Julian may have been the writings of continental women visionaries, many of whom, like Julian, suffered serious illnesses and integrated these into a way of sharing in the sufferings of Christ. Because of the close connections that I have already noted between Norwich and the Low Countries, it is quite possible that such texts were known to Julian even though, as we have seen, quasi-Beguine groups may not have settled in the city until the 1430s.[30] Rather more controversial are links between Julian and the tradition of the so-called *Brautmystik*, or "bridal mysticism," influential among the Rhineland mystics Eckhart, Tauler, and Suso as well as among the Beguines, with its idea of union with God as a "mystical marriage" often expressed through erotic imagery. There are undoubtedly some similarities in the themes. For example, Julian briefly refers to "God's son" as the "spouse" of the soul towards the end of the Long Text, chapter 51. She uses the image of God as spouse at the start of chapter 52, "and God rejoices that he is our true spouse, and that our soul is his beloved wife." Finally, in chapter 58 the spousal imagery is explicitly linked to Julian's major theme of God's meaning as love. Thus, "...he is our very true spouse and we his beloved wife and his fair maiden, with which wife he was never displeased; for he says: I love you and you love me, and our love will never divide in two." That said, any direct links between Julian and the "bridal mysticism" tradition are inconclusive.[31]

Otherwise, English spirituality as inherited by Julian of Norwich had several notable characteristics. First of all it was deeply biblical. This was often mediated through the monastic tradition of meditative biblical interpretation, known as *lectio divina*, which across time was "translated" for the benefit of non-monastics such as clergy or laypeople. Anglo-Saxon England had originally been evangelized by the arrival of Benedictine monks from Rome, and monastic culture subsequently dominated English religion far more than Continental Europe. For example, half of the English cathedrals (for example, Norwich) during the Middle Ages were run by monastic personnel. There were no parallels on the Continent.

Second, the English spiritual tradition was strongly grounded in affective piety, especially devotion to the humanity of Christ, not least to Jesus' Passion. A notable example is the Benedictine Anselm of Canterbury's *Prayers and Meditations.* This affective strain also resulted in countless meditations, poems, hymns, and prayers that sought to inspire intense and intimate love. One particular theme that is closely associated with Julian of Norwich is Jesus as Mother. However, it is important to note that while Julian employs the theme in original ways, devotion to Jesus as Mother is not original to her. Nor, indeed, is it limited to women writers. For example it appears in Anselm of Canterbury and among Cistercian writers.[32] The originality of Julian's approach to the image will be outlined in Chapter 4.

Third, there was a preference for the solitary life. A separate section on this follows. In general terms, the solitary life was ascetic and penitential in that it explicitly confronted worldly dangers and temptations, not least the solitary's own frailties. The link between holiness and heroism led to a strong emphasis on spiritual warfare and the quest for singleness and purity of heart. Finally, within the solitary life the practice of virginity especially among women became linked particularly to the notion of being brides of Christ. Various forms of the solitary life seem to have been more popular and idiosyncratic in Celtic Christianity and later in Anglo-Saxon and Medieval England than in the rest of Europe. Aelred of Rievaulx's *Rule of Life for a Recluse*, already mentioned, has relatively little on external rules of life and mostly concerns interior dispositions. The aim was to inspire single-hearted devotion.

Fourth, medieval English spirituality developed an emphasis on the "mixed life," *vita mixta*, which not only sought to combine contemplation and action but was also increasingly aimed at both secular clergy and laypeople outside the monastic cloister. A notable example is Walter Hilton's *The Scale* [or *Ladder*] *of Perfection* which appeared during Julian's lifetime. Book 2 of *The Scale* suggests that spiritual transformation is inherent to the life of all the baptised as opposed merely to the monastic or the solitary life. This echoes Julian's emphasis on her message being addressed to all her "fellow Christians."

Finally, the English spiritual tradition placed a strong emphasis on the importance of "balance" – between affectivity and the speculative, between divinely given insights and loyalty to the Church, in terms of ascetical moderation, a preference for the grounded as opposed to the abstract and with a pastoral emphasis.[33]

The Anchoritic Life

The strong presence of the solitary life within English spirituality, and Julian's own existence as an anchoress, needs some further explanation. The solitary life in various forms seems to have characterized four of the five major English fourteenth-century mystical writers, leaving aside Margery Kempe. Richard Rolle (*c.*1300–1349) pursued the solitary life after studying at Oxford. He was never ordained and ended up at Hampole in Yorkshire next to a monastery of Cistercian nuns. Rolle is the most prolific of the English mystics, writing in both Latin and English, and producing treatises, spiritual meditations and poetry.[34] Walter Hilton (died 1395/1396) ended as an Augustinian Canon of Thurgaton

Priory in Nottinghamshire. However, apart from his studies at Cambridge, he lived for some time as a solitary before entering the Augustinians. In a sense, therefore, his spiritual life was a mixed one and this is perhaps reflected in his most famous work, *The Scale of Perfection* mentioned above.[35] Finally, the anonymous author of the famous and still influential book, *The Cloud of Unknowing* (1380s), and related works, was probably a Carthusian monk who therefore led a partly solitary life.[36]

Originally the terms "anchorite" and "hermit" were synonymous and referred to the quest to be solitary or to withdraw to the *eremos*, the desert. This could imply total seclusion and stability or allow freedom of movement and social interaction. Early desert solitaries, for example in Egypt, while geographically distant from towns and while emphasizing withdrawal, had a degree of interchange with visitors. They saw charity and hospitality as virtues – even providing food and clothes to villagers in times of famine. They also visited towns to sell their work in the markets.

Only in the Western European Middle Ages did the terms "hermit" and "anchorite" or "anchoress" become more distinct. The "hermit" was more general, indicating "the one alone." Hermits were not necessarily secluded. Many lived in towns or villages. Thus, for example, Richard Rolle called at local houses to eat and drink. The point was that the true hermit lived alone and vowed obedience to God alone, not to a monastic rule or to an abbot or abbess. Some solitaries engaged in external works. They might be guides to travellers or offer their cells as overnight hostels. Others acted as bridge or toll keepers. In England, some looked after coastal beacons, as evidenced by the remains of a medieval hermitage and chapel linked to the beacon on St Aldhelm's Head in Dorset.

The title of "anchorite" or "anchoress" was restricted to those who were recluses, enclosed and stable. Some of those who felt called to this life were already members of religious communities. Thus, quite a number of monasteries in England, whether of men or women, had responsibility for one or more recluses. Some of these lived close to the main community but others such as the Benedictines of Durham Cathedral Priory maintained a hermitage on the islands of Farne off the Northumberland coast. Also, on the edge of the moors above the Carthusian monastery of Mount Grace in Yorkshire are the remains of an isolated hermitage where it is thought that a monk from the Priory below could retire.

However, and importantly in the context of Julian of Norwich, in England there were many recluses with no previous connections to a monastery. Thus, famous figures such as Godric of Finchdale, Wulfric of Haselbury, and Christina of Markyate had not previously been monastics. The best-known English rule for the anchoritic life, the early thirteenth-century *Ancrene Wisse (A Guide for Anchoresses)*, was written explicitly for three women living outside traditional monastic structures.[37] This text tells us something about the way of life of an anchoress. The solitary life was considered the highest form of the Christian life because it combined asceticism and contemplation. The way of life was particularly popular with women and gave them a status and role aside from clerical life.

Anchorholds were familiar features of late medieval life, often attached to parish churches, as at St Julian's in Norwich. They could be single rooms or larger complexes with courtyard and garden. In the case of the latter, a secluded area was set aside for the anchoress and a reception area housed a maid who organized the food and protected the privacy of the solitary. Here guests might also sit and speak to the anchoress. The maid also has certain rules because she too was to lead a life of dedicated devotion with some austerity. The anchoress probably had access to three windows: one onto the church, one into the reception area and one directly onto the street. In the case of the latter, there should be a curtain so that the anchoress could neither see, nor be seen by, any visitor. It is not certain what style of anchorhold Julian occupied. It is noted in the book by Fr John-Julian that during the post-war reconstruction of St Julian's Church in 1953 the foundations of an anchorhold destroyed by the bombing were discovered and the space was tiny: some nine and a half feet by eleven and a half feet. This does not seem consistent with the multiple occupancy of the anchorhold in Julian's time implied in a surviving will of 1404, noted above. However, in the Introduction to their translation of Julian's texts, Edmund Colledge and James Walsh indicate that the "cell" destroyed during the Second World War was actually a reconstruction. Further, in the Introduction to their scholarly edition of Julian's texts, they cite a comment by the eighteenth-century Norfolk antiquarian, Francis Blomefield, in the second volume of his 1745 text, *Norfolk*, that the original anchorhold had been demolished at the dissolution of the monasteries.[38]

Leaving aside questions of lifestyle, it is instructive to compare the radically different spiritual ethos of the *Ancrene Wisse* with Julian's writings and their essentially positive vision and also concern for all her fellow Christians. The two visions of life are not very compatible. Thus the *Ancrene Wisse* does not portray a romantic vision of the solitary life although it does see the anchoress as a kind of spiritual "aristocrat." It emphasizes the anger of God set against the spiritual dangers of the world. It portrays solitude as the medium for saving one's soul. Indeed, the initial ceremony of enclosure strongly symbolized death to the world. The anchorhold was a kind of tomb and anchoresses were to meditate frequently upon death. There is to be a round of prayer from waking to sleeping in order to ward off evil. Plus, a devotional routine keeps the solitary's attention away from other things that might encourage idleness. The day is largely silent. The emphasis is on the weakness of an anchoress – essentially sinful and thus committed to the solitary life as if it were imprisonment. There is no sense of an anchoress being able to offer spiritual insight to others; rather, such people are unworthy of fellowship. Self-disgust is a spiritual value. There should be meditation on the vileness of the body. This approach contrasts strongly with Julian's positive imagery of embodiment in Long Text, chapter 6, where the process of defecation underlines God's loving providence! The text of the *Ancrene Wisse* manifests a strain of deep anxiety and its language is that of frailty plus the just anger of God.[39]

Conclusion: Context and Julian's Teachings

Julian makes no direct reference to any of the social, political, or religious problems of her troubled times. However, there seem to be echoes of these problems in both the tone and the content of her teachings. In the context of such a difficult world, Julian's assertion that "all shall be well" must have raised as many questions as it offered comfort. Indeed, Julian's visions focus on the bleeding, suffering Christ on the cross as God's response to sin and suffering. Thus Julian's own human instinct is to ask how all shall end up well when such harm is done by human sin. In that sense, her eventual acceptance of God's message is born of deep interior struggle. "All shall be well" is not offered as a cheap and easy response to the troubles of the world and of her fellow Christians. To ask her fellow Christians to believe that, as the final chapter of the Long Text affirms, love was God's meaning would have been deeply challenging.

The first sentence of the chapter suggests that "this boke" was begun by God's grace but is not yet "performed"; that is, fully perfected. Perhaps this does refer in part to the imperfection of Julian's own understanding of God's revelations, and therefore to the incompleteness of her teaching in the written text. However, Julian adds: "For charity, let us all join with God's working in prayer, thanking, trusting, rejoicing." In the end what has been taught on the basis of what was revealed to Julian must be performed by all her fellow Christians in some way in the midst of the imperfections of everyday living in a fractured world. Humans are called to participate as best they can in God's working and "performance" and not simply be passive recipients.

There are some hints about what is demanded by this human sharing in God's "performing." In at least one way, it seems to me that this speaks radically to the conditions of Julian's times, characterized by war, human enmity, rebellion, accusations of heresy, and rejections of "otherness," for example, attitudes to the Jews. As a footnote, in her one reference to the Jews (chapter 33), Julian is ambiguous. She admits to seeing nothing "specified" about them in her visions but "nonetheless" follows the conventional assumption that that they were collectively responsible for Jesus' death and therefore were condemned, unless "converted by grace." Returning to the notion of humanity sharing in God's "performing," in the Short Text, chapter vi, Julian affirms the vital importance of the practice of love among Christians. This would, at the very least, have directly countered the schism in the Church and other expressions of mutual condemnation.

> It is in this unity of love that the life consists of all men who will be saved. For God is everything that is good, and God has made everything that is made, and God loves everything that he has made, and if any man or woman withdraws his love from any of his fellow Christians, he does not love at all, because he had not love towards all. And so in such times he is in danger, because he is not at peace; and anyone who has general love for his fellow Christians has love towards everything which is. For in mankind which will be saved is comprehended all, that is, all that is made and the maker of all; for God is in man, and so in man is all. And he who thus generally loves all his fellow Christians loves all, and he who loves thus is safe.

Notes

1 For an overall study of context and interpretation in relation to the history of Christian spirituality and classic texts, see Philip Sheldrake, *Spirituality and History: Questions of Interpretation and Method*, Revised edition, London: SPCK/Maryknoll, NY: Orbis Books, 1995, especially Chapters 3 and 7.

2 I am grateful to Fr Christopher Wood, the current parish priest of St Julian's Church, for informing me about the contemporary consensus in Norwich about Julian as a widow and bereaved mother as well as for information about the Carrow Psalter and devotion to St Julian of Le Mans.

3 Both the Colledge & Walsh and the Watson & Jenkins scholarly editions agree on 13 (xiii) May whereas the recent edition by Windeatt reads it as 8 (viii) May. This remains unclear and depends on which manuscript you read.

4 See the comments in Nicholas Watson & Jacqueline Jenkins, eds., *The Writings of Julian of Norwich*, University Park, PA: The Pennsylvania State University Press, 2006, Introduction, p 4.

5 See Norman Tanner, *The Church in Late Medieval Norwich 1370–1532*, Toronto: Pontifical Institute of Medieval Studies: Studies & Texts 66, 1984.

6 See Watson & Jenkins, *The Writings of Julian of Norwich*, Appendix B, pp 431–435.

7 For the most commonly used modern translation from the Middle English, see B.A. Windeatt, ed., *The Book of Margery Kempe*, London: Penguin Classics, 1985.

8 See Conrad Pepler, *The English Religious Heritage*, London: Blackfriars, 1958, p 306.

9 See Edmund Colledge & James Walsh, eds., *A Book of Showings to the Anchoress Julian of Norwich*, Toronto: Pontifical Institute of Mediaeval Studies, 1978. For the list of scriptural citations and allusions, see Part Two, pp 779ff. For a more general overview of Julian's supposed scriptural and theological sources, see Part One, pp 43–59.

10 For these speculations and their justification, see the extensive book by the founder of the Episcopalian monastic Order of Julian, Fr John-Julian OJN, *The Complete Julian of Norwich*, Brewster, MA: Paraclete Press, 2009, especially pp 21–27. For Tanner's comments about bequests continuing until 1429, see his *The Church in Late Medieval Norwich 1370–1532*, Appendix 7, p 200, note 29.

11 See A. Barratt, "Lordship, Service and Worship in Julian of Norwich" in E.A. James, ed., *The Medieval Mystical Tradition in England*, Exeter Symposium VII, Cambridge: D.S. Brewer, 2004, pp 177–188.

12 See, for example, Kim Phillips, "Femininities and the Gentry in Late Medieval East Anglia: Ways of Being," in Liz Herbert McAvoy, ed., *A Companion to Julian of Norwich*, Cambridge: D.S. Brewer, 2008, pp 19–31.

13 See Phillips, p 27.

14 See E. A Jones, "Anchoritic Aspects of Julian of Norwich," in McAvoy, ed., *Companion to Julian of Norwich*, pp 75–87, especially p 78.

15 Tanner, p 27.

16 See Benedicta Ward, "Julian the Solitary," in Kenneth Leech & Sister Benedicta Ward, *Julian Reconsidered*, Oxford: SLG Press, 1988, pp 11–29.

17 I am grateful to Nicholas Watson for pointing out to me the conventional nature of this image.

18 On this point see, for example, Barry Windeatt, "Julian's Second Thoughts: The Long Text Tradition," in Liz Herbert McAvoy, ed., *A Companion to Julian of Norwich*, Cambridge: D.S.Brewer, 2008, pp 101–115.

19 See Nicholas Watson, "The Composition of Julian of Norwich's Revelations of Love," in *Speculum* 68, 1993, pp 637–683. See also the Introduction to Watson & Jenkins, eds., *The Writings of Julian of Norwich*, pp 1–4.

20 For general historical overviews, see A.R. Myers, *England in the Late Middle Ages*, London: Penguin Books, 1981; Rosemary Horrox & W. Mark Ormrod, *A Social History of England 1200–1500*, Cambridge:

Cambridge University Press, 2006; W. Mark Ormrod, *Political Life in Medieval England 1300–1450*, London: Macmillan, 1995; Miri Rubin, *The Hollow Crown: A History of Britain in the Late Middle Ages*, London: Penguin Books, 2005; Gerard Harris, *Shaping the Nation: England 1360–1461*, Oxford: Clarendon Press, 2005. For specific connections between this period and the English mystics, including Julian, see Joan M. Nuth, *God's Lovers in an Age of Anxiety: The Medieval English Mystics*, London: Darton, Longman & Todd/ Maryknoll, NY: Orbis Books, 2001, Chapter 1 "The Historical Framework," pp 13–33.

21 See Barry Windeatt, ed., *Julian of Norwich: Revelations of Divine Love*, Oxford: Oxford University Press, 2016, p xvi.

22 See Ritamary Bradley, *Julian's Way: A Practical Commentary on Julian of Norwich*, London: Harper Collins, 1992, p 95.

23 See Windeatt, *Julian of Norwich*, pp xvii–xviii.

24 For an extensive overview of religion in medieval Norwich, see the thorough and reliable book by the English Jesuit medieval historian, Norman Tanner, *The Church in Late Medieval Norwich 1370–1532*, Toronto: Pontifical Institute of Medieval Studies, 1984. For a more general overview, see Cariole Rawcliffe & Richard Wilson, eds., *Medieval Norwich*, London/New York: Hambledon (Palgrave Macmillan), 2004. For specific details of the monastic and other religious houses in Norwich, see David Knowles & R. Neville Hadcock, *Medieval Religious Houses, England & Wales*, Harlow: Longman, 1971.

25 See Mavis Mate, *Women in Medieval English Society*, Cambridge: Cambridge University Press, 2001. See also Judith M. Bennett & Ruth Mazo Karras, eds., *Oxford Handbook of Women and Gender in Medieval Europe*, Oxford: Oxford University Press, 2010.

26 See Anne Savage & Nicholas Watson, eds., *Anchoritic Spirituality: Ancrene Wisse and Associated Works*, Mahwah, NJ: Paulist Press, 1991, especially pages 68–69 and 77.

27 For this quotation from Gerson's *De examinatione doctrinam*, see Caroline Walker Bynum, *Jesus as Mother: Studies in the Spirituality of the High Middle Ages*, Berkeley, CA: University of California Press, 1982, pp 135–136.

28 See, for example, Frances Beer, *Julian of Norwich: Revelations; Motherhood of God*, Cambridge: D.S. Brewer, 1998, Interpretive Essay, pp 71–80; also her *Women and Mystical Experience in the Middle Ages*, Woodbridge: Boydell & Brewer, 1992, Introduction pp 1–13; also Grace Jantzen, *Julian of Norwich*, 2nd edition, London: SPCK, 2000, pp xi–xiv.

29 For details of both of these possible influences on Julian see Denise Nowakowski Baker, *Julian of Norwich's Showings: From Vision to Book*, Princeton, NJ: Princeton University Press, 1994, Chapter 2 "From Visualisation to Vision: Meditation and the Bodily Showings," pp 40–62.

30 On this point, see Nuth, *God's Lovers in an Age of Anxiety: The Medieval English Mystics*, p 101. For a broad study of continental women visionaries, see Elizabeth A. Petroff, ed., *Medieval Women's Visionary Literature*, Oxford: Oxford University Press, 1986.

31 For some positive but tentative comments, see Jantzen, *Julian of Norwich*, pp 61–70.

32 See Caroline Walker Bynum, *Jesus as Mother: Studies in the Spirituality of the High Middle Ages*, Berkeley: University of California Press, 1984, Chapter IV "Jesus as Mother and Abbot as Mother: Some themes of Twelfth-Century Cistercian Writing," pp 110–169.

33 On English spirituality, see Nuth, *God's Lovers in an Age of Anxiety*, pp 15–23 & Gordon Mursell, *English Spirituality: From Earliest Times to 1700*, London: SPCK/Louisville, KY: Westminster John Knox Press, 2001, especially Chapter 4 "The Quest for the Suffering Jesus: Late Medieval Spirituality (1300–1500)."

34 For a modern translation of Rolle's English writings, see Rosamund S.Allen, ed., *Richard Rolle – The English Writings*, Mahwah, NJ: Paulist Press, 1989.

35 For a modern translation, see John P.H. Clark & Rosemary Dorward, eds., *Walter Hilton – The Scale of Perfection*, Mahwah, NJ: Paulist Press, 1991.

36 For a modern translation of these works, see James Walsh, ed., *The Cloud of Unknowing*, Mahwah:NJ: Paulist Press, 1981 and James Walsh, ed., *The Pursuit of Wisdom and Other Works*, Mahwah, NJ: Paulist Press, 1988.

37 For a modern translation, see Savage & Watson, *Anchoritic Spirituality – Ancrene Wisse and Associated Works*.

38 On the post-war reconstruction, see John-Julian, *The Complete Julian of Norwich*, p 38. On the demolition of the original anchorhold, see also Colledge & Walsh, *Julian of Norwich: Showings*, Introduction p 18, and for a full reference to the work of Francis Blomefield, see their *A Book of Showings to the Anchoress Julian of Norwich*, volume 1, pp 11–12.

39 For an overview of the anchoritic life, see Jantzen, *Julian of Norwich*, Chapter 3, "The Life of an Anchoress."

Chapter 2

Julian's Theology

Why should Julian be considered as a theologian rather than simply as a spiritual writer or as a "mystic"? The famous mid-twentieth century monastic writer Thomas Merton was clear that Julian of Norwich was not only the greatest of the fourteenth-century English mystics but was also, in his judgment, one of the greatest English theologians of all times.[1] Scholars nowadays acknowledge that Julian's texts are neither solely a record of her mystical visionary experiences nor essentially devotional in tone and purpose. Rather, particularly in her Long Text, Julian offers substantial, innovative, and important theological reflections aimed at teaching a wide audience of her fellow Christians.

Apart from developing my judgment that Julian is to be considered as an important theological writer, in this chapter I also wish to underline the difference between exploring theological themes provoked by reading Julian and offering a study of Julian's own theology. The purpose of this book is to do the latter. My aim, in a positive sense, is to provide a critical study of the range of Julian's theology rather than a purely descriptive survey. What is the nature of Julian's theology, its genre, purpose, and projected audience? The questions of purpose and intended audience are central to this issue.

In her book of essays *The Kindness of God*, Cambridge theologian Janet Martin Soskice notes that, in the continuing popular enthusiasm for Julian as a great mystical writer, the importance of her text as a work of theology is frequently underplayed or even entirely overlooked. This suggests that many people are instinctively reacting against a widespread perception that theology is simply "sclerotic pronouncements."[2] Soskice also implicitly outlines the difference between Julian and classic systematic or philosophical theology. Julian's style may appear to be "rambling" but it is deliberately so. Indeed, Soskice prefers the term "recursive." The point is that Julian's writing in her Long Text is not meant to be a logical, architectonic exposition of doctrine. Rather she seeks to draw the reader into the text and its purpose in such a way as to make the reader a "fellow traveller into the mystery of the love of God."[3]

Julian of Norwich: "In God's Sight" – Her Theology in Context, First Edition. Philip Sheldrake.
© 2019 John Wiley & Sons Ltd. Published 2019 by John Wiley & Sons Ltd.

The Forms of Medieval Theology

During the Western European Middle Ages, there were broadly three major styles of theology. First there was scholastic theology, or the theology "of the schools" (that is, the new universities) of which arguably the best-known exponent is Thomas Aquinas.[4] This drew a great deal upon classical philosophy and on philosophical categories more broadly and was tightly structured in a similar way to contemporary styles of systematic theology. The scholastic style of theology, as a method of learning, placed a strong emphasis on philosophical reasoning. Its conceptual analysis was rigorous and dialectical with a careful use of distinctions. The pedagogical process classically involved what was known as "disputation" through a logical sequence of questions and speculative debate leading to a final conclusion. In contemporary terms, systematic theology is also an orderly, rational, and highly structured exposition of Christian doctrines often drawing upon philosophical method as well as on scripture and history. No contemporary scholars interpret Julian in these terms.

The second Western medieval theological style was what is known as monastic theology. "Monastic" refers both to the setting within which this theological reflection took place and to its particular approach or method. Monastic theology arose from an inner contemplative life within a monastic setting and the spiritual practices or ascetic disciplines that nurtured the contemplation of God. Monastic theologians existed within the lifestyle of monasteries where their theology was rooted in an experience of the rhythm of worship and daily meditative reading of scripture and reflection upon scripture, known as *lectio divina*. Monastic theology was therefore based primarily on a meditative approach to scripture so that its method was not one of detached, objective speculation but of committed participation.[5] One or two scholars have suggested that Julian partly fits into this theological category. However, as I shall explain briefly in a moment, I seriously question this understanding of Julian.

The third approach to theology, inherited originally from the Patristic period and developed further in the Middle Ages, is known as mystical theology. As I will suggest, I believe that this is one of the most important categories for understanding the basis of Julian's theology and her theological style.

Julian's Theological Style

If we describe Julian's writing as theological, a central question concerns the genre of theology that we are dealing with and the degree to which Julian explicitly draws upon earlier theological sources. Judgments about these questions vary.

In their ground-breaking 1978 two-volume critical edition of Julian's texts, the scholars Edmund Colledge and James Walsh were convinced that, first, Julian not only extensively cited or alluded to large numbers of scriptural passages but also showed evidence of having made her own translations from the Latin Vulgate (thus indicating a good grounding in Latin). In their second volume, they offer an extensive list of scriptural citations. They also suggested that Julian knew the theology of Augustine and Gregory the Great well and was explicitly influenced by William of St Thierry's *The Golden Epistle* and more generally by Cistercian writings.[6] Other contemporary scholars are more cautious about Julian's direct scriptural or theological sources. However, to be fair, in the description of her visit to Julian for spiritual counsel, Margery Kempe does suggest that Julian referred to biblical texts and alluded to St Jerome and St Bernard on the gift of tears.[7]

In more recent studies of Julian's theology since the days of Colledge and Walsh, opinions about her theology and her possible sources vary. Here I will summarize five important contributions. First, in the Preface and Introduction to their relatively recent scholarly edition of Julian's writings, Nicholas Watson and Jacqueline Jenkins describe Julian as one of the greatest "speculative" theologians of the Middle Ages. In their judgment, Julian (not least in her exemplum of a Lord and a Servant) radically rethinks the nature of sin and goodness in "speculative leaps." In their words, Julian offers "an unprecedented speculative vernacular theology." I will discuss the important category of vernacular theology later in this chapter. However, I believe that we need to be careful about how we use the word "speculative" in relation to Julian's theology. The notion of speculative theology has frequently been employed to describe a theological style founded upon metaphysical philosophy. It seems pretty clear that Julian's somewhat meandering approach does not correspond to the philosophically influenced, analytically precise, and dialectical approach of medieval scholastic theology. However, my sense is that by using the word "speculative," Watson and Jenkins are not reflecting this technical definition. Rather, they are actually implying that Julian's theological style is an imaginative and highly original rereading of the nature of God, the created order, human identity, and how God interacts with humanity.[8]

In her illuminating study of Julian's theology, Joan Nuth describes it as womanly, synthetic, sensitive to pastoral needs, and based on life rather than on abstract thought. In other words, Julian's theology is not in the style of medieval scholastic theology based on formal questions and disputations. Rather, the foundation of Julian's theology is essentially intense and careful reflection over many years on her spiritual experiences. Nuth describes this as a theology of integration in which Julian's experience of God in the midst of her sickness and suffering, sophisticated reflection, and a trajectory of pastoral concern are brought together. Nuth also judges that Julian wrote a style of monastic theology in which scriptural reflection and resulting spiritual insight are the core. I have questions about this judgment because she does not base her theological reflections explicitly on the monastic style of meditative scriptural exegesis. Nor, as we have already noted, does Julian make any other references to monastic values or to a monastic lifestyle. Nuth suggests that Julian's theology may be tentatively described as "systematic" in the broad sense that Julian focuses on the chief Christian doctrines and has an original theological system, involving rigorous speculation. However, it is certainly not systematic in contemporary terms because it does not have a predominantly philosophical basis. Nuth believes that Julian had a thorough grasp of key aspects of Augustine's theology although this does not necessarily mean that she had direct access to Augustine's writings or had read them. I agree with both aspects of this judgment.[9]

In another important study of Julian and her writings, the late Grace Jantzen notes that no aspect of Julian's theology is divorced from her original vision of the crucified Christ (the First Revelation) that she experienced while on her sickbed. Jantzen is clear that everything else about Julian's teachings is based on this central theme of Christ's Passion. I will return to this insight later. Like Nuth, Jantzen judges that Julian does not employ the medieval scholastic theological method. Rather, hers is an "integrated theology" that brings her religious experiences, the concerns of daily life, and theological reflection together into an integrated whole. The organizing thread, developed from her vision of the Passion, is that love is God's meaning. The essential link to the cross means that Julian's understanding of love is not sentimental but robust and gritty. Julian's Long Text understands theological doctrines in the context of three criteria. The first of these is natural reasoning ("in my sight"). Then there is what is commonly taught by the Church ("Holy Church teaches"). Finally, there is the inward – and challenging – operation of God's Spirit within Julian's process of understanding. For Julian, the intellect is never separated from love. Reason is natural in the sense of being part of our nature but this is not contrasted with "the spiritual," which is also a dimension of our nature, grounded in God. Finally, Jantzen describes Julian's theology as practical theology in the sense of placing a clear emphasis on practicality.[10]

In his more recent book of theological and philosophical reflections provoked by reading Julian, Denys Turner agrees with Nuth and Jantzen that Julian's approach is very different from the medieval scholastic method of *quaestio* and *disputatio*. However, he also suggests that Julian's method is unlike monastic theology, whose starting point and method are explicitly scriptural, based on *lectio divina* which embraces meditative "rumination" upon scripture. In contrast, Julian's theological reflections are "a process of progressive intensification and complex elaboration of particular and personal experience."[11] Turner also underlines that Julian's theology is intentionally incomplete because, theologically speaking, only the eschatological vision can "complete" our understanding of God.[12] This incompleteness is a subject to which I shall return at the end of this book. Finally, Turner interestingly describes Julian as an "anchoritic theologian." That is, her theology is inextricably linked to a place of unlikeness or exile. In that sense it is liminal theology conceived on a boundary or a "between place." Of course, this notion depends on believing that Julian's Long Text was not completed before she became an anchoress. Unfortunately Turner does not substantially discuss Julian in relation to her historical context and so this issue is not addressed. As with everything else about Julian we have no certainty about the date when she entered the anchorhold. The earliest evidence of her status as an anchoress is in a will dating to 1393–4. However, the contemporary scholarly consensus is that, whether or not she began the first draft of the Long Text before entering the anchorhold, Julian's text probably went through several revisions and developments and may not have been completed until the second decade of the fifteenth century. On this basis, Turner's description of Julian as "anchoritic theologian" seems reasonable and illuminating.[13]

Bernard McGinn, in the fifth volume of his major project on the history of Western Christian mysticism, is clear that Julian of Norwich is deeply theological.[14] He highlights her remarkable theology of the Trinity, her distinctive theodicy, a soteriology that undercuts "satisfaction" models of redemption, and a nuanced understanding of our union with God ("oneing" in Julian's language). This union originates in humanity's eternal existence in God and human destiny is the completion of this "oneing" by enjoying endless bliss. Denys Turner also gives a great deal of attention to Julian's theodicy. Personally, I have some questions about using the term "theodicy" in its classic sense in relation to Julian. I believe it can be misleading. I will explain this further in Chapter 5, Love is God's Meaning, where I will discuss Julian's creative theology of the Trinity and her Christology. McGinn is cautious about the designation "systematic" in relation to Julian's theology, although this depends on how we define "systematic." He is certainly clear that she does not write medieval scholastic theology and he also does not believe that Julian writes monastic theology because she does not present her teaching as meditative exegesis of scripture. Rather, McGinn sees Julian's theology as "relational" in the sense of holistic. He also makes reference to Jantzen's description of Julian's "integrated theology." Each aspect of her thought interlocks with and implies the others. Clearly, McGinn understands Julian's theology as mystical. He also describes it as vernacular theology in the fullest sense – that is, not only written in the English vernacular but also addressed to an everyday audience. Indeed, it is the earliest significant theological text in Middle English rather than in Latin. However, it is also addressed to, and focused upon, the needs of a "vernacular" (that is, everyday) audience of spiritually minded literate Christians rather than at professional theologians, clergy, or monastics.

Finally, in his 2014 Julian Lecture given in Norwich, the theologian and former Archbishop of Canterbury, Rowan Williams, interestingly refers to Julian's "anti-theology." That is, Julian's theology is intended to lead the reader into contemplative theological awareness rather than focus on abstract theological formulae or argumentation. Williams is not suggesting that Julian is essentially a devotional writer or that she is uninterested in Christian doctrines. Rather, her deeply reflective "anti-theology" counters what Williams refers to as "unthinking theology." That approach suggests that the purpose of theology is essentially to establish straight-forward "answers." However, in contrast, the foundations of Julian's theological reflections are "revelations." These imply that "we have been impelled by the act of God into this unfolding process of reflection and growth."[15]

In terms of my own interpretation of Julian's theological style, I agree with other scholars that Julian was neither a scholastic theologian nor a monastic theologian. Rather, I believe that it is more useful to think of Julian's theology in three other important ways. First, it is mystical theology in the classic sense. Second, it is vernacular theology that is symptomatic of an emerging "age of the vernacular." This notion has a number of dimensions which I will explain further. Finally, in describing Julian's theological style we need to give prominence to Julian's own stated purpose in relation to her urgent and transformative theological message. In this context, Julian's theological method should also be considered as a form of practical-pastoral theology, no doubt responding, albeit implicitly, to the complex cultural, social, and religious realities of her immediate audience.

However, before briefly exploring these categories, it is important to underline that Julian's theology was thoroughly embedded in scripture.

Scriptural Sources

Scripture is part of the very texture of Julian's thinking. In her description of a visit to Julian for spiritual counsel, Margery Kempe notes that Julian cited the scriptures. As Julian herself says in the Long Text, chapter 32, "Our faith is founded on God's word." Julian does not simply refer to biblical characters or to scriptural anecdotes, for example David, Mary Magdalen, Peter and

Paul, and the apostle Thomas (chapter 38). Many of these could have come from listening to popular preaching or from the religious art with which Julian was familiar. There are also occasional quotations. For example in chapter 15 she says "And in the time of joy I could have said with St Paul: Nothing shall separate me from the love of Christ; and in the pain I could have said with St Peter: Lord save me, I am perishing."

At other moments, Julian embeds scriptural phraseology or allusions in her texts in an apparently seamless way. A particularly rich example is her exemplum known as the parable of a Lord and a Servant (chapter 51). Clearly her reference to the story of Adam and the Fall echoes the Book of Genesis, chapter 3. The figure of the servant is both rich and ambiguous. The image of falling into a ditch and being wounded immediately suggests the story of Adam. However, the image of the servant as beloved and chosen also seems to echo the servant songs and image of a "suffering servant" in the Book of Isaiah, especially the chapters now known as Deutero-Isaiah. For example, there is "Here is my servant, whom I uphold, my chosen, in whom my soul delights" (Isaiah 42, 1–7). There is also the ambiguity and pain of being Yahweh's servant in Isaiah 49, 1–7. The servant was "a man of suffering and acquainted with infirmity" yet will "be exalted and lifted up" (see Isaiah 52, 13 to Isaiah 53, 12). The "man of sorrow" in 53, 3 echoes the experience of Julian's servant but also points to the connection in the Christian mind between Isaiah's suffering servant and the person of Christ, God's servant who must suffer and be rejected (Gospel of Luke 9, 22). It is now thought by scholars that Julian's chapter 51 may have significant Pauline echoes. The willingness of the servant to leave himself aside to do the will of his lord may be an allusion to the kenotic hymn in Philippians 2 where Christ Jesus, though at one with God, the Lord ("in the form of God," verse 6), emptied himself, taking the form of a servant. This fits with the fact that in chapter 51 Julian's servant is shown to be both Adam and Christ. There also seem to be a number of allusions to the Letter to the Ephesians, chapter 5 and to 1 Corinthians, chapter 12 and to Christ as the head of the body and Christians as his members. More controversially, the inability of the servant in the ditch to see the lord who has followed him or to feel the lord's continuing love may be an echo of Jesus Christ on the cross crying "My God, my God why have you forsaken me?" (Gospel of Matthew 27, 46 and Gospel of Mark 15, 34).

Mystical Theology

If we are to describe Julian's theology as mystical, what exactly does this imply? The eminent Belgian Catholic philosopher, Louis Dupré, who developed an interest in what might be called a mystical experience of "the self," suggested that "The mystics start their spiritual journey from within, and that is the only place where the believer *must* begin, whether he wants to or not."[16] As we shall see in a later chapter, this inwardness does not compromise the essence of Christian theological anthropology, which involves self-giving rather than self-focused interiority. This inwardness is also radically open to a mysterious God who draws human beings into the unknown. What Dupré critiqued is the failure of conventional theology to be touched by the reality of God rather than limiting itself to abstract and systematic attempts to analyse God's nature. In that sense, Dupré's "from within" is not self-preoccupation but implies the courage actually to encounter God and to be radically changed by this encounter. What is conventionally termed "mystical theology" is an alternative (and subversive) approach to theological reflection based not simply on intellectual thought but also on the vulnerable practice of contemplation. This means taking seriously the witness of those theological thinkers like Julian of Norwich who in their engagement with the immediacy of God risk the experience of "rupture"; that is, in the words of Bernard McGinn, the "surprise and amazement that opens up new possibilities in spiritual experience."[17]

Julian's rich theological reflection is founded upon her deep mystical-visionary experience and, according to her own testimony, intense ongoing spiritual reflection over a period of many years. This led Julian to a transformed perception of God, and of God's relationship with humanity. Without her deep encounter with God, and the sense that she had been "shown" vitally important insights through that encounter, Julian would not have been inspired to write theology at all.

From its patristic origins, not least in the central figure of the anonymous sixth-century theologian known as Pseudo-Dionysius, mystical theology has consistently sought a different approach to theological reflection from one founded purely upon analytical-philosophical ways of thinking.[18] This is partly a process, as with Julian, of engaging the process of theology with a lived experience of God and with the on-going practice of the Christian life including exposure to the scriptures, participation in the liturgy and sacraments, and through belonging to "the fellowship of the mystery"; that is, the Church. The very heart of all theology was mystical. "Doctrinal theology" arose from this basis rather than from speculative reasoning in isolation.[19]

From the patristic period until the development of the so-called "new theology" of scholasticism around the twelfth century, theology was a single unified enterprise. By unified I do not simply mean that there was an absence of the later distinctions between theological disciplines, such as doctrine, moral theology (ethics), Church history, sacramental theology, and so on. Rather, the unity of theology overall implied that intellectual reflection or speculation, the practice of contemplation, living the Christian life, and pastoral practice were ideally a seamless whole. Critically, to be "a theologian" meant that a person (for example, Julian of Norwich) had contemplated the mystery of God and had an experience of faith and practice (especially exposure to scripture and participation in the liturgy) on which to reflect. Knowledge of divine things was inseparable from the love of God, deepened in prayer. For Augustine, for example in his *De Trinitate*, Books XII–XIV, God is known not by *scientia* (analytical knowledge) but by *sapientia* (a contemplative knowledge of love and desire). This approach to theology is richly illustrated in the writings of Julian.

It is important to underline that the notion of "mysticism" as a distinctive reality based on purely subjective experience is not overtly present in patristic and medieval contexts, including Julian. The French Jesuit interdisciplinary scholar and important historian of Christian mysticism, Michel de Certeau, can be credited with establishing that such a distinct category associated with subjective religious experience, largely detached from the wider Christian life and from Church teaching, originated only in the later sixteenth century and the seventeenth century. It was associated with the major religious, social, and cultural changes of the time.[20]

Julian of Norwich is a mystical theologian in the sense that her theology expresses an *intelligentia amoris*, a knowledge born of loving God and experiencing the love of God. Julian's theological journey depends on her pursuit of a deeply contemplative Christian life which led at some stage to her becoming a solitary or anchoress. The starting point of Julian's theology, as with so much medieval mystical writing, is her experience of God in the midst of sickness and suffering and her sense that the essential icon of God is the figure of the suffering Jesus on the Cross.

As a consequence, Julian's mystical theology maintains an ambiguous balance of a theology of "knowing" ("positive" or kataphatic theology) and a theology of "unknowing" ("negative" or apophatic theology) both in relation to the transcendent mystery of God-as-Trinity and in relation to the core of human identity which is irrevocably united with God. These themes will be developed further in later chapters.

Vernacular Theology

The historical context within which Julian of Norwich wrote her texts is often described as "the age of the vernacular." This was a century when, as I noted in the previous chapter, there was a gradual shift from writing literature only in Latin or Norman-French to using Middle English as a literary language rather than simply the spoken language of the lower social classes. It was also a time when there was a growing interest in religious ideas and greater access to the bible and other religious literature among an increasingly literate laity, particularly the new merchant classes in the expanding world of commercial towns and cities like Norwich.

However, Julian may be described as a vernacular theologian not simply because she used Middle English prose rather than Latin but also because her vision and projected audience is democratic rather than limited to a spiritual or theological elite. In her own words, "In all this I was greatly moved in love towards my fellow Christians ['mine evenchristen'], that they might all see and know the same as I saw, for I wished it to be a comfort to them, for all this vision was shown for all men" (chapter 8).

The phrase "fellow Christians" or "my fellow Christians" appears regularly throughout Julian's text. The first mention of this key word is at the end of chapter 6 where Julian underlines that the lesson of God's tender love for us is the foundation of everything that was revealed to her. Her teaching addressed to everyone is that this knowledge should provoke "the soul" – that is, each human being – to be less self-preoccupied and to be filled with love for its fellow Christians. In chapter 8 Julian is very clear that her intention in writing is that all her fellow Christians "might see and know the same as I saw" and that "everything that I say about me I mean to apply to all my fellow Christians."

This additional dimension of the concept of "vernacular" is defined by Denys Turner as "demotic" theology – that is, non-formulaic, non-hierarchical in tone, and in a language intelligible to ordinary people.[21] This demotic style is underlined by Julian's frequent use of everyday images. Thus, in chapter 6 (as it appears in the Paris manuscript) God's providential care is shown even in the physical provision in the human body of a means of expelling food waste; in other words, defecation. Her vision of the copious bleeding of Jesus in chapter 7 is compared to the drops of water that fall from the eaves of a house during rain showers and also to the herring scales that would have been familiar to people living in a fishing port such as Norwich. The following chapter 8 echoes the imagery of chapter 5 in suggesting that all that is made is "little" when compared to God. Yet Julian also firmly underlines that the world that we know and all creation is beautiful and good. Again, perhaps echoing the familiar experience of the fishermen and other sailors of the port of Norwich, chapter 10 uses the imagery of being in the depths of the sea. Whatever its origins, this imagery was intended by Julian as a way of reassuring people that wherever they are, God is continually with them and they are wholly safe. The imagery of "bountiful waters" on the earth is also used in chapter 12 as a reminder of God's care. A final example is the use of the word "poynte" or "pointe" in chapter 11: "I saw God in a pointe." While Colledge and Walsh translate this as "an instant of time," it seems clear from the wider context of the chapter that this is a spatial image. As Julian herself comments, "by which sight I saw that he is in al thing." God is present in everything, however small it may be. God is the "within" of all things. This develops Julian's vision of existence first stated in chapter 1. God "has made everything that is…," "He does and brings about all that is done." As noted in the previous chapter, in her practical commentary on Julian of Norwich, Ritamary Bradley also suggested that Julian may have been thinking of needle-point or lace-point. The metaphor of "a pointe" would then suggest God's presence in even the smallest stitch that goes towards making up the final pattern of the cloth.[22]

Pastoral Theology

Finally, in describing Julian's theological style we need to give prominence to Julian's own stated purpose in relation to her urgent and transformative theological message. In this context, Julian's theological method should also be considered as a form of practical-pastoral theology, responding to the needs of her readers in their cultural, social, and religious contexts. Julian's vernacular theology has a clear pastoral purpose. In broad terms, its goal is to underline for her readers, all her "fellow Christians," a new understanding of human living in the everyday world as well as a revolutionary understanding of the nature of God and how God engages with this world, particularly through Christ. Her initial vision is of the Passion: God in Christ suffering for all humanity on the cross. However, later in her text she develops the rich imagery of Christ as Mother. The interrelated Christological and Trinitarian dimensions of this theology will be developed more substantially in Chapter 4, Love is God's Meaning.

The foundation of Julian's pastoral theology is her explanation of the work of Christ our Mother. The work of Christ our Mother is developed particularly in Long Text chapters 60, 61, and 63. All this was added to Julian's writings after she was led to understand the meaning of the exemplum of a Lord and a Servant which became chapter 51 of the Long Text. Essentially, the theme of motherhood expresses the essence of Christ's action for humankind. That is, it expresses why he took on human nature in the Incarnation, and also the "economy" of redemption. In chapter 60 Christ's motherhood is described in terms of mercy and grace.

> Our Great God.....arrayed and prepared himself in this humble place [Mary's womb], all ready in our poor flesh, himself to do the service and the office of motherhood in everything.

Equally important:

> The mother's service is nearest, readiest and surest.... No one ever
> might or could perform this office fully, except only him.

In general, Mother Jesus' love for humans is compared to the tenderness
and compassion that a human mother has towards her child.

Also in chapter 60, Julian compares the nourishment of the human soul
through the Eucharist to the nurturing function of motherhood. Mother
Jesus feeds us (as a human mother suckles her child) with the blessed
sacrament of the Eucharist. A mother also lays her child tenderly on her
breast while Mother Jesus opens up his wounded side to draw us in.
Overall, Julian compares Jesus's suffering in the Passion with the pains of
childbirth. In this selfless act, Mother Jesus had "born us for bliss."

Yet in chapter 61, a mother may sometimes suffer a child to fall for its
own learning and benefit. Yet Mother Jesus never suffers "any kind of
peril to come to her child." Equally, Mother Jesus "may never suffer us
who are his children to perish." Mother Jesus wants us to act like children
with a human mother: running to him in need and calling for help.

In chapter 63, the idea of Christ our Mother taking on human fleshli-
ness and giving of himself is compared to the human mother giving of
her bodily self to the fetus in the womb. Overall, the "office" of Mother
Jesus is to ease us and to save us.

By way of conclusion, I think that it is important to underline that, as
Grace Jantzen suggests, we may describe Julian's theology as "practical"
in that there is a clear emphasis on the practicalities of human life.
However, in her writings Julian does not fall into the trap of seeking to be
simplistically "relevant."

The Heart of Julian's Theology

What is the heart of Julian's theology? Classic approaches to what may be
called "doctrinal theology" are not really present in Julian in any organized sense. In terms of the dimensions of theology on which Julian
reflects, she explores profoundly the nature of God-as-Trinity but in
ways that are founded upon her Christology at the heart of which lies her
visions of Christ's suffering on the cross. Other important themes are
those of sin and salvation, her theology of human identity (theological
anthropology), and her distinctly non-apocalyptic eschatology. While
Church and sacraments are mentioned, these themes are not developed
at length. Ecclesiology is only important to Julian in relation to the
authority of Holy Church and its teachings in the light of Julian's

challenging visions and alternative insights. She battles away with the tension between orthodoxy (what "Holy Church" teaches) and what she believes she has been led to see by God. Notable examples are her reflections in the Long Text chapters 9 and 10. Thus in chapter 9 she affirms that "I am sure that there are many who never had revelations or visions, but only the common teaching of Holy Church, who love God better than I." And again, "in everything I believe as Holy Church preaches and teaches." Julian does not deal with Church organization, hierarchical order, or sacramental theology in any technical sense. However, there is an extensive consideration in the Fourteenth Revelation of the nature of prayer as a relationship with God, but with no mention of actual spiritual practices.

The Centrality of Christ's Passion

In my judgment, in terms of describing the heart of Julian's theology there are three vital keys. First of all, Julian's initial visionary experience of Jesus' suffering and Passion is the provocation for her theological reflections and for everything that she subsequently writes. Towards the beginning of her Long Text (chapter 3), Julian describes how she lay gravely ill and apparently dying aged thirty and a half. Her local priest was sent for and he brought a crucifix to place by her bed in order to comfort her. This led her to be filled with a recollection of the Passion. In chapter 4, she describes seeing blood running from under the crown of thorns, "hot and flowing freely and copiously, a living stream." Yet, she says, suddenly the Trinity "filled my heart full of the greatest joy." This leads her to affirm the Trinitarian nature of God as our lover, joy, and bliss. Here is the first of a series of rich reflections on God-as-Trinity that permeate her text and which I will develop further in Chapter 4 on Julian's theology of God. Her imagery of the suffering Christ continues in subsequent chapters. Thus in chapter 5, at the same time as she continues to see the bleeding from Christ's head, she is shown "a spiritual sight" of God's love. She uses the image of clothing – God is our clothing wrapping us in love. She is also shown the famous image of something small, "no bigger than a hazelnut," which she is led to understand is creation, "everything which is made." This is created, loved and preserved by God. In chapter 6 Christ's passion and wounds are intimately linked to an insight about God's goodness and providence. In subsequent chapters Julian's spiritual vision – in other words, the heart of her spiritual insights and the source of her teaching – continues to be linked to the "bodily" imagery of bleeding as she explicitly affirms in chapter 7. "And during all the time that our Lord showed me this spiritual vision which I have now described, I saw the bodily vision of the copious bleeding of the head persist." What is critically important here is her further comment in chapter 4 that "where Jesus appears the blessed Trinity is understood, as I see it." In her vision of the suffering Christ lies the source of all that she needs to see and know about God, about created reality, and about the human condition. In chapter 18 she comes to understand in the image of the suffering Christ the "great unity between Christ and us." In other words, in Christ's pain is his identification with human suffering.

In chapter 19 Julian describes how she wanted to look away from the crucifix. She felt secure contemplating the cross but she experienced an apparently friendly suggestion "to my reason" that she should take her eyes off the crucifix by her sickbed to "look up the heaven to his Father." She rejects this option because, as she addresses Jesus on the cross, she affirms powerfully "No, I cannot, for you are my heaven." She does not desire to come to heaven "any other way than by him." In the following chapter, chapter 20, Julian effectively states that she came to understand that all she needed to know about God, "the glorious divinity," was to be found in the image of the suffering Christ.

Julian's Triadic Theology

A second vital key to Julian's theology is her regular use of various triads. Beyond Julian's explicit Trinitarian theology, it is worth noting in reference to her broader theological style that she employs three-fold imagery (that is, triads) in a range of other ways. Without question her overall use of three-fold imagery echoes her rich theology of the Trinity as the in-built meaning of everything. Indeed, it is reasonable to describe Julian's theology as in some sense triadic overall. A brief summary of examples will serve to illustrate this point.

Thus, in chapter 2, Julian describes how, before her revelations, she had desired three graces – a recollection of the Passion, bodily sickness, and, by God's gift, three wounds. These wounds were true contrition, loving compassion, and a longing for God. In chapter 5, Julian describes being shown "something small, no bigger than a hazelnut, lying in the palm of my hand." This proves to be "everything which is made." Julian notes that this image of all creation had three properties: that God made it, that God loves it, and that God preserves it. In chapter 7 when Julian had a "bodily vision of the copious bleeding of the [that is, Christ's] head" she notes that three things occurred to her. First, the drops were round like pellets. Second, "they were round like herring's scales as they spread" and, finally, "they were like raindrops off a house's eaves, so many that they could not be counted." In chapter 9, Julian notes that her revelations were "shown" in three parts – bodily vision, words formed in her understanding, and spiritual vision. Towards the end of chapter 10, Julian affirms that God desires that we receive three gifts: that we should seek joyfully and happily, that we wait for God steadfastly, and, third, that we have great trust. In chapter 13 after being shown how the fiend [the devil] is overcome by the Passion, Julian says to her companions around her sickbed that in this process she sees three things: sport and scorn and seriousness. In chapter 14 God shows Julian the "three degrees of bliss" which every soul will have in heaven: honor and thanks from God, that this honor will be revealed to everyone else in heaven, and joy that will last for evermore. In chapter 39 Julian affirms that all souls will come to heaven by three means: by contrition in which they are made clean, by compassion by which they are made ready, and finally by true longing for God in which they are made worthy. Finally, in chapter 58 Julian explicitly links her theology of the Trinity to human existence. "For all our life consists of three: In the first we have our being, and in the second we have our increasing, and in the third we have our fulfilment. The first is nature, the second is mercy, the third is grace."

Love as God's Meaning

The third vital key to the heart of Julian's theology appears at several points in her Long Text, for example in chapter 6, but most clearly in the final chapter 86. On one level these references indicate that after many years of struggle and questioning, she was given the spiritual understanding that "our Lord's meaning is love," and only love. For Julian, theologically speaking, everything is subordinated to the nature of God as love, the nature of human beings as irrevocably loved and just as irrevocably united to God in their essential substance. In particular, as we shall see in later chapters, Julian's insights into sin, salvation (soteriology), and eschatology are predicated on this fundamental vision of a God of love. Having said this, Julian is clear that this message of love is not easy to grasp. In chapter 73, she notes that God wants us "in all things to have our contemplation and our delight in love." However, "it is about this knowledge that we are most blind, for some of us believe that God is almighty and may do everything, and that he is all wisdom and can do everything, but that he is all love and wishes to do everything, there we fail." Running through Julian's theological reflections is a deep sense of reassurance. This pervades the whole of the Thirteenth Revelation and is further reinforced in the Fifteenth and Sixteenth Revelations. As chapter 1 of the Long Text summarises the matter, "Here [that is, in the Thirteenth Revelation] he says: Behold and see, for by the same power, wisdom and goodness that

I have done all this [creating all things], by the same power wisdom and goodness I shall make all things well which are not well, and you will see it."

Julian's Apophatic and Eschatological Theology

Finally, on another level, the final chapter 86 of Julian's Long Text also suggests that her teachings are necessarily open-ended. "This book is begun by God's gift and his grace, but it is not yet performed, as I see it." Julian's theological journey is necessarily incomplete because authentic theology takes us to the boundaries of the knowable: "a marvellous great mystery hidden in God," as Julian suggests in chapter 27. This is both a reference to Julian's incomplete understanding and also to the necessarily on-going process of God's relationship with humanity which will find completion only in "heavenly joy."

For all its emphasis on her God-given visions and her rich use of imagery, Julian's theology is at the same time a theology of "seeing" (that is, of knowing) in a new way but also a theology of "unknowing" at the deepest level. In short, Julian's writings are a balance of positive (kataphatic) theology and negative (apophatic) theology. Julian's writings are famously fully of imagery and she is also clear in making certain affirmations about the nature of God. However, Julian is also clear that in her revelations she has not been given any complete or definitive knowledge about God. As we have seen, Julian's overall theological process is not a form of analytical reasoning and her affirmations about God are not a matter of reaching certain conclusions through logical deduction. Rather, in her revelations Julian senses what might be called a "surplus of meaning" that she cannot conclusively understand but which she feels the need to return to again and again over many years. In Julian's own words, after she received her revelations "I desired many times to know in what was our Lord's meaning." As her final chapter 86 makes clear, more than 15 years later she received further spiritual insight. "Know it well, love was his meaning.... Remain in this and you will know more of the same. But you will never know different, without end."

As a revelation of love, Julian's text is not a consecutive and highly structured narrative. On the contrary, it is a meditative circling around the key themes of her teaching that are aimed at all her fellow Christians. For Julian, any one theme she presents immediately calls up other important issues. In addition, there is an on-going connection between the themes of time and eternity in her text. What does it mean to learn that "all manner of thing will be well"? God continually reminds her that God does not see things in sequential terms or in terms of sharp distinctions between past, present and future. Consequently, there is necessarily an open-ended, unfulfilled, and eschatological core to Julian's theology and to what she seeks to teach her audience of fellow Christians. As Julian had herself been told by God, so she affirms that every one of her audience were to "remain in this" (that is, the realization that love is God's meaning) while "more of the same" was offered throughout life and finally given conclusively at the end of time.

Conclusion

It is true that Julian's Long Text does not merely describe her religious experiences but explains their theological meaning and implications. In the process, Julian touches on many of the most important themes and dimensions of Christian theology including the Trinity, Christology, grace, creation, anthropology, sin and redemption, and eschatology. However, she is not compiling a theological textbook. Julian reflects on various theological areas in order to communicate a multi-faceted and vital message to her fellow Christians about the true nature of God and of human beings "in God's sight."

Notes

1 See Thomas Merton, *Mystics and Zen Masters*, New York: The Noonday Press, Reprinted 1993, p 140.
2 See Janet Martin Soskice, *The Kindness of God: Metaphor, Gender, and Religious Language*, Oxford: Oxford University Press, 2008, p 126.
3 Soskice, *The Kindness of God*, p 131.
4 See, Brian Davies, *The Thought of Thomas Aquinas*, Oxford: Oxford University Press, 1993; Mary Clark, ed., *An Aquinas Reader: Selections from the Writings of Thomas Aquinas*, New York: Fordham University Press, 2000.
5 For a classic exposition of monastic theology, see Jean Leclercq OSB, *The Love of Learning and the Desire for God: A Study of Monastic Culture*, 3rd edition, English translation, New York: Fordham University Press, 1982, especially Chapter 9 "Monastic Theology."
6 See Edmund Colledge & James Walsh, eds., *A Book of Showings to the Anchoress Julian of Norwich*, Toronto: Pontifical Institute of Mediaeval Studies, 1978, Part One, Introduction Part IX "Theological Content of the Revelations," pp 59–198. Colledge & Walsh also offer a massive list of scriptural citations or echoes in Part Two, pp 779–788.
7 See Barry Windeatt, ed., *The Book of Margery Kempe*, London: Penguin Books, 1985, Chapter 18.

8 See Nicholas Watson & Jacqueline Jenkins, eds., *The Writings of Julian of Norwich*, University Park PA: The Pennsylvania State University Press, 2005, Preface, p ix and Introduction, pp 2–3.

9 Joan M. Nuth, *Wisdom's Daughter: The Theology of Julian of Norwich*, New York: Crossroad, 1991, Chapter 2 "Julian's Theology."

10 Grace Jantzen, *Julian of Norwich*, 2nd edition, London: SPCK 2000, Chapter 6 "Love was his meaning": Julian's Theological Method.

11 See Denys Turner, *Julian of Norwich, Theologian*, New Haven, CT: Yale University Press, 2011, p xi.

12 Turner, p xii.

13 See Turner, Chapter One "Julian the Theologian."

14 See Bernard McGinn, *The Varieties of Vernacular Mysticism: 1350–1550*, New York: Crossroad, 2012, Chapter 12 "Julian of Norwich: 'Love is oure lordes mening'."

15 See Rowan Williams, *Holy Living: The Christian Tradition for Today*, New York: Bloomsbury Continuum, 2017, Part Five: Ways of Knowing, Chapter 12: Julian of Norwich's Way.

16 Louis Dupré, "Spiritual life in a secular age," in *Daedalus* volume III, 1982, pp 21–31, quote from p 25.

17 See Bernard McGinn, "The future of past spiritual experiences," *Spiritus: A Journal of Christian Spirituality*, volume 15, issue 1, Spring 2015 pp 1–17, especially p 3. In using the term "rupture," McGinn draws explicitly upon the important writings on mysticism by Michel de Certeau, particularly his late work, *The Mystic Fable, Volume One: The Sixteenth & Seventeenth Centuries*, ET Chicago: University of Chicago Press, 1992.

18 For an accessible modern translation of the works of Pseudo-Dionysius, see C. Luibheid & O. Rorem, eds., *Pseudo-Dionysius: The Complete Works*, Classics of Western Spirituality, New York: Paulist Press, 1987. For further remarks on the approach of Pseudo-Dionysius to mystical theology, not least the balance between kataphatic and apophatic approaches, see Philip Sheldrake, *Spirituality and History: Questions of Interpretation and Method*, Revised edition, London: SPCK/Maryknoll, NY: Orbis Books 1995, pp 199–206.

19 For a brief summary of this approach to and understanding of theology as it would have impacted on Julian of Norwich, see Philip Sheldrake, *Spirituality and Theology: Christian Living and the Doctrine of God*, London: Darton, Longman & Todd, 1998/Maryknoll, NY: Orbis Books 1999, Chapter 2 "The Divorce of Spirituality and Theology," pp 33–64.

20 For a summary overview of de Certeau's approach to mysticism, see Philip Sheldrake, *Explorations in Spirituality: History, Theology and Social Practice*, Mahwah, NJ: Paulist Press, 2010, Chapter 6 "Mysticism and Social Practice: The Mystical and Michel de Certeau." For Michel de

Certeau's own writings on mysticism, see "'Mystique' au XVIIe siècle: Le probleme du language mystique," in his *L'Homme Devant Dieu: Mélanges offerts au Père Henri du Lubac*, Paris: Aubier, 1964, 2: 267–291; also de Certeau's essay in English translation "Mystic Speech" in his *Heterologies: Discourse on the Other*, Minneapolis, MN: University of Minnesota Press, 1995; and most importantly the first volume of de Certeau's *The Mystic Fable: The Sixteenth and Seventeenth Centuries*, Chicago, IL: University of Chicago Press, 1992.

21 Turner, p 3.

22 See Ritamary Bradley, *Julian's Way: A Practical Commentary on Julian of Norwich*, London: Harper Collins, 1992, pp 94–97.

Chapter 3

Parable of a Lord and a Servant

As a way of understanding some of the central theological themes in Julian's Long Text, I will first of all explore her famous parable of a Lord and a Servant as it is narrated and explained in chapter 51.[1] This is by far the longest chapter of the Long Text. In my view this parable is in important ways the heart of the Long Text and the key to Julian's major theological insights and teachings in what we must presume was the final, definitive version of her *A Revelation of Love*.

In chapter 45, Julian outlines her background problem, as a result of her visionary experience, of how to reconcile the "judgment of Holy Church" that "sinners sometimes deserve blame and wrath" with the fact that "I could not see these two in God." However, "to all this I never had any other answer than a wonderful example of a lord and a servant, as I shall tell later, and that was very mysteriously revealed." By "example" Julian means an *exemplum* of the kind that medieval preachers used to illustrate their message.

The Exemplum and Lordship

The genre of *exempla*, or "examples," was a rhetorical device and a legacy of the classical world. There, the category of "examples" or illustrations, was originally used by political or legal orators and writers such as Suetonius and Plutarch. Up to the early thirteenth century, the use of an *exemplum* tended to be by Christian moralists and was an instrument of edification. This usually revolved round the imitation of an individual, particularly Jesus Christ, whose life story was the quintessential "example" for Christians of virtue and religious practice. Thereafter, the genre became associated more with a new style of preaching that suited the needs of a society and culture increasingly dominated by the expanding urban classes. Collections of *exempla* were produced to assist preachers. An "example" might be an anecdote, whether brief or extensive, like

Julian of Norwich: "In God's Sight" – Her Theology in Context, First Edition. Philip Sheldrake.
© 2019 John Wiley & Sons Ltd. Published 2019 by John Wiley & Sons Ltd.

Julian's chapter 51. It might sometimes be a real story or perhaps it was an allegorical fable or parable; again, as in chapter 51. Either way, such rhetorical devices were used to inform, edify, persuade, and motivate the listeners. "Examples" were instruments of recollection and memory aimed at helping those who listened to them or who read them, as was the case with the parable of a Lord and a Servant, to recall a nourishing lesson that pointed forwards towards salvation. In that sense, the ultimate horizon of such spiritual or moral "examples" was eschatological. Indeed, such a horizon of ultimacy characterizes the conclusion to Julian's parable.[2]

A specific feature of Julian's *exemplum* or parable is the imagery of lordship and of service. This imagery is present only in the Long Text and is anticipated in earlier chapters. It also echoes important social values in Julian's changing times. As early as the First Revelation (chapter 7), through the medium of her bodily vision of the "copious bleeding of the head" of Jesus on the cross, Julian found strength through her realization that the Lord God, while rightly revered and feared, "is so familiar and so courteous." Julian goes on to reflect that the greatest gift a great lord can offer a servant is to be familiar. "See, what greater honour and joy could this noble lord give me than to demonstrate to me, who am so little, this wonderful familiarity?" The point is that this is a greater joy than being given "great gifts" in the sense of money or other material presents. This thought is echoed strongly in the parable. Again in chapter 14, Julian's "understanding was lifted up into heaven." There she sees God as a lord "in his own house" – yet, a lord who despite his status appears to take no position of rank but hosts a splendid banquet for "all his friends," "very familiarly and courteously."

The themes of familiarity and courtesy on the part of a lord, rather than mere exploitation of servants, were beginning to become aspects of Julian's surrounding social culture. In my judgment, it is likely that this had some impact on Julian's theological insights and imagery. The status of nobility increasingly moved from the older feudal, rural, warrior class to an increasingly urban – and one might say, urbane – aristocracy and gentry. "Courtesy," a word used regularly by Julian in relation to God and not merely in reference to the lord of the parable, connects with "courtliness" – the new code of good manners that was becoming more apparent in urban life. This is not just a matter of being polite but also involved respect, kindness, and consideration. Courtesy also has the implication of generosity of spirit because until shortly before Julian's time it would not have been expected of lords in their relationship with servants. The exploitation of servants was slowly being replaced by a culture of care. Conversely, the ideal for servants was that their relationship with a lord should be one of attachment, even love, albeit shown appropriately according to one's social station.

Yet, in the parable of a Lord and a Servant, it may be thought that Julian is somewhat unconventional in idealizing some kind of personal and unbreakable bond between the lord and the servant. So, when the servant fails to return from his errand, he is searched for rather than simply replaced. In that sense, reflecting the equality of the servant Son (the second Adam) with the Lord God, the social inequality of a human lord and servant is radically transgressed. Importantly, therefore, it is the inner Trinitarian relationships and the way these are reflected in the status of humankind before God that become the hermeneutical key to the parable.

The Parable

It seems that the narrative of lord and servant formed part of Julian's original visions and inner experience. However, it perplexed her so much that she did not include it in what is known as the Short Text. Julian's perplexity is provoked most strongly by the previous Thirteenth Revelation where she is led to a new insight about sin and how God views sin. However, having said this, Julian appears to have been challenged as early as her First Revelation or showing, for example as expressed in her chapter 9: "For in mankind which will be saved is comprehended all, that is to say all that is made and the maker of all." Julian's ambiguous reaction is abundantly clear. "I speak of those who will be saved, for at this time God showed me no one else. But in everything I believe as Holy Church preaches and teaches." Later, in chapter 32 Julian struggles to hold onto God's promise that "Every kind of thing will be well." This contrasts with her perception that "there are many deeds which in our eyes are so evilly done and lead to such great harm that it seems to us impossible that any good result could ever come of them." Equally, there is "one article of our faith…that many creatures will be damned" such as fallen angels and people who either "die out of faith of Holy Church" or "who live unchristian lives and so die out of God's love."

In the section before the parable, chapter 50, Julian returns to the subject of her continual struggle to balance her consciousness that we sin with her visions and inward understanding (which she believed was given by God) that God imputes no blame to humankind. Apart from the fact that this insight clearly went against her own assumptions, Julian is deeply concerned about how such an understanding fits with the formal teaching of the Church. Chapter 50 ends with Julian's anguished cry for help. "Ah, Lord Jesus, king of bliss, how shall I be comforted, who will tell me and teach me what I need to know, if I cannot at this time see it in you?"

According to the beginning of chapter 51, Julian was answered "very mysteriously" by a "wonderful example of a lord who has a servant." God also "gave me sight for the understanding of them both." Julian indicates that this was shown "doubly"; that is, it was manifested to her on two levels. There was a spiritual vision in bodily form, that is an imaginary vision. Then there was a more spiritual vision without bodily form – a deeper intellectual and spiritual understanding. Equally, Julian summarizes three stages of her understanding and therefore, presumably, of her composition of a final version of the text. "And therefore I must now tell of three attributes through which I have been somewhat consoled." The word "attributes" as used in the Colledge and Walsh modern English edition translates the Middle English words "thre properties," or ways of learning or modes of knowing. The first is the beginning of the teaching received at the time of Julian's original visions. The second is the inward instruction that Julian had received since then. Finally, there is the capacity to see as a whole the essential insight revealed in the parable, "from beginning to end." That is, Julian is enabled to reach a unified sense of the parable and its meaning.

Julian's parable narrates a story of actions but in which every detail of, for example, the stance of the characters, their way of gazing, and their appearance has a specific meaning. The two central characters are a lord and a servant. The lord sits "in rest and in peace" while the servant stands respectfully before the lord, ready to do his bidding. The parable proceeds with the lord sending his servant off on an errand, "to do his will." Out of love the servant rushes away at great speed. However, in his haste he promptly falls into "a slade"– that is a ditch or a hollow. As a result the servant is seriously hurt but "the most mischefe" (the worst damage) that Julian sees in him is that he could not turn his face to look up to see his loving lord who was close by and therefore there was a "failing of comfort." Instead, the servant acted as someone who for the moment was "ful febil and unwise" – that is, weak and stupid – because he could only focus on how badly he felt and the fact that it persisted. This resulted in seven great pains. These are described in physical and psychological terms and do not appear to echo references in other medieval texts to the seven deadly sins.[3] The pains experienced by the servant are severe bruising, clumsiness of his body, weakness caused by these two, being blinded in his reason and perplexed in his mind so that he almost forgot his own love, the fact that he could not rise, the pain of lying alone with no apparent help at hand, and, finally, that the ditch was narrow and comfortless.

Interestingly, the medieval theologian Anselm of Canterbury also used the image of a servant and a ditch in his work *Cur Deus Homo*. This has led some people to speculate about whether Julian had read the writings of Anselm. Whether she had or not, Anselm and Julian treat the image in wholly different ways. According to Anselm:

> Suppose one should assign his slave a certain piece of work and should command him not to throw himself into a ditch, which he points out to him and from which he could not extricate himself; and suppose that the slave, despising his master's command and warning, throws himself into the ditch before pointed out, so as to be utterly unable to accomplish the work assigned; think you that his inability will at all excuse him for not doing his appointed work?[4]

Not only does the language offer a radically different understanding from Julian both of the nature of God and humanity as well as of their relationship, but in Anselm the servant's fall is an act of disobedience that makes him incapable of performing his tasks. The tone is one of moral culpability and guilt. Julian takes a completely different stance. In her parable the fall into the ditch is not an act of disobedience but the result of excessive desire to please. In that sense, Julian and Anselm also disagree about how they interpret the narrative of Adam's Fall in the Book of Genesis, chapter 3, and its implications for the status before God of humanity in general.[5]

Julian could not detect any fault in the servant. Nor did the lord impute any kind of blame. The only cause of the servant falling into the ditch was his good will and great desire to serve the lord out of love. Although he failed, fell, and was deeply wounded, "in spirit" the servant remained as fundamentally good as when he stood before the lord ready to do his will. As Julian notes, during all this time the "loving lord" looks on the servant tenderly rather than with judgment or condemnation. The way the lord looks at the fallen servant has two dimensions. Outwardly it is with compassion and pity. The deeper, inward, level of insight brought Julian to see how the lord rejoices over the noble restoring to which he will bring the servant. Julian then hears the lord put the injuries of the servant in the context of his loving service and ask rhetorically whether it is not reasonable that he should reward the servant for his fright and fear. Indeed, such reward would be better and more honorable for the servant than "his own health could have been." What Julian refers to as "an inward spiritual revelation" of the lord's meaning then led her to understand that the servant's eternal reward would be "above what he would have been if he had not fallen." Present woe will be turned into endless bliss.

Julian remains in a quandary about how to interpret what she understands to have been revealed to her as the answer to her struggles and uncertainties. However, a sufficient appreciation of the parable, its meaning, and its importance was not immediately clear. As she notes in chapter 51:

> For twenty years after the time of the revelation except for three months, I received an inward instruction, and it was this: You ought to take heed to all the attributes, divine and human, which were revealed in the example, though this may seem to you mysterious and ambiguous.

In this "instruction" Julian is granted an understanding that is not purely intellectual but is a deep spiritual insight that involved an ability to accept what she has been shown on all its levels. In summary, Julian is led to a wholly new perception about God, about human identity and about eternal union.

On this basis, the "inward instruction" and new insights which helped to clarify the parable or *exemplum* and therefore enabled her to include it in the Long Text took place around 1393. It would seem that, as a result of this new insight and instruction, Julian not only inserted the parable into the Long Text but may also have revised earlier parts of her text and also have been led to reflect on the famous image of the Motherhood of Jesus (and of God overall) in the chapters that follow on from the parable.

The Teaching of the Parable

The new "inward instruction" to Julian on the part of God leads her to understand the full implications of the parable narrative. She comes to see that the lord is God and that the servant, in the first instance, is Adam. She also came to see that in this one symbolic man and his fall is embraced how God regards all of humankind and their failings. "For in the sight of God all men are one man, and one man is all men." Her critical insight is that while the servant was "injured in his powers" his will (parallel to the "godly will" in chapter 37) is preserved in God's sight. Because of his injury the servant was prevented from knowing this will. The implication is that human sinfulness, the capacity to fall into ditches, is its own punishment. This punishment consists of our pain at an apparent separation from God and also an introspective self-loathing. "And then I saw that only pain blames and punishes, and our courteous Lord comforts and succours, and always he is kindly disposed to the soul, loving and longing to bring us to his bliss."

Then Julian sees the lord sitting on the ground, alone in the barren wilderness, rather than sitting on a throne. It eventually becomes clear as

Julian's chapter further unfolds that this image signifies that God seeks no alternative dwelling place except the human soul which was created to be God's own city and dwelling. Indeed, Julian comes to see that the human soul is the most pleasing of all God's works. Therefore, upon the ground, God waits "until the time when by his grace his beloved Son had brought back his city into its noble place of beauty by his hard labour." Later in the chapter when the Son has restored the city of the human soul to its true beauty, the lord once again sits down but now "in his noblest seat." The image of the lord waiting for humanity is also echoed in chapter 78 when Julian suggests that our Lord wishes us to know four vital things in relation to sin. "The fourth is how steadfastly he waits for us, and does not change his demeanour, for he wants us to be converted and united to him, as he is to us."

Julian initially sees the servant as Adam (and, in Adam, all of humanity) wearing laborer's clothes and wishing to do the one thing that would pay honor to the lord. This was to obtain a treasure "in the earth" which the lord loved. Julian wonders what this might be and is led to understand that "it is a food which is delicious and pleasing to the lord." Consequently, the servant was "to do the greatest labour and the hardest work there is." This is to be a gardener, digging and toiling, planting and making streams to run. Then the servant was to bring the fruit of his labor to the lord and to serve him. In a sense the lord has everything apart from the treasure in the earth. This treasure was founded in the lord but would only be really "to his honour" when the servant (humanity) had cultivated it and then brought it to him.

Thereafter, Julian comes to understand that the servant also represents the Son, the second person of the Trinity. So, when Adam (humanity) fell, God's Son also fell.

> Because of the true union which was made in heaven, God's Son could not be separated from Adam, for by Adam I understand all mankind. Adam fell from life to death, into the valley of this wretched world, and after that into hell. God's Son fell with Adam, into the valley of the womb of the maiden who was the fairest daughter of Adam, and that was to excuse Adam from blame in heaven and on earth.

The critical key to Julian's insight and teaching is that "in all this our good Lord showed his own Son and Adam as only one man."

When Julian affirms that "our good Lord Jesus" has taken upon himself all our blame she is not reproducing in some simple way a classic medieval "satisfaction" or "restitution" theory such as that proposed by Anselm of Canterbury. In that approach human sin defrauds God of the honor God is rightly due. However, Christ, through his death, takes on the role of "satisfying" our debt to God and of restoring God's honor. Without this we would merit punishment. However, in Julian it is quite clear that God is neither angry nor feels dishonored nor assigns blame to humanity. This is reinforced by her image of the lord sitting patiently in the wilderness. The only "blame" is our own self-blame in the context of a deep sense of failure. Thus, in Julian's narrative, the servant in the ditch can only feel pain and failure because he is self-preoccupied and therefore unable to see the lord looking on him with pity. "Blame" is part of our self-preoccupation and destructive self-image. This prevents us from seeing ourselves truly or from seeing God truly. In short, I am a failure, I am guilty, I am worthless. Thus, when Julian says "And so has our good Lord Jesus taken upon him all our blame," this is not the blame that God lays upon us. It is the unproductive sense of guilt and worthlessness that we lay upon ourselves and which makes us feel that we are unlovable, not least in the sight of God. Thus, the Son taking "upon him all our blame" is the redemption of our blinded sight and the healing of our false confusions that stand between us and God's love. In that sense, without being reductionist, redemption is an act of healing and compassion rather than simply God-as-judge showing clemency in response to human evil and sin.

Interestingly the double understanding of the servant in Julian's parable has the Son take on Adam's tunic (meaning his clothing) and take on "all our charge" – that is, all humanity's burden and responsibility as gardener of the earth. In medieval society, clothing was not merely a practical matter but had great social significance. What was worn differentiated each social class. In that sense, clothing was a form of uniform. Thus, in reference to the lord sitting in the wilderness Julian says that "His clothing was wide and ample and very handsome, as befits a lord." She also notes that the colour of the lord's clothing was azure blue. Culturally and socially this may reflect the fact that, while in the early Middle Ages poor-quality blue dyes were associated with the underclass, by the twelfth and thirteenth centuries ultramarine blue from lapis lazuli and also azurite blue became the dominant colours of the clothes of the rich. Both in clothing and in art, blue was used more and more as a noble or royal colour. In addition, with the appearance of blue in images of the Virgin Mary (seen as Queen of Heaven) as the colour of her mantle the colour also became an image of faithfulness and of what is truly spiritual. Consequently, in the light of a specifically spiritual symbolism, the blue clothing of the lord sitting on the ground in the wilderness stood for his faithfulness to humanity and his humility.[6]

The image of clothing continues to be used creatively in the parable. The Son wears Adam's "tunic." This becomes the image of the Son of God taking on human flesh and being permitted "to suffer all man's pain." "By his tunic being ready to go to rags and to tear is understood the rods and the scourges, the thorns and the nails, the pulling and the dragging and the tearing of his tender flesh, of which I had seen a part." This refers back to Julian's original vision of the suffering of Jesus on the cross when she was seriously ill. There is also a graphic parallel between the Son's suffering on the cross and the original narrative of the servant trapped in the ditch.

> And by the tossing about and writhing, the groaning and moaning, is understood that he could never with almighty power rise from the time that he fell into the maiden's womb until his body was slain and dead, and he had yielded his soul into the Father's hand, with all mankind for whom he had been sent.

Then, in the resurrection, "Adam's old tunic" was "made lovely." At the end of the chapter, as already noted, the lord no longer sits in the wilderness but on a noble seat. The servant-as-Son now stands immediately before the Father not as a servant "pitifully clothed" but "richly clothed in joyful amplitude" with a rich crown on his head. This crown is humankind. "We are his crown." Subsequently, the Son does not stand to the left of the Father as if he were a common laborer but "sits at the Father's right hand in endless rest and peace."

By comprehending in the image of the servant both Adam (humanity) and the Son of God, Julian understands not simply that the Fall and redemption are a single event "in God's sight" but that the creation and redemption of humanity are a simultaneous process. The first implies and contains the second.

The parable of a Lord and a Servant is presented as God's answer to Julian's various anxieties and questions about the experience of daily sinfulness yet her growing sense of God's lack of blame. The underlying problem or question is how these two realities of sinfulness and of God's lack of blame are compatible. In many respects this chapter and its narrative are pivotal to Julian's theological teaching and to her urgent sense of what needs to be understood by her fellow Christians. The focus of the parable is not so much on the classical theodicy question in a philosophical sense as on a radical realignment of Julian's understanding of the nature of God as our lover rather than our wrathful judge, of the meaning and value of creation as well as of human identity and of her radical soteriology or theology of sin and salvation. These themes will be explored in subsequent chapters.

Ways of Seeing

What Julian comes to understand is that there are two ways of seeing (that is, understanding) reality – "in my sight" and "in God's sight." As she suggests in chapter 10, in reference to her vision of the Passion, her "seeing" is natively partial and incomplete. "So I saw him [God] and sought him, and I had him and lacked him; and this is and should be our ordinary undertaking in this life, as I see it."

Following on from the ambiguities of chapter 32, already noted, in the following chapter 33 Julian still desires to see hell and purgatory. This is not to question her inherited beliefs but to understand them more clearly and therefore to live better. "But for all that I could wish, I could see nothing at all of this, except what has already been said in the fifth revelation." This refers to the devil being scorned by God. However, Julian also learns that she must be content both with what God conceals and what God reveals. If we do anything else "the further we shall be from knowing."

A key feature of the parable is that the fallen servant sees neither his loving lord "nor does he truly see what he himself is in the sight of his loving lord." One of the effects of the Fall is that we cannot see ourselves truly. Indeed, as Julian suggests in the next chapter (chapter 52) "God sees one way and man sees another way." Alternatively, as in the Watson and Jenkins Middle English edition, "For otherwise is the beholding of God, and otherwise is the beholding of man." That is why the deep implications of the parable of a Lord and a Servant were initially unclear to Julian. Like the servant in the parable, she can neither see herself truly nor see the wider story of humankind. Therefore Julian needed to be shown the reality of the Fall as it is "in God's sight."

The notion of "beholding" – that is, an immediacy of God's presence and being in a state of connection with the divine – is a recurring theme in Julian's Long Text. As we shall see in the final chapter of this book, it is an important dimension of Julian's teaching on prayer and on spiritual growth. However, in the present context, Julian's remarks in chapter 9 about the three "parts," or levels, of beholding are highly relevant. "All this [that is, the revelations] was shown in three parts, that is to say, by bodily vision and by words formed in my understanding and by spiritual vision." Initially, Julian "sees," in her limited human way (bodily vision), the narrative of the parable which she struggles to comprehend. Subsequently, 20 years or so later, she receives "inward instruction." It seems to me that this corresponds to the second level of beholding, "words formed in my understanding." This then leads Julian on to the critical level of beholding, that is, "spiritual vision." This level of "spiritual vision" does not merely refer to a depth of awareness but also to the challenging nature of God's "inward instruction" or "inward spiritual revelation." Thus, what becomes Julian's chapter 51 contains radical theological insights that take her way beyond her own capacity to reach through either the intellectual or contemplative reflections that presumably played an important role in her life.

Mystics make truth claims in the sense that their writings attempt to express what they have come to know inwardly about God. In quite singular ways, a mystic such as Julian of Norwich embodies God's presence. What she seeks to articulate from her experience is not only something of what God is but also something of how God sees. Because of this, she offers a radically alternative vision of created reality, including human existence. We might think of this as Julian having been shown, albeit momentarily, "the world seen through God's eyes."

It is this perspective, among other things, that differentiates Julian's approach to the Passion from the more common medieval expressions of Passion devotion. Essentially her experience of God is centered on the cross of Jesus. However, she does not simply see the Trinity through the cross. She also sees the cross through the eyes of the Trinity. For this reason she can write of the cross as the Trinity's joy or bliss. The most concise statement is in chapter 1 in which Julian summarizes all of the revelations in turn.

> The ninth revelation is of the delight which the blessed Trinity has in the cruel Passion of Christ, once his sorrowful death was accomplished, and that he wishes that joy and delight to be our solace and happiness, as it is his, until we come to glory in heaven.

Interestingly it is while Julian contemplates the blood running down Jesus' face (chapter 4) that "*in the same revelation*, suddenly the Trinity filled my heart full of the greatest joy" (the italics are mine). It was precisely in "this sight of his blessed Passion" that Julian understood the ultimate sense of security and comfort that was God's desire for all humanity.

Julian is led to view the world and especially human nature through God's eyes.[7] This results in two striking assertions. First, there is neither blame nor wrath in God (chapters 45–49). Secondly, and related to it, sin is "nothing" (Short Text chapter viii) or "no deed" (Long Text chapter 11). In seeing God in everything (Long Text chapter 11) Julian also sees all things in God and therefore "in all this sin was not shown to me." Later, as she considers how sin hinders her longing for God (chapter 27) she is taught that she could not see sin as she contemplated the Passion because "it has no kind of substance, no share in being, nor can it be recognized except by the pain caused by it." As we shall see in Chapter 6, sin is the cause both of human pain and of the Passion and yet "sin is necessary" (in Middle English *behovely*, that is "fitting" or "opportune"). In an echo of the liturgy of the Easter Vigil, sin is the *felix culpa* that reveals so great a redeemer or, in Julian's teaching, enables us to experience more profoundly the reality of God's being as love.

In the end, as the *exemplum* in chapter 51 underlines, God does not "see" sin but only the bliss that will be ours. In God's vision this is the ultimate truth and so Julian, in her perception of God's eye view, cannot see sin even though humanly she knows its effects in her life and in the world. This is not to deny the reality of sin in the world of human actions and experiences. However, it is to say that the centrality of sin in human experience and theology is not reproduced on the level of God's essential relationship with humanity. Julian expresses this in terms of paradox at the end of chapter 34: "When I saw that God does everything which is done, I did not see sin, and then I saw that all *is* well. But when God did show me about sin, then he said: All *will* be well" (the italics are mine). One might say that in her God's eye view Julian has a realized eschatology but that from the point of view of experience she necessarily has a proleptic eschatology. This is what saves her teaching from the accusation that it is unrealistic about the reality of sin and evil.

The two assertions are based on God's "great endless love" (chapter 45). "God is that goodness which cannot be angry, for God is nothing but goodness" (chapter 46). However, as the parable of a Lord and a Servant makes clear, it all depends on a difference of seeing. The parable is really a response to Julian's questions and concerns about sin and why she cannot see it when she contemplates all reality in God. God looks on human beings and their failings with compassion and love and not with blame. Interestingly, the only time that Julian suggests that God acts robustly towards humanity seems to be in reference to the tribulations of Holy Church (chapter 28). In order to combat the dangers of "'the pomps and pride and the vainglory of this wretched life" God says "I shall completely break down in you your empty affections and your vicious pride." This is likely to be a contemporary reference to divisions in the Church, probably to the controversies surrounding a divided papacy and perhaps to the fears of heresy in England.[8]

In the parable, Julian is led to understand that essentially God cannot but see humanity in the light of his Son. "When Adam fell, God's son fell [into Mary's womb]; because of the true union which was made in heaven, God's Son could not be separated from Adam, for by Adam I understand all mankind." Julian finally understands the parable when she begins to see matters from God's perspective. From this standpoint, the story of the Adam (the Fall) and of Christ (the Incarnation) are somehow the same. The moment of Adam's fall becomes the moment of salvation as well. The parable is an exposition of salvation history from God's viewpoint. God looks upon us as we are in Christ and sees us in our final integrity: healed, sinless, and glorified. That is how God "sees" the fallen servant in the ditch which contrasts so radically with the servant's own experience of himself and his failure. In the light of eternity we are ever in union with God and always have been. This has already been implied in the phrase, "I saw God in a point," whether this is an "instant of time" or the smallest physical space (chapter 11). All that exists in both time and space is but a single "point" for God. "And for the great endless love that God has for all mankind, he makes no distinction in love between the blessed soul of Christ and the least soul that will be saved" (chapter 54).[9]

In the Sixteenth Revelation, chapter 68, Julian is led from her contemplation of the Lord's realm to seek where the Lord dwells.

> And then our good Lord opened my spiritual eye, and showed me my soul in the midst of my heart. I saw the soul as wide as if it were an endless citadel, and also as if it were a blessed kingdom and from the state which I saw in it, I understood that it is a fine city. In the midst of that city sits our lord Jesus, true God and true man.

Julian's anthropology is complex and depends on understanding two dimensions to human existence, "substance" and "sensuality" (developed especially in chapters 54–59). These are not easy to define as the words have a number of implications. They will be examined in detail in Chapter 5.[10] However, one aspect of them is to describe "substance" not simply as the dimension of ourselves that, by nature, is irrevocably united to God. It is also the self that God sees. "Sensuality," therefore, may stand for the self that we see. Neither is exclusively true and neither is untrue. The paradox of the self is somehow caught in the image of "the crown." We are God's crown. That is a crown of thorns as Jesus Christ suffers for our sins (chapter 4) and a crown of glory "which crown is the Father's joy, the Son's honour, the Holy Spirit's delight, and endless marvellous bliss to all who are in heaven" (chapter 51).

While Julian's theology is not architectonic or systematic in the classical sense, it is produced by a central image which holds together within it various "doctrinal realizations," to borrow a phrase from Joan Nuth. This central image is that of Julian's original vision (or "sight") of the suffering Christ, "his precious crowning with thorns"; that is, the cross and Passion. However, the original vision of the Passion of Christ reveals in a single moment the Trinity, the union of our humanity with God, and God's eternal and irrevocable love. In other words, this key image contains all when it comes to understanding Julian's theology.

God, Time, and Place

A fundamental aspect of Julian's parable of a Lord and a Servant is that there are four "fallings" that become one in her inner understanding. First, there is the surface narrative of the servant who falls into a ditch. Then, Julian comes to see that this story represents Adam's Fall as portrayed in the Book of Genesis. Third, because Julian understands Adam to represent all of humanity, the Fall of Adam expresses the human situation of continually falling into sin. Finally, the fourth "fall" is that of the Son of God. The Son "falls" into "the womb of the maiden," meaning Mary. The Son of God enters into the human condition in the Incarnation which therefore becomes the medium of human redemption. Thus, beyond the four "fallings" there is effectively a collapsing of the sense of time and historical sequence in the "sight" (that is, in the understanding) of human beings into a single eternal event "in God's sight." The Bible, across both the Hebrew and the Christian scriptures, portrays a sequential narrative of creation, fall and sinfulness, salvation, and then an ultimate eternal destiny with God. This supposed sequence is shown to Julian to be a single moment, a single act, a single willing, and a single "sight" from the perspective of God. In this singleness Julian's parable is shown at the end to be an eschatological narrative in which the Son finally stands before the Father "with a rich and precious crown upon his head." It was then revealed that "we are his crown." Equally, the lord, God as Father, no longer sits "on the ground in the wilderness" of fallen human existence. Rather the Father now sits "in his rich and noblest seat" in his own city which we have already come to understand from earlier in chapter 51, reinforced in later chapters, is the human soul.

There can be no more striking image of God's courtesy and familiarity than to see the Lord and King dwelling in the humble state of the human soul. That is what Julian does. God's home, God's place, God's heaven is imaged as being within the human soul, understanding "soul" as the core of human identity.

> For I saw very surely that our substance is in God, and I also saw that God is in our sensuality, for in the same instant and place in which our soul is made sensual, in that same instant and place exists the city of God, ordained for him from without beginning. He comes into this city and will never depart from it, for God is never out of the soul, in which he will dwell blessedly without end.
> *(Chapter 55)*

As already noted from her chapter 68, Julian sees her soul "as wide as if it were an endless citadel, and also as if it were a blessed kingdom" in which sits "Our Lord Jesus, true God and true man." Here, the Lord Jesus in the human soul rules heaven and earth.

There is a tension within Julian between her sense that God is "in place" within created reality and a sense that her experience drew her beyond the limits of physical, time-bound, contingent space. Her "place" was with an eternal transcendent God. God was within her soul and God was within the created world. Yet, at the same time, God transcends the limits of the physical and material. Therefore, Christians must not believe that contingent reality can satisfy human desires. This tension is perhaps most sharply expressed in chapter 5. The image of all created reality as "something small, no bigger than a hazelnut'" affirms God's creation in love and continual preservation of all things. Yet Julian goes on in the same chapter to suggest that human beings should "despise as nothing everything created." In the full context of Julian's teaching the word "despise" is not a rejection of created reality but an affirmation that human beings will not ultimately be satisfied if they mistakenly think that the created order is the ultimate reality. The overall theme of creation will also be explored more extensively in Chapter 5.

In her First Revelation, Julian indicated that she was astonished that God could be "at home" (or "familiar") with a sinful creature.[11] She initially interpreted the great joy that she was given as a form of temporary spiritual consolation because "our Lord Jesus wanted, out of his courteous love, to show me comfort before my temptations began" (chapter 4). In a way it was true that God desired to comfort her. However, she came to see that this revelation also revealed a teaching about the "humility" of God-in-Christ. This insight echoes the sentiments of Paul's Letter to the Philippians 2, 6–8, regarding Christ Jesus:

> Who, though he was in the form of God did not regard equality with God as something to be exploited, but emptied himself, taking the form of a slave, being born in human likeness, and being found in human form, he humbled himself and became obedient to the point of death, even death on a cross.

Because God is "humble," Julian's perfectly conventional desire to be immediately with God in heaven (chapter 19) was converted. This was a defining moment in the teaching she received and then sought to communicate to others. Julian found that she did not need to go to a heaven elsewhere to be with God. For God was already "at home" in the flesh of Jesus Christ and therefore with us in this life. God's "homeliness" towards us is an extension of "being at home" in material creation. The divine love was revealed to Julian not simply as willing to suffer on the cross but also as at home in the human condition.

Conclusion

As I have already suggested, the parable of a Lord and a Servant in chapter 51 is in important ways central to Julian's text and to her theology. As the parable affirms, God cannot see Adam (humankind) except through the Son's Incarnation and death. That is why Julian is briefly shown reality as God sees it. "I did not see sin" (chapter 27). Julian's key premise is that there is no human nature (Adam) independent of the Son who united our substance and our sensuality. Hence, from all eternity, God-as-Trinity has created human nature in the Son to be God's crown.

The story of the lord and the servant is presented as God's answer to Julian's various anxieties and questions about her daily experience of sinfulness yet her growing sense of God's lack of blame. As I have already indicated, I believe that in a deep sense this chapter with its *exemplum* narrative is pivotal to the teachings that Julian felt bound to direct at her "evenchristen." The parable offers the key to Julian's sense of meaning about the true nature of God and of human existence that she has slowly and painfully come to understand and which she now seeks to communicate through the text. Julian's fundamental concern had been to find an answer to the question of how the two realities of her experience of sinfulness and yet of God's lack of blame are to be harmonized. As I have already indicated, in my view, the focus here is not so much on providing a response to the classical theodicy question as on a radical realignment of Julian's understanding of God as lover rather than wrathful judge, of how creation and human identity are understood "in God's sight" and, consequently, of the true nature of sin and salvation. Julian's whole theology – of the Trinity and of God's Motherhood, not to mention her theology of human nature – follows from this parable and depends upon it.[12] The chapters that follow will now consider these three important theological themes: Julian's understanding of God, her theology of human identity, and her soteriology; that is, her theology of sin and salvation.

Notes

1 Key features of this chapter originally appeared as an essay in the international journal *Spiritus: A Journal of Christian Spirituality* volume 17, issue 1, Spring 2017, pp 1–18, "Two Ways of Seeing: The Challenge of Julian of Norwich's Parable of a Lord and a Servant."

2 See, for example, the French historian and medievalist Jacques Le Goff, *The Medieval Imagination*, Chicago, IL: University of Chicago Press, 1988, Part Two "Space and Time: The Time of the *Exemplum* (Thirteenth Century)," pp 78–80.

3 See Nicholas Watson & Jacqueline Jenkins, eds., *The Writings of Julian of Norwich*, University Park, PA: The Pennsylvania State University Press, 2006, p 274.

4 See *Cur Deus Homo*, Book First, Chapter XXIV, in S.N. Deane, ed., *Saint Anselm: Basic Writings*, 2nd edition, LaSalle, IL: Open Court Publishing, 1962, p 233.

5 For further comments on the contrast between Julian and Anselm, see Denise Nowakowski Baker, *Julian of Norwich's Showings: From Vision to Book*, Princeton NJ: Princeton University Press, 1994, pp 92–94.

6 For example, see Jacques Le Goff, *Medieval Civilisation*, Oxford/ Cambridge, MA: Basil Blackwell, 1990, pp 358–359; also M. Pastoureau & M.I. Cruse, *Blue: The History of a Color*, Princeton, NJ: Princeton University Press, 2001.

7 See for example, Jay Ruud, "Nature and Grace in Julian of Norwich'" in *Mystics Quarterly* volume XIX, issue 2, June 1993, pp 70–81.

8 The so-called heresy of the Free Spirit was the object of a great deal of fear by Church authorities across Europe during the fourteenth century. The findings of Robert Lerner in *The Heresy of the Free Spirit in the Later Middle Ages*, Berkeley, CA: University of California Press, 1972, have not been substantially revised by more recent scholars. Lerner convincingly demonstrates that the "heresy" was substantially a projection of institutional fear rather than a significant reality. It was, however, one of the accusations levelled at Beguines and women mystics and perhaps known to Julian. The argument in Nuth, *Wisdom's Daughter*, p 19, that Julian's references cannot be to Wycliffe and his followers is dependent on dating the Short Text to as early as *c.*1373. As we have already seen, some scholars now argue for a much later date.

9 See Brant Pelphrey, *Christ our Mother: Julian of Norwich*, Wilmington, DE: Michael Glazier, 1989, pp 113–118.

10 They certainly do not mean "spirit"/soul and "matter"/body. They bear some, but not total, resemblance to the Augustinian concept of higher and lower parts of the soul. See, for example Jantzen, *Julian of Norwich*, pp 137–139 and Nuth, *Wisdom's Daughter*, pp 104–116.

11 For example, in the Long Text, chapter 5, Colledge and Walsh use the word "familiar" in their modern English translation when the Middle English text uses the word "homely."

12 See, for example, Denise Nowakowski Baker, *Julian of Norwich's Showings: From Vision to Book*, Princeton, NJ: Princeton University Press, 1994, Chapter 4 "The Parable of the Lord and Servant and the Doctrine of Original Sin," pp 83–106.

Chapter 4

Love is God's Meaning

As I suggested in Chapter 2, I believe that the Christian mystical tradition offers a vital resource for renewing theology. However, when we approach spiritual texts with a theological frame of reference, we need to exercise some care. The great classical texts are not concerned primarily with ideas about doctrine but about the practice of the Christian life. What I am implying is that it is all too easy to identify an abstract infrastructure of theological concepts and ideas in a text such as Julian's *A Revelation of Love* and yet miss its essentially spiritual-pastoral character. If it is true that mystical theology offers a source for the overall renewal of theology it will not be purely in terms of better conceptual frameworks. The writings of the great mystics introduce a way of knowing and seeing that is different from the path offered by traditional theological method. It is a knowledge that arises from a journey of love and engagement with God rather than something that depends on purely rational enquiry. Mystical "knowing" never loses sight of the essential ineffability of God and so it concentrates on seeking images of God to express the passionate and the poetic rather than concentrating on abstract concepts. The mystical tradition in fact invites theologians to cultivate a degree of conceptual "silence" and to re-engage their analysis with contemplation and the use of imagination.

The writings of Julian are particularly rich from the point of view of the theology of God. As we have already noted, *A Revelation of Love* or Long Text is among the most theological of medieval mystical texts. In particular, Julian is profoundly Trinitarian in tone. In addition, her approach to God-as-Trinity echoes many of the substantial questions raised in contemporary explorations of the doctrine. How does the inner relational and personal life of God connect with God's relationship with the world? How is salvation related to the inner life of God? Is the Trinity affected by creation and human history? Is the cross related only to one aspect of God, the eternal Word, or to the Trinity as such?

Julian of Norwich: "In God's Sight" – Her Theology in Context, First Edition. Philip Sheldrake.
© 2019 John Wiley & Sons Ltd. Published 2019 by John Wiley & Sons Ltd.

A Practical Theology of the Trinity

In one sense, Julian's "showings" and her reflections upon them are a form of theological inquiry. She asks many questions about the nature of God, about creation and human nature, about sin and salvation, and about the ultimate meaning and fulfilment of all things – that is, eschatology. However, at the same time, the "showings" may be understood as an extended prayer because Julian's questions are directed at God. They are not simply an expression of her own ability to intellectualize in relation to what she has asked.[1] In that sense, Julian's theology of God is fundamentally practical-spiritual rather than concerned purely with the language and concepts we use about God. Her aim is to emphasize the love of God in such a way as to liberate her fellow Christians from all that prevents them growing into the life of God. Our ignorance of God's love keeps us in sin and despair (chapter 73). In the end, therefore, there is only one "showing" or "revelation" and that is God's love as the meaning of everything. As Julian herself says in chapter 1, "This is a revelation of love which Jesus Christ, our endless bliss, made in sixteen showings."

The basis for Julian's teachings about God is her visions of the Passion and yet in the very first "showing" she comes to understand that "where Jesus appears the blessed Trinity is understood, as I see it" (chapter 4). Two things follow from this. First, the fundamental "showing" touches the inner reality of God in a direct way. "And in the same revelation suddenly the Trinity filled my heart full of the greatest joy" (chapter 4). The starting point of Julian's experience of and theology of God is the Trinity. "For the Trinity is God, God is the Trinity." Second, the suffering Jesus is revealed as the ground of hope. Julian experienced an inclination to "look up to heaven to his Father" but she is drawn to say "No, I cannot, for you are my heaven."

> So I was taught to choose Jesus for my heaven, whom I saw only in pain at this time. No other heaven was pleasing to me than Jesus, who will be my bliss when I am there. And this has always been a comfort to me, that I chose Jesus by his grace to be my heaven in all this time of suffering and of sorrow. And that has taught me that I should always do so, to choose only Jesus to be my heaven, in well-being and in woe.
>
> *(Chapter 19)*

The understanding Julian received was not only for the sake of herself, "the simple, unlettered creature" (chapter 2) who is granted the sight, a woman who at the time was on the margins of the institutional Church without teaching authority or status. The message delivered through

Julian is for all those people who seek to love God, whatever their lack of hierarchical status.

> In all this I was greatly moved in love towards my fellow Christians, that they might all see and know the same as I saw, for I wished it to be a comfort to them, for all this vision was shown for all men.
>
> *(Chapter 8)*

Julian's teaching about God and God's relationship with human beings is rich and complex. Because her Long Text has pastoral and spiritual teaching always in mind, her approach to the doctrine of God is woven throughout her teaching and is expressed in a variety of images that underline its practical and spiritual focus. At the heart of Julian's vision of God lies the Trinity – but the Trinity as expressed most graphically in the figure of a suffering and humble Jesus Christ. It is difficult to be precise or certain about connections between Julian's images and her cultural experience or theological background. Any comments must be tentative. As we have already seen, there is no substantial evidence for Julian's sources beyond her own language. She does not explicitly quote any theological or spiritual sources nor does she make clear references to historical events. Again, as we have seen, the degree to which Julian was even aware of theological influences in an explicit way is contested among scholars. What is not a matter of dispute is that Julian's theological "method" is inductive. She proceeds by reflecting on her foundational visionary experiences, rather than by using the deductive, dialectical, and systematic approach of the theology of the "schools."

The Passion as the Measure of God-as-Trinity

A major aspect of Julian's religious culture and of her own "showings" was the Passion of Jesus Christ. Devotion to the Passion of Jesus was widespread by the fourteenth century and so the visionary basis for Julian's teaching is not unusual. It is worth noting, however, that Julian is not unhealthily obsessed with the details of Jesus' sufferings as were some of her contemporaries.[2] The visions are simply starting points for her teaching about God's love for humanity.

However, modern readers are frequently disturbed by Julian's admission (chapter 2) that she not only desired a vision of the Passion but also a bodily sickness that would bring her to the verge of death. Her own explanation is that the third gift she prayed for, the wounds of contrition, compassion, and longing, was far more important. She only desired the vision and the sickness conditionally if it was God's will and she stated that the motive was "because I wanted to be purged by God's mercy, and afterwards live more to his glory because of that sickness." Strange though it may seem to us, the illness had a Christological trajectory. It was part of Julian's deep desire to participate more deeply in the Passion of Jesus. The text shows quite clearly that this was not merely a question of physical illness but of the spiritual temptation and desolation that she presumed was the experience of Jesus on the cross. This is part of the overall piety of *imitatio Christi* that was characteristic of the great evangelical spiritual and reform movements that swept the Western Church from the twelfth century onwards. The particular desire for illness as a symbol of solidarity with Jesus seems to have been more common among women than men.[3]

Julian's foundational experience on which she bases her theological reflections consists of visions focused primarily upon the Passion of Jesus. Julian recognizes that everything she was taught was grounded in the First Revelation (chapters 2–9). That is, the whole of Julian's theology finds its focus in the Passion. Her teaching on God as Trinity and on the creation and Incarnation are ultimately measured by the standard of the cross. The Passion is understood fundamentally as the supreme revelation of the love of God. Love is God's nature and this love is directed outwards towards creation and humanity. Love itself, whether divine or human, is to be measured by the standard revealed in the Passion.

God's love is not an emotion. Nor is it one characteristic of God or simply related to God's external action. For Julian, love is God's very being or reality. Julian does not provide simple definitions to help us to understand what this means. Her pedagogical approach is to begin with the Passion as her foundation, expressed in visionary form, and then to proceed by means of other images and stories. In this way, Julian is able to teach a deeper wisdom beyond the language of logic. The Long Text begins with an overwhelming image of self-giving love in the face of the crucified Jesus. Julian recognized that as she was apparently dying, she was being invited to contemplate the face of Jesus and to observe his crown of thorns and suffering. The details, while not extended or excessive compared to other contemporary piety, are nonetheless graphic.

> I saw his sweet face as it were dry and bloodless with the pallor of dying, and then deadly pale, languishing, and then the pallor turning blue and then blue turning brown, as death took more hold in his flesh.
>
> *(Chapter 16)*

The point of the visions was to find in this broken figure the reality that this is God. Julian fully experienced God's presence in the crucified Jesus. Yet, at the same time, to see God only in the flesh of Jesus or through God's "working" also serves to preserve the otherness of God: transcendence even in the immanence.

I perceived, truly and powerfully, that it was he who just so, both God and man, himself suffered for me, who showed it to me without any intermediary.

(Chapter 4)

Thus in Jesus Christ all humanity, creation, life, and eternal future are caught up with him into the very life of God as Trinity.

And in the same revelation, suddenly the Trinity filled my heart full of the greatest joy, and I understood that it will be so in heaven without end to all who will come there. For the Trinity is God, God is the Trinity. The Trinity is our maker, the Trinity is our protector, the Trinity is our everlasting lover, the Trinity is our endless joy and our bliss, by our Lord Jesus Christ and in our Lord Jesus Christ.

(Chapter 4)

On the cross, the relationship of God to humankind is shown to be identical with the love relationship within the Trinity – a dynamic and mutual indwelling in which each person of the Godhead is constantly giving to and sharing with the others. This way of being is also revealed as afflicted love, united through suffering to all humanity.

At the same time as I saw this sight of the head bleeding, our good Lord showed a spiritual sight of his familiar [or homely] love. I saw that he is to us everything which is good and comforting for our help. He is our clothing, who wraps and enfolds us for love, embraces us and shelters us, surrounds us for his love, which is so tender that he may never desert us.

(Chapter 5)

From the vision of Christ on the cross Julian learned, and teaches through a mixture of complementary images, that everything is filled with God and enclosed by God. Through the cross, God offers intimacy, "familiar love." Julian does not suggest directly that God suffers. Yet there are hints that God is not untouched by our condition. In the Incarnation, God is indissolubly joined to the human condition and longs for us. Indeed, Julian is careful to say that,

in his divinity he [Christ] is supreme bliss, and was from without beginning, and he will be without end, which true everlasting bliss cannot of its nature be increased or diminished.

(Chapter 31)

Julian regularly employs paradoxical language. As second person of the Trinity, as God, Christ is impassable. And yet, as united to the human condition, Christ is still said to have the thirst and longing that he had upon the cross. This will remain the case "until the time that the last soul which will be saved has come into his bliss." Then Julian is bolder still. There is longing and desire within God and this quality is part of God's everlasting goodness. Somehow, in Christ, God is touched by suffering out of love.

> For as truly as there is in God a quality of pity and compassion, so truly there is in God a quality of thirst and longing.... And this quality of longing and thirst comes from God's everlasting goodness.
>
> *(Chapter 31)*

Because of God's indwelling, this image of God's thirst explains our own desire. God in Christ thirsts and because of our union with God we also thirst. Just as Christ's spiritual thirst is God's painful longing for us, so the longing and yearning we feel is our unsatisfied desire for God.

> God's thirst is to have man, generally, drawn into him, and in that thirst he has drawn his holy souls who are now in bliss. And so, getting his living members, always he draws and drinks, and still he thirsts and he longs. I saw three kinds of longing in God, and all to the same end, and we have the same in us, and from the same power, and for the same end.
>
> *(Chapter 75)*

Julian is imaginative in her theology of God. Although she sometimes assigns traditional "roles" to one or other of the persons of the Trinity, it is fair to suggest that she breaches the boundaries that have sometimes artificially separated the persons of the Trinity in terms of their outward movement and action. Rather than the Father being the creator, the Son the redeemer, and the Spirit the sanctifier, all persons of the Trinity (God as God) manifest creative, redemptive, and sanctifying qualities.

For Julian the simple fact is that, in her understanding of the Passion, the Trinity as a whole participate in all activities relating to salvation even if only the "virgin's Son" may be said to suffer. "All the Trinity worked in Christ's Passion, administering abundant virtues and plentiful grace to us by him; but only the virgin's Son suffered, in which all the blessed Trinity rejoice" (chapter 23). The participation of the Trinity in salvation is also strongly implied in chapter 11 of the Long Text where she sees God "in a pointe."[4] Here God is seen to be in all things, doing all things, and bringing them to their ordained conclusion.

And therefore the blessed Trinity is always wholly pleased with all its works; and God revealed all this most blessedly, as though to say: See I am God. See, I am in all things. See, I do all things. See, I never remove my hands from my works, nor ever shall without end. See, I guide all things to the end that I ordain them for, before time began, with the same power and wisdom and love with which I made them; how should anything be amiss?

(Chapter 11)

Julian uses a range of triads in reference to the Trinity. These include might, wisdom, love; joy, bliss, delight; maker, keeper, lover; fatherhood, motherhood, lordship.[5] Julian especially and classically links power or might with the Father, wisdom with the Son and goodness or love with the Spirit. Yet these qualities are not to be limited to specific persons of the Trinity. They are "properties" in God. Equally, in her teaching on God as Mother (imaging generativity and loving-kindness) she is radically Trinitarian. As we shall see, Jesus as Mother is not distinguished from the Father as Ruler or Judge – ultimately, the Trinity is our Mother. Julian maintains a delicate balance between distinguishing the persons of the Trinity from each other and, on the other hand, depersonalizing matters so as to deal only with abstract "attributes." Thus, as Julian "contemplated the work of all the blessed Trinity" (chapter 58) she saw the three "properties" of fatherhood, motherhood, and lordship "in one God." Our essential human nature (substance) dwells equally in each person and in all the persons together. "And our substance is in our Father, God almighty, and our substance is in our Mother, God all wisdom, and our substance is in our Lord God, the Holy Spirit, all goodness, for our substance is whole in each person of the Trinity, who is one God." Julian is clear about the fundamental unity of God as Trinity. "For the Trinity is God, God is the Trinity. The Trinity is our maker, the Trinity is our protector, the Trinity is our everlasting lover, the Trinity is our endless joy and our bliss, by our Lord Jesus Christ and in our Lord Jesus Christ" (chapter 4). This early statement is further underlined in chapter 23 concerning our salvation. "All the Trinity worked in Christ's Passion, administering abundant virtues and plentiful grace to us by him."

The mutual indwelling of the persons of the Trinity one in the other (*perichoresis*) is affirmed at a number of points including at the end of the famous parable of a Lord and a Servant.

Now the Son, true God and true man, sits in his city in rest and in peace, which his Father has prepared for him by his endless purpose, and the Father in the Son, and the Holy Spirit in the Father and in the Son.

(Chapter 51)

This "city" is the human soul, redeemed and restored, which is from creation joined to God. Creation and especially human nature is God's "native place" in which God indwells. The image of the Son's crown as he now stands "richly clothed" before the Father is no longer the crown of thorns, the image of suffering. Rather, as Julian is shown, humanity is his crown.

> For it was revealed that we are his crown, which crown is the Father's joy, the Son's honour, the Holy Spirit's delight, and endless marvellous bliss to all who are in heaven.

The famous phrase, "all will be well, and all will be well, and every kind of thing will be well" is first introduced in the Thirteenth Revelation in the context of sin and the pain that it brings to humanity (chapter 27). It is in the Passion of Jesus that the promise is made. Julian understands in these words that this is part of the mystery at the heart of God. This mystery of God's desire will ultimately issue in a "deed" and the deed that will be done to make all things well is an action of the Trinity. In a further exposition of the phrase the Trinitarian nature of salvation is explicitly stated. The making well of all things relates to salvation and all who are saved "will be saved in the blessed Trinity" (chapter 31). Julian assures her readers that on "the last day" the Trinity will perform a deed that will make "all things well." At the same time God will reveal how this is so. Until then it is concealed (chapter 32). It is clear from the remainder of the chapter that Julian is struggling with her sense that this may imply universal salvation and with how this accords with the Church's teaching about the existence of hell.[6] The central point, however, is that the ultimate deed is the work of the Trinity. "For just as the blessed Trinity created all things from nothing, just so will the same blessed Trinity make everything well which is not well" (chapter 32).

Grace

Julian's approach to the theology of God is performative rather than simply informative. In Christian theology, God's action towards humanity is classically referred to as "grace." There have been a range of approaches to the concept of grace in Christian tradition. However, most importantly, grace is not an abstract "something." Rather, in broad terms the word stands for God's action in relation to creation and especially towards humanity. This shows itself particularly as love and mercy and as the giving of gifts.[7] As Julian puts it in chapter 59, God affirms that "I am he, the light and the grace which is all blessed love."

Julian uses the word "grace" on many occasions throughout her Long Text. For Julian, grace is God's work in us and for us. Grace is regularly linked to mercy and therefore to that changeable and contingent dimension of human identity referred to as our "sensuality." We shall explore this further in the exploration of Julian's binary anthropology of "substance" and "sensuality" in the next chapter. For example, chapter 62 notes that we are bound to God by nature ("kind") in our fundamental "substance" and "we are bound to God by grace" – by implication in our changeable "sensuality." In chapter 52 our human lives are described by Julian as a mixture of well-being and woe. We endeavour to wait for God and to trust that God will give us grace and mercy. "And this is his own working in us." In chapter 57 mercy and grace are explicitly said to bring our sensuality to completion.

Love was His Meaning

By focusing everything on the Passion (that is, on Jesus Christ) Julian is offering a strong signal that everything she has to say about God has a connection to our way of understanding human life. Thus, the various triads of properties that Julian uses in writing about the Trinity refer outwards to God's active being; that is, God's relationship with creation. For this reason some scholars suggest that Julian concentrates on the "economic" Trinity.[8] It would be better to say that Julian's approach refuses to separate an economic from an immanent Trinity. For Julian, God is as God does. She is concerned to establish that the "meaning" of God is love but that this "substantial" (i.e. natural) meaning is inherently related to God's deeds.

> Know it well, love was his meaning. Who reveals it to you? Love. What did he reveal to you? Love. Why does he reveal it to you? For love. Remain in this, and you will know more of the same. But you will never know different, without end. So I was taught that love is our Lord's meaning. And I saw very certainly in this and in everything that before God made us he loved us, which love was never abated and never will be, And in this love he has done all his works, and in this love he has made all things profitable to us, and in this love our life is everlasting. In our creation we had beginning, but the love in which he created us was in him from without beginning.
>
> *(Chapter 86)*

As we have seen, Julian is assured that God the Trinity has the power to perform "on the last day" a great deed whereby "all that is not well will be made well" (chapter 32). Yet, this powerful God who can and will accomplish more than we can imagine is, for Julian, revealed totally and essentially as love. Love is not only God's meaning but the whole teaching of Julian's book. Everything else (including, for example, God's Lordship) is to be interpreted in the light of love. God may be thought of as all-powerful and all-knowing but the deepest truth about God is love. For it is love that unites the Trinity. Love is the inner life of God.

> Though the three persons of the blessed Trinity be all alike in the self, the soul received most understanding of love. Yes, and he wants us in all things to have our contemplation and delight in love. And it is about this knowledge that we are most blind, for some of us believe that God is almighty and may do everything, and that he is all wisdom and can do everything, but that he is all love and wishes to do everything, there we fail.
>
> *(Chapter 73)*

As an aside, it is important to underline that the notion of God's meaning as love is not merely a comfortable and comforting message. First of all, it runs against the conventional Christian teaching of Julian's day that, in the words of her chapter 45, "Sinners sometimes deserve blame and wrath" and that, as she suggests in chapter 46, humans may merit pain for the many evil deeds they have done. That there is neither anger nor blame in God also challenges the frequent violent anger of human beings towards other humans who do evil. However, as created in the image of God-as-love, we humans are called upon to be agents of love in our own world. This is frequently a deeply uncomfortable message.

It is widely thought that Julian's approach echoes, whether consciously or unconsciously, Augustine's *De Trinitate*, XV. There it is the reciprocal love of each person for the others that unites the Trinity. For Julian, this love of the Trinity is never purely inward or introspective. It necessarily overflows into love for creatures or, perhaps better, it overflows itself as creation.

Julian is clear in her teaching about the fundamental unity of God-as-Trinity.

> For the Trinity is God, God is the Trinity. The Trinity is our maker, the Trinity is our protector, the Trinity is our everlasting lover, the Trinity is our endless joy and our bliss, by our Lord Jesus Christ and in our Lord Jesus Christ.
>
> *(Chapter 74)*

This early statement is further underlined in chapter 23 concerning our salvation, as we have seen: "All the Trinity worked in Christ's Passion, administering abundant virtues and plentiful grace to us by him." Again it is repeated near the beginning of the Sixteenth and final revelation in reference to our creation,

> for as well as the Father could create a creature and as well as the Son could create a creature, so well did the Holy Spirit want man's spirit to be created, and so it was done.
>
> *(Chapter 68)*

God as Mother

What I have suggested implies, among other things, that the image of motherhood, while used at first of Jesus Christ, is in fact a property of God-as-Trinity. Julian's reference to God's Motherhood appears only in the Long Text, chapters 52–63. This is because it is part of her reflections that follow on from her coming to understand the parable of a Lord and a Servant which also appears only in the Long Text.[9] Julian is not alone among female and male writers in the Middle Ages in using the imagery of motherhood in God.[10] She is unique, however, in the sophistication and complexity with which she relates the image both to the reality of God and to God's relationship with human nature. Julian's thought has been compared with the use of Motherhood imagery in, for example, the *Ancrene Wisse* (or *Ancrene Riwle*) written in the thirteenth century for female hermits like Julian.[11] The comparison is unhelpful because the hermit rule portrays the tender Mother Jesus as standing between us and the stern angry Father God who threatened to strike us.

It is interesting to note that Julian does not suggest that God is *like* a mother but that God *is* our mother. The choice of metaphor over simile is important because in this way Julian avoids projecting conventional notions of human motherhood onto God. On the contrary, the Motherhood of God is the measure of true human motherhood: "it is not that God is like a mother, but mothers make visible a function and relationship that is first and foremost in God."[12] Thus Jesus Christ is "where the foundation of motherhood begins" (chapter 59). Also,

> This fair lovely word "mother" is so sweet and so kind in itself that it cannot truly be said of anyone or to anyone except of him [Jesus] and to him who is the true Mother of life and of all things.
>
> *(Chapter 60)*

In summary,

> The mother's service is nearest, readiest and surest; nearest because it is most natural, readiest because it is most loving, and surest because it is truest. No one ever might or could perform this office fully, except only him [Mother Jesus].
>
> *(Chapter 60)*

Of course the additional effect of Julian suggesting that true motherhood *begins* in God is to underline to her contemporaries that the identity and work of women are as much in the image of God as the identity and work of men.

Julian may begin her reflections on motherhood with conventional human images such as nurturing and sustaining but she quickly moves divine motherhood onto another level. Thus, the human mother feeds a child with milk, which in medieval theory derived from her blood. This was seen as the mother's very life force. This belief reflected various biblical texts such as the Book of Leviticus: "You shall not eat the blood of any creature, for the life of every creature is its blood (Leviticus 17, 4)." So, Jesus as Mother also feeds the Christian with his very life but in the Eucharist: "The mother can give her child to suck of her milk but our precious Mother Jesus can feed us with himself, and does, most courteously and most tenderly with the blessed sacrament, which is the precious food of true life" (chapter 60). Further, the wound in Christ's side is a kind of parallel to the human mother's breast but in this case it nurtures us to the "inner certainty of endless bliss."

Julian's image of mothering is not passive but is seen as a work. Again this echoes medieval theory that the lining of the mother's own uterus provided the material for the fetus. In giving birth, a mother literally gave of herself.[13] In reference to God as Mother, Julian highlights the process of giving birth in both our natural creation and in the rebirth of salvation. "And our saviour is our true Mother, in whom we are endlessly born and out of whom we shall never come" (chapter 57). This is linked by Julian to the motherhood of our Lady. She is not merely the mother of Jesus but also of redeemed humankind. "So our Lady is our mother, in whom we are all enclosed and born of her in Christ, for she who is mother of our saviour is mother of all who are saved in our saviour" (chapter 57).

Julian compares the pain of a human mother giving birth to the suffering and death of our Mother Jesus.

> We know that all our mothers bear us for pain and for death. O, what is that? But our true Mother Jesus, he alone bears us for joy and for endless life, blessed may he be. So he carries us within

him in love and travail, until the full time when he wanted to suffer the sharpest thorns and cruel pains that ever were or will be, and at the last he died.

(Chapter 60)

In chapter 60 Our Lord is both "our Mother in nature, our Mother in grace."

So in our true Mother Jesus our life is founded in his prescient wisdom from without beginning, with the great power of the Father and the supreme goodness of the Holy Spirit. And in accepting our nature he gave us life, and in his blessed dying on the Cross he bore us to endless life.

(Chapter 63)

There is also nursing and nurturing as dimensions of God's loving. However, motherhood is not merely a matter of loving protection. There is also a motherhood of wisdom and knowing: "To the property of motherhood belong nature, love, wisdom and knowledge" (chapter 60). This guiding role brings the human soul to its proper fulfilment. The mother guards her child tenderly "as the nature and condition of motherhood will have" (chapter 60). As the child grows up, a mother never changes her love but acts differently. When the child is even older, a mother allows it to be chastised to destroy its faults. Sometimes she also allows the child to fall and to be upset in various ways "for its own benefit" (chapter 61) but she never allows any real danger to harm the child. No mother wants her child to flee. So children, when distressed, run to their mothers and call for help. The basic point that Julian makes about both human mothers and God as Mother is that children do not naturally despair of a mother's love (chapter 63).

What is particularly important is that Julian takes the image of Jesus as Mother (and, through this, of God as Mother) to a new level of significance beyond previous writers who used such imagery. In the end, the image of motherhood summarizes Julian's whole theology of sin and redemption and becomes an essential attribute of God.[14]

God as Teacher

The image of Jesus as Mother may be important but it is equally important to note that one of the most common images Julian uses for Jesus Christ throughout her Long Text is "teacher." Thus, "This is a revelation of love which Jesus Christ, our endless bliss, made in sixteen showings...with many fair revelations and teachings of endless wisdom and love" (chapter 1). Julian is always being gently taught the truth of God's love, often in answer to her questions or worries. This is part of Christ's Motherhood and intimacy. God as revealed in Christ is not a remote pedagogue. Teaching is yet another dimension of love. It has as its purpose a deepening of the kind of knowing that is founded on love. "Our precious lover helps us with spiritual light and true teaching, in various ways from within and from without, by which we may know him" (chapter 71). Given that Julian's strongly Christological framework is used to present her fundamental teaching about God-as-Trinity, the notion of "teacher" becomes one of her strongest images for God. Sometimes this is quite explicit. "He [God] is the foundation, he is the substance, he is the teacher, he is the end, he is the reward for which every loving soul labours" (chapter 34).

In the first place, to image God as teacher turns our attention away from Julian's own importance to the source of her teaching which is God's revelation. In this context, "revelation" implies teaching rather than simply visionary experiences.[15] No doubt, Julian's further purpose is to encourage all those who desire to be Christ's lovers to allow themselves to be drawn into him so that they may be taught spiritually as she has been taught. Teaching and learning are presented as something that takes time. Dramatic experiences such as visions are a starting point not an end in themselves. True teaching and deep learning involve years of further contemplation, reflection, and thought. However, it seems likely that another purpose in writing about God as the teacher is to deflect any criticisms that Julian is claiming theological or spiritual authority at a time when lay people, and women in particular, were not permitted to undertake that role in the Church. Julian's writings are aimed at all her fellow Christians. She feels compelled to teach and yet the Church says that she cannot. So the image of God as teacher is a rhetorical device to communicate the message without fear. In the meantime she safely remains one who has simply been taught, and continues to be, by God but also by "Holy Church." Thus, Julian frequently uses the phrase "as Holy Church teaches me to believe" (for example in chapter 32).

Lordship and Familiarity

The image of the Lordship of God also appears throughout Julian's writings. Sometimes the word "lord" refers to God as such, at other times specifically to Jesus Christ. As we saw in the last chapter, it seems likely that "lordship" in Julian is not merely a scriptural image but reflects the fourteenth-century experience of feudal and hierarchical relations, albeit in a paradoxical and challenging way. While necessarily speculative, it may even be that Julian's challenge to traditional concepts of lordship reflects the serious questions being raised in her time concerning the established social order. The rapid growth of cities like Norwich and the expansion of urban industry and trade that we have already noted was an important sign of the new world that was coming to birth. Historic feudalism, based on land ownership and the obligations of military service, was essentially a rural concept and was in decline. This was further exacerbated by the decimation of the traditional peasantry by the Black Death and famine as well as by a growing cynicism with the system as a result of the interminable wars with France. As we have seen, the impact of both was sharply expressed in the Peasants' Revolt of 1381.

We might reasonably expect an image of lordship based on the world of feudalism to have produced an understanding of God as dominating and domineering. This is not the case with Julian. Overall, her life-giving experience of the Trinity is attractive and convincing. It challenges both a distant, hierarchical relationship between God and creation and also the classic image of an angry Lord God generating a fear of damnation. One aspect of the teaching that "all shall be well" is shown to Julian as an indication of God's homeliness and humility. "He wants us to know that he takes heed not only of things which are noble and great, but also of those which are little and small, of humble men and simple, of this man and that man" (chapter 32).

Early in her Long Text (chapter 7) Julian anticipates the parable of a Lord and a Servant. God shows her the example of "a majestic king or a great lord" welcoming a poor servant into his presence with familiarity (another of Julian's favorite images for God's way of behaving) and in front of others. Julian contrasts this with merely showering a person with material gifts while remaining personally distant. Later, Julian is "lifted up into heaven." There, God is imaged as the lord who entertains all his friends to a great feast (chapter 14). The language Julian uses is almost lyrical:

> I saw him reign in his house as a king and fill it all full of joy and mirth, gladdening and consoling his dear friends with himself, very familiarly and courteously, with wonderful melody in endless love in his own fair blissful countenance, which glorious countenance fills all heaven full of the joy and bliss of the divinity.

As we have seen, the parable of a Lord and a Servant in chapter 51 is central to Julian's overall teaching. It provides a key to understanding the nature of God's faithful love and God's union with humanity through suffering. While the language reflects feudal hierarchies, the context and dynamic of the story and its teaching contrasts sharply with social realities. For one thing, God is not simply the lord but also the servant who is identified not only with Adam and humankind but with Christ, second person of the Trinity and equal to the Father. Then as we have also seen, the explanation of the parable in chapters 52–63 is dominated by Julian's imagery for God as Mother. This not only redefines our images of God but also our notions of "lordship" or authority.[16]

The language of "courtesy" is chivalrous and courtly. The humility and reverent fear of "our Lady St Mary" standing before God is commended (chapter 7). However, "our good Lord, who is so to be revered and feared, is also familiar and courteous." The image of Jesus Christ as "courteous Lord" is regularly repeated throughout Julian's text. God's "royal dominion" is closely linked to his "wonderful courtesy" (for example, in chapter 48). As we saw in Chapter 3 "courtesy" was an important attribute in the society of Julian's day. It involved polite behavior in which one deferred to another; in other words, put the convenience or desires of another person before one's own.[17] So God defers to us and finds pleasure especially in giving us pleasure. So courtesy implies familiarity but it is an unexpected (and unearned) familiarity that implies the crossing of conventional boundaries.

> So it is with our Lord Jesus and us, for truly it is the greatest possible joy, as I see it, that he who is highest and mightiest, noblest and most honourable, is lowest and humblest, most familiar and courteous.
>
> *(Chapter 7)*

The Stability of God

In chapter 5, Julian also describes God's love as "homely" (translated as "familiar" by Colledge and Walsh). Although the Middle English word "homely" indicates intimacy, it also has linguistic resonances of "at home," "permanent," or "habitual." There is, therefore, an interesting connection between God's "homeliness" and the virtue of "stability." This not only implies a commitment to make one's home permanently in a particular context but the virtue of sticking at it "for better or for worse." Julian suggests that this is an important quality of God's dwelling among us. In the historical context of the late fourteenth century, the notion of permanence or stability had a particular force and poignancy. Not only was the Church and civil society wracked by instability and insecurity but there was a widespread failure of trust in the social and religious structures that should have provided an image of stability and faithfulness. Bishops such as Henry Despenser of Norwich spent little time in their dioceses, preferring to be in London and in the service of the crown. Feudal lordship, based originally on a stable relationship with a specific place and with a defined group of dependent people, was in serious decline. In this context the "stability of God" offered a very different model of authentic lordship.[18]

The stability that Julian described in terms of God's relationship with humanity and with all created reality reflects God's inner stability. Julian's description of God-as-Trinity is in terms of God being supremely active in creation and in human lives. The inner life of God-as-Trinity involves a constant movement of relationships. Yet, at the same time, the Trinity also dwells in peace and stillness whether in heaven or the human soul. "Now the Son, true God and true man, sits in his city in rest and in peace" (chapter 51).

Conclusion

In summary, Julian's theology of God-as-Trinity is fundamentally "practical" as is the whole of her theological teaching. The image of the Trinity in Julian is, as it were, the answer to the question of whether and how God is engaged with humanity and the world. The God of Julian's revelations is joyfully and purposefully involved in human history, in the smallest of human events, and in the lives of all of her "fellow Christians." While God's inherent freedom demands that this involvement be a matter of God's own choice, it is nevertheless, for Julian, an aspect of God's happiness and fulfilment. In that sense, God's saving action in the world is not simply a revelation of God's inner nature as a community of persons. It is also the vehicle for mutual Trinitarian interaction. In this way, Julian draws together the immanent Trinity and the economic Trinity. God's action *is* God's Trinitarian way of being.

A final question remains. Is the purpose of the "showings" merely to reassure Julian's fellow Christians that their own, individual status before God is secure? Interestingly, the image of God (in Jesus Christ) dwelling in the human soul may be interpreted as encouraging a self-absorbed interiority. It is generally accepted that Julian's theology of God owes something to the legacy of Augustine. Augustine focused on the "traces" of the Trinity (*vestigia Trinitatis*), particularly in the soul of the individual human being. The question is whether this theme of interiority effectively undermines a theology and spirituality of engagement with the outer world. This is not the flavor of Julian's writings. Throughout these Julian is moved by compassion for all her fellow Christians. That is her fundamental motive for writing. Consequently, the effect on Julian of her theology of God is not to drive her into self-indulgent reverie but to empower her with an urgency to pass on those teachings to a wider audience. The implication is that the compassion of God for us will lead to our growing compassion for others as we are drawn ever more deeply into the life of God-as-Trinity.[19] By implication the hope is that the impact on all those touched by Julian's teaching will be a similar deepening of compassion for God's creation and for fellow humans within each of whom, without exception, dwells the divine presence.

Notes

1 See, for example, Brant Pelphrey, *Christ Our Mother: Julian of Norwich*, Wilmington, DE: Michael Glazier, 1989, p 103.

2 See Ewart Cousins, "The Humanity and Passion of Christ," especially pp 386–389, in Jill Raitt, ed., *Christian Spirituality: High Middle Ages and Reformation*, London: Routledge & Kegan Paul/New York: Crossroads Publishing, 1987.

3 See Caroline Walker Bynum, *Holy Feast and Holy Fast: The Religious Significance of Food to Medieval Women*, Berkeley, CA: University of California Press, 1987, pp 120, 199–200, 207, 209, 211–212.

4 Although the Middle English "pointe" is translated by Colledge & Walsh as "an instant of time" (p 197) the chapter overall is more suggestive of a spatial image. "By which vision I saw that he is present in all things." "For he is at the centre of everything."

5 See the helpful analysis in Joan M. Nuth, *Wisdom's Daughter: The Theology of Julian of Norwich*, New York: Crossroad, 1991, pp 89–94.

6 Of course it may also be the case that Julian was perfectly clear about the implications of the "showing." The struggle to maintain a balance with the Church's teaching may have been a rhetorical device to avoid accusations of heresy.

7 See, for example, Roger Haight, *The Experience and Language of Grace*, New York: Paulist Press, 1979.

8 For example, Elizabeth Dreyer, "The Trinitarian Theology of Julian of Norwich," in *Studies in Spirituality* volume 4, 1994, pp 79–93.

9 Julian uses the Middle English words "moder" or its associated terms "moderhede" and "moderly" some 83 times in the Long Text. Of these, nine refer to Mary and four to "Holy Church." The remainder refer to Jesus Christ, God, or the Trinity. See Jennifer P. Heimmel, *"God is Our Mother": Julian of Norwich and The Medieval Image of Christian Feminine Divinity*, Salzburg: Instituut für Anglistik und Amerikanistik, 1982, pp 50–51.

10 See, for example, Caroline Walker Bynum, *Jesus as Mother: Studies in Spirituality of the High Middle Ages*, Berkeley, CA: University of California

Press, 1982, Chapter 4 and the listing of other sources in the critical edition of Julian, Colledge & Walsh, eds., *A Book of Showings*, pp 151–162.

11 See Jantzen, *op. cit.*, pp 117–118. The original reference is to "Ancrene Wisse," in Anne Savage & Nicholas Watson, eds., *Anchoritic Spirituality*, The Classics of Western Spirituality, New York: Paulist Press, 1991, Part IV, p 132 & Part VI, p 182.

12 Ritamary Bradley, *Julian's Way: A Practical Commentary on Julian of Norwich*, London: Harper Collins, 1992, p 146.

13 On the medieval understanding of blood as a person's life and on the mother giving literally of her own flesh in giving birth, see Caroline Walker Bynum, *Fragmentation and Redemption: Essays on Gender and the Human Body in Medieval Religion*, New York: Zone Books, 1992, Chapter III "The Body of Christ in the Later Middle Ages," p 97.

14 See, for example, Kerrie Hide, *Gifted Origins to Graced Fulfillment: The Soteriology of Julian of Norwich*, Collegeville: The Liturgical Press, 2001, Chapter 7.

15 On this point see Julia Lamm, "Revelation as Exposure in Julian of Norwich's *Showings*," in *Spiritus: A Journal of Christian Spirituality* volume 5, issue 1, 2005, pp 54–78.

16 While the connection Julian makes between the lordship image and the motherhood of God is noted by several scholars, the "feminization" of lordship and authority does not seem to have been explicitly drawn out. See, for example, Catherine Innes-Parker, "Subversion and Conformity in Julian's *Revelation*: Authority, Vision and the Motherhood of God," in *Mystics Quarterly* volume XXIII, issue 2, March 1997, pp 7–35 at p 21.

17 Nuth, pp 74–79, suggests that Julian's usage is closer to texts such as the *Ancrene Riwle* (or *Wisse*) that designate "courtaysye" as a Christian virtue of giving pleasure to others. This is perhaps to miss the point that the conventions of courtly love and of spiritual love were not unconnected!

18 See the comments of Brant Pelphrey in *Love Was His Meaning: The Theology and Mysticism of Julian of Norwich*, Salzburg: Instituut für Anglistik und Amerikanistik, 1982, p 106 & n 5.

19 See Margaret Ann Palliser, *Christ Our Mother of Mercy: Divine Mercy and Compassion in the Theology of the Showings of Julian of Norwich*, Berlin: de Gruyter, 1992, Chapter 5 (B) "Jesus Christ: The Compassion of God and Our Compassion."

Chapter 5

Creation and Human Nature

The themes of God's relationship with material creation and the status of humankind before God are central to the theological vision of Julian of Norwich and her teachings in the Long Text. I suggest that the rich imagery employed by her in chapter 5 offers an evocative and appropriate starting point for considering her understanding of both creation and her theology of human nature.

Creation

In terms of God's relationship to material creation, I will begin with one of Julian's most famous images, that of "something small, no bigger than a hazelnut." Without being pedantic, it is worth noting that Julian's language is comparative whereas some popular writings and icons of Julian are more literal, suggesting that the "something small" actually *was* a hazelnut!

> And in this he [our good Lord] showed me something small, no bigger than a hazelnut, lying in the palm of my hand, as it seemed to me, and it was as round as a ball. I looked at it with the eye of my understanding and thought: What can this be? And I was given this general answer: it is everything which is made.[1]
>
> *(Chapter 5)*

Julian wonders how creation could survive, given that it is so little and therefore fragile. "I thought that because of its littleness it would suddenly have fallen into nothing." However, the answer she receives is that it is simply God's love that is the cause both of creation's existence and of the survival of everything that is other than God. Julian then summarizes her understanding of the three essential "properties" of creation, "this little thing." First, God made it, then God loves it, and finally God preserves it.

Julian of Norwich: "In God's Sight" – Her Theology in Context, First Edition. Philip Sheldrake.
© 2019 John Wiley & Sons Ltd. Published 2019 by John Wiley & Sons Ltd.

However, in the following sentences Julian declares that an appreciation of creation as the gift of God's love must never be allowed to come between us and God. Here we need to be careful about how we understand what Julian says. On the face of it, we are asked to "delight in despising as nothing everything created" – in Middle English, "that us liketh to nought all thing that is made." However, Julian qualifies this potential contradiction of the value and goodness of creation. "Despise" is arguably an unhelpful translation. The point Julian seeks to make is that if we mistakenly focus our "liking," that is our ultimate satisfaction, on created things rather than on God ("if we seek rest in this thing which is so little") we cannot truly love God or be "substantially united" to our uncreated God.

Overall, in reference to Julian's teaching, both Watson and Jenkins in their scholarly edition of the Middle English text, as well as Bernard McGinn in the chapter on Julian in his volume on late medieval mysticism, detect echoes in Julian's imagery of the deutero-canonical book of the Old Testament, The Wisdom of Solomon 11, 22–25.[2] Here the littleness of creation is portrayed as "a speck that tips the scales" and "a drop of morning dew." Yet "you [God] love all things that exist."

More strikingly, the image of a nut is also used in relation to creation, albeit in a different way, in a text by another of the fourteenth-century English mystics, Walter Hilton (mid-1340s–1396). This is specifically in his *The Scale* [or *Ladder*] *of Perfection*. Hilton's text consists of two Books, apparently written some years apart, and addressed to an anchoress. These probably date from the late 1380s and the early 1390s. Of course, as with everything else about Julian's sources and influences, we have no way of knowing whether she knew Hilton's text let alone whether she had read it. However, its intended audience and its likely dates make this theoretically feasible. In his Book 2, chapter 33, Hilton refers to Jesus being "within all creatures but not in the way that a kernel is hidden inside the shell of a nut…he is within all creatures as holding and keeping them in their being."

Interestingly, in her reference to Julian's image the Australian theologian Kerrie Hide refers to an "active kernel of growth" within a hazelnut. In this way she notes that Julian's image suggests an evolutionary view of creation rather than a static one. Beyond "making," the images of God's "preserving" or keeping creation and "loving" creation suggests both God's continuous involvement in renewing creation and also the dynamic nature of creation itself.[3]

What Julian portrays in chapter 5 is that the whole of creation is a manifestation of divine love. There is a radical contingency to everything that is not God. That is, in relation to God's "Being" created reality is infinitesimal. Yet God is nevertheless always active in the world of time and space which God loves eternally. Julian makes no overt reference to the creation myth in the Book of Genesis but her parable of a Lord and a Servant in chapter 51, which we explored in depth in Chapter 3, can be seen as an image of God's restoration and renewal of creation. The servant of the parable is also identified as the second Adam, God's Son. The servant is thus imaged as "a gardener, digging and ditching and sweating." He waters plants, and makes streams to flow and fruit to grow. In summary, Julian's understanding of the created universe is Christocentric both in terms of its making and also in terms of its renewal through Christ, the second Adam, in his embodied suffering and death. The critical point is that the work of salvation carries on God's work of creation. In Julian's theology there is a unity and continuity between them that underlines the irreversible value of material creation, including human nature. The theme of salvation will be developed further in the next chapter.

A second evocative image of God in relation to creation appears in chapter 11. "I saw God in a pointe...by which sight I saw that he is in al thing." From the wider context of the passage, I have already suggested that this "pointe" is a spatial image rather than a reference to "an instant of time" as in the translation by Colledge and Walsh.[4] In other words, for Julian, God is unquestionably the center of everything that exists and does everything in the functioning of creation. Indeed, God alone is the "doer."

In chapter 11, the image of "a pointe" also suggests God's presence and action in even the smallest conceivable thing. "Everything which exists in nature is of God's creation, so that everything which is done has the property of being God's doing." Further, "the smallest of deeds which is done is as well done as the best and the greatest." Again, as in chapter 5, the image of God "in a pointe" is used at the end of the chapter to underline God's continuous involvement in preserving creation. Julian expresses this by having God say:

> See, I am God. See I am in all things. See, I do all things. See I never remove my hands from my works, nor ever shall without end. See, I guide all things to the end that I ordain them for, before time began, with the same power and wisdom and love with which I made them.

Both images, "like a hazelnut" and "in a pointe," offer a vision of a created universe wholly dependent on God, originating in God, and also destined to return to God. All things finally converge in God. Julian's vision of, and subsequent meditation upon, the bleeding head of Christ leads her to see creation as a whole as the ultimate expression of the self-giving love of God. Her chapter 8 clearly states that one of the important things she came to understand from this powerful vision of the bleeding Christ was both that "heaven and earth and all creation are great, generous and beautiful and good" and that God "created everything for love, and by the same love is it preserved, and always will be without end."

The proper Christian attitude towards creation is summarized in Julian's chapter 75. God's presence is to be affirmed in the smallest part of what is created.

> But it is proper to God's honourable majesty so to be contemplated by his creatures, trembling and quaking in fear, because of their much greater joy [literally, "mekehede of joy," meekness of joy] endlessly marvelling at the greatness of God, the Creator, and at the smallest part [literally, "litilhede," littleness] of all that is created.

While in Julian's mind even "the smallest of deeds which is done is well done," she has a hierarchical approach to the created order that is typical of a medieval world view. Thus, she affirms that "man's creation is superior to all God's works" (chapter 1) and that God "wants us to know that the noblest thing which he ever made is mankind" (chapter 53).

Human Nature

Turning now to Julian's theology of human nature and identity, or theological anthropology, it is important to underline at the outset that Julian's understanding of the value of human nature in God's eyes makes no distinction between women and men. As already noted, her more conventional, and apologetic, portrayal of womanhood in the Short Text, chapter vi, as ignorant, weak, and frail disappears in the Long Text. Here, Julian's confident voice addresses her teachings, a woman's teachings, to all her fellow Christians, both men and women.

A rich starting point for considering Julian's anthropology is a second image employed by her at the very beginning of the Long Text, in chapter 5. Here she describes how God showed her a spiritual sight of his "familiar love." The closeness of God to humankind is described in terms of clothing. "He is our clothing, who wraps and enfolds us for love, embraces us and shelters us, surrounds us for his love, which is so tender that he may never desert us." By describing God as our clothing, Julian does not merely offer an image of closeness and loving intimacy but also one of care and protection. It is important to note that Julian does not express any dichotomy between male and female in the chain of being. All humanity is equally loved and protected.

It is interesting to note that later in the same chapter Julian appears to use human nakedness as an image of innocence when she added that God also revealed that "it is very greatly pleasing to him that a simple soul should come naked, openly and familiarly." The notion of a "simple soul," or "sely soule" in Middle English, may validly be translated as an "innocent soul." The image of being clothed in God is repeated in the following chapter 6 immediately after the graphic image of human excretion (as it appears in the Paris manuscript) where God's care is shown in "the simplest natural functions of our body." From this, Julian concludes that "we, soul and body, are clad and enclosed in the goodness of God."

Taken together, Julian's images of God as our "clothing" and "being clad" by God in love appear to contrast with the imagery of nakedness and clothing as they appear in the Book of Genesis, chapter 3. There, the narrative of humanity's original disobedience and "fall" has Adam and Eve lose their innocence, become aware of their nakedness and seek to cover themselves up. Subsequently, in the Eden story, God clothes Adam and Eve in garments of skins before expelling them from the Garden of Eden. The contrast between Genesis and Julian's text is that, in the first, being covered up by clothing is a sign of human degradation whereas in Julian's text being clothed by and in God is an image of love and protection. In this regard, there is also a striking contrast between Julian and the other fourteenth-century English spiritual writer Walter Hilton. In Book 1, chapter 84 of his *The Scale of Perfection*, Hilton has a more negative view of human embodiment as a symbol of our sinful state.

> Our Lord made clothes of beasts' hide for Adam and his wife as a sign that for his sin he was misshapen like a beast. With these bestial clothes we are all born, wrapped up and disfigured from our natural shape.

In her Seventh Revelation (as in the Long Text chapter 15, also summarized in chapter 1), Julian suggests that she (and no doubt her intended audience) was caught between an experience of well-being, which she understood as being enlightened by God's grace, and what she refers to as woe. She suggests that this is caused by "the heaviness and weariness of our mortal life" (chapter 1). However, this sense of depression is to be understood as a temptation.

The Influence of Augustine

The probable influence, directly or indirectly, of the theology of Augustine of Hippo (354–430 CE) on Julian's thinking about human nature has been noted frequently. Augustine was, and continues to be, a major figure in Western theology, not least in relation to theological anthropology. Augustine adopted the symbol of the heart as a way of expressing "the self." In the mind of Augustine our inner selves are where we are also united with the whole of creation and with God. For Augustine, God created humans with the divine image (*imago Dei*) in their hearts. This *imago Dei* is the true self although sin may disconnect us from it. The concept of the *imago Dei* points to humanity being inherently united to God, a theme strongly underlined in Julian of Norwich. Humanity in this image also reflects the triune nature of God, expressed by Augustine and later mystical theologians in the three-fold structure or "powers" of human identity, the soul, in terms of memory, understanding, and will. As I shall explain in a moment, Julian appears to modify and expand Augustine's three-fold schema.

Augustine's notion of the *imago Dei* in which we are created and which is imprinted on the heart must be read alongside his overall doctrine of human creation. In Augustine's *Commentary on Genesis*, Adam's sin was precisely to please himself and to live for himself (*secundum se vivere, sibi placere*). Thus the unity or mutual communion that should be at the heart of everything is ruptured; whether this is our union with God, our solidarity with other people, or our harmony with our true selves. Self-seeking pride is the archetypal sin (*Commentary on Genesis* XI.15.19–20). In Augustine's mind, the original Garden of Eden and his "City of God" were based on "the love that promotes the common good for the sake of the heavenly society" (*Commentary on Genesis* XI.15.20). For Augustine, in the Heavenly City there is to be the fullness of sharing.[5]

In terms of the foundations of Augustine's theological anthropology, there is a tension that should not be resolved between a clear sense of a personal self and an equally clear sense of the fundamentally collective nature of human existence. It is possible to detect echoes of this viewpoint in Julian's strong sense of responsibility for, and solidarity with, her "evenchristen." "The heart" for Augustine is where a true integration of our inner and outer lives takes place. In Book 10 of his *Confessions* Augustine refers to "my heart, where I am whatever it is that I am" and in his *Tractates on the Gospel of John* (Section 18.10) Augustine exclaimed "return to your heart!" However, Augustine is clear that if anything is claimed to be in the heart but does not show itself outwardly in love and community, it is illusory.

Julian's Anthropology

The Augustinian theme of returning to the heart connects strongly with how Julian of Norwich approaches her theology of human identity. While the question of what we are as humans is important, equally challenging is precisely how we come to know ourselves deeply rather than superficially. As Julian underlines, this is not a self-driven intellectual or psychological process but involves a contemplative journey inwards. As we shall see, in Julian's way of thinking, for us to come to know our own soul (or self) demands that we first come to know God.

In Julian's theological vision, her complex binary (but not dualistic) portrayal of human identity in terms of the dimensions of "substance" and "sensuality" also echoes Augustine's anthropology to some degree. However, the fundamental source of Julian's highly original theological reflection in *A Revelation of Love* is what she believes was revealed to her by God initially through her visions and then through her subsequent contemplative reflection. Julian's doctrine of human nature and human destiny is expressed particularly in her chapters 53–63.

As I suggested in Chapter 2, I believe that Julian's overall theological approach may be partly placed within the category of mystical theology. This equally applies to her theology of human identity or theological anthropology. In patristic and medieval mystical theology the theological style, including the approach to theological anthropology, takes broadly two forms. There is a "positive" or kataphatic approach that focuses on what we may legitimately affirm about human identity. The second approach, known as "negative" or apophatic theology, emphasizes that the human soul or "self" in its deep union with the divine is, like the all-embracing reality of God, ultimately beyond our capacity to know definitively. It is important to emphasize that while these two theological approaches have distinctive features they are not mutually exclusive. Rather, they complement each other and, indeed, may intersect in the writings of specific mystical thinkers such as Julian of Norwich.

Two interrelated elements run through the writings of Julian of Norwich and underpin her mystical anthropology. The first element is that "the mystical" involves a process of self-forgetfulness rather than the pursuit of self-preoccupied interiority. Second, as a consequence, Julian's mystical reflections remind us that the core of a theology of human identity necessarily involves a risky openness to a God who draws Julian, and all her "evenchristen," forward into the unknown. In that sense, human identity is not a static reality but is a dynamic and open-ended process. These interrelated elements of self-emptying and a divinely guided process of becoming are presented in a range of ways in Julian's mystical theological writing.

Here, I suggest that Julian modifies Augustine's three-fold scheme of memory, understanding, and will. Julian adopts the more dynamic, process-focused, categories of "being," "increase," and "fulfilment."

> I had a partial touching, and it is founded in nature, that is to say: Our reason is founded in God, who is nature's substance. From this substantial nature spring mercy and grace and penetrate us ["spredeth into us"] accomplishing everything for the fulfilment of our joy. These are our foundations, in which we have our being, our increase and our fulfilment. This is three properties in one goodness, and where one operates all operate in the things which now pertain to us.
>
> *(Chapter 56)*

Later, Julian expounds her triadic process of human existence further in relationship to the nature and work of the Trinity. Thus, "being" is nature, "increase" is mercy, and "fulfilment" is grace (chapter 58).

In general, in Julian's theology, how she comes to understand human identity engages directly with her mystical theological understanding of God-as-Trinity. The mutual indwelling of God in us and us in God permeates her theological vision. Indeed, according to Julian we cannot truly know our self unless we first cease to be self-preoccupied and contemplate God.

> For our soul is so deeply grounded in God and so endlessly treasured that we cannot come to knowledge of it until we first have knowledge of God, who is the Creator to whom it is united. But nevertheless I saw that we have, naturally from our fullness, to desire wisely and truly to know our own soul, through which we are taught to seek it where it is, and that is in God.
>
> *(Chapter 56)*

Indeed,

> God is closer to us than our own soul, for he is the foundation on which our soul stands, and he is the mean which keeps the substance and the sensuality together, so that they will never separate.
>
> *(Chapter 56)*

Julian bases her theological reflections on her foundational experience of sixteen visions. As we have already underlined, the visions, "showings," or "revelations" focus primarily upon the Passion of Jesus. Julian recognizes that everything she was taught was grounded in the first revelation of Jesus' suffering and bleeding on the cross (chapters 2–9). As a result, the whole of Julian's theology of human identity finds its focus in the self-emptying of Christ's Passion. Her teachings on God-as-Trinity, on creation, and on Incarnation are ultimately measured by the standard of the cross and flow naturally into her anthropology. The Passion of the incarnate Christ is understood fundamentally as the supreme revelation of the love of God.

Love is not something God "does" or "has." Rather, love is God's very nature and this love is directed outwards towards creation and towards humanity in particular. In other words, for Julian, self-giving love is God's entire reality. Julian does not provide simple definitions or a systematic structure to help us to understand what this means. Her pedagogical approach is to begin with the Passion, expressed in visionary form, and then to proceed by means of other images and stories. In this way, Julian is able to teach a deeper wisdom beyond the language of logic. Julian's *A Revelation of Love* begins with an overwhelming image of self-giving love manifested in the face of the crucified and suffering Christ and which is to be the measure of all human existence. The cross is both an indication of humanity's need for healing and radical transformation and also of humanity's continued worth "in God's sight."

The point of the visions was to find the transcendent reality of God in this broken human figure of the crucified Jesus. Yet, at the same time, to see God mediated essentially through the suffering flesh of Jesus and through God's "working" in all contingent things also paradoxically serves to preserve the otherness of God. That is, God's transcendence is inextricably linked to God's immanence. "I perceived, truly and powerfully, that it was he [Christ] who just so, both God and man, himself suffered for me, who showed it to me without any intermediary" (chapter 4).

Thus, in Jesus Christ the creation, life, and eternal future of humanity are caught up into the life of God-as-Trinity.

> And in the same revelation, suddenly the Trinity filled my heart full of the greatest joy, and I understood that it will be so in heaven without end to all who will come there. For the Trinity is God, God is the Trinity. The Trinity is our maker, the Trinity is our protector, the Trinity is our everlasting lover, the Trinity is our endless joy and our bliss, by our Lord Jesus Christ and in our Lord Jesus Christ.
>
> *(Chapter 4)*

On the cross, the love of God for humankind is shown to be a parallel of the love relationship within the Trinity – a dynamic and mutual indwelling in which each person of the Godhead is constantly giving to and sharing with the others. This way of being is also revealed as afflicted love, united through suffering to all humanity. From the vision of Jesus Christ on the cross Julian learned that everything is filled with God and enclosed by God. Through the cross, God offers intimacy or "familiar love." Julian does not suggest directly that God suffers. Yet there are hints that God is not untouched by our condition. In the Incarnation, God is indissolubly joined to the human condition and longs for us.

As we saw in the last chapter, within God there is a longing and desire as part of God's everlasting goodness. Also because of God's indwelling within the human soul, God's thirst underpins our own deep longing and desire. God in Christ thirsts for us and because of our union with God we also thirst for God.

For Julian the simple fact is that, in her understanding of the Passion, the Trinity as such participates in all activities relating to salvation. This is part of the eternal economy of God even if only the "virgin's Son" may be said to suffer. "All the Trinity worked in Christ's Passion, administering abundant virtues and plentiful grace to us by him; but only the virgin's Son suffered, in which all the blessed Trinity rejoice." Further, concerning our salvation, "All the Trinity worked in Christ's Passion, administering abundant virtues and plentiful grace to us by him" (chapter 23).

The participation of the Trinity in salvation is also strongly implied earlier in chapter 11 where, as we have already noted several times, Julian sees God "in a pointe." Here, God is seen to be in all things, as doing all things and as bringing them to their preordained conclusion.

> And therefore the blessed Trinity is always wholly pleased with all its works; and God revealed all this most blessedly, as though to say: See I am God. See, I am in all things. See, I do all things. See, I never remove my hands from my works, nor ever shall without end. See, I guide all things to the end that I ordain them for, before time began, with the same power and wisdom and love with which I made them; how should anything be amiss?
>
> *(Chapter 11)*

As we have seen, in the three "properties" of fatherhood, motherhood, and lordship "in one God" our essential human nature (what Julian refers to as our "substance") dwells equally in each person of the Trinity and in all the persons together. "And our substance is in our Father, God almighty, and our substance is in our Mother, God all wisdom, and our substance is in our Lord God, the Holy Spirit, all goodness, for our substance is whole in each person of the Trinity, who is one God." In chapter 58 Julian also explicitly links her theology of the Trinity to human existence. "For all our life consists of three: In the first we have our being, and in the second we have our increasing, and in the third we have our fulfilment. The first is nature, the second is mercy, the third is grace." In other words, in relation to human existence, God's love has three effects, corresponding to the persons of the Trinity. First, God's love performs a work of nature by creating us in God's image and sustaining us in existence. Second, God's love performs a work of mercy by healing the damage caused by our failing and falling (that is, by sin). Finally, God's love performs a work of grace, fulfilling human existence by bringing it into union with the life of God. This begins now in time and space but is to be finally completed in heaven.

The mutual indwelling of the persons of the Trinity one in the other (*perichoresis*), as affirmed at a number of points including at the end of the famous parable of a Lord and a Servant, is related to the human condition. "Now the Son, true God and true man, sits in his city [the human soul] in rest and in peace, which his Father has prepared for him by his endless purpose, and the Father in the Son, and the Holy Spirit in the Father and in the Son" (chapter 51). We are drawn into this mutual indwelling, into an intimacy with God that is Julian's version of deification. She expresses this as a mutual enclosure. We are enclosed in God and God is enclosed in us:

> And I saw no difference between God and our substance, but, as it were, all God; and still my understanding accepted that our substance is in God, that is to say that God is God, and our substance is a creature in God. For the almighty truth of the Trinity is our Father, for he made us and keeps us in him. And the deep wisdom of the Trinity is our Mother, in whom we are enclosed. And the high goodness of the Trinity is our Lord, and in him we are enclosed and he in us. We are enclosed in the Father, and we are enclosed in the Son, and we are enclosed in the Holy Spirit. And the Father is enclosed in us, the Son is enclosed in us, and the Holy Spirit is enclosed in us, almighty, all wisdom and all goodness, one God, one Lord.
>
> *(Chapter 54)*

Also, "Our soul sits in God in true rest, and our soul stands in God in sure strength, and our soul is naturally rooted in God in endless love" (chapter 56).

Because Julian seeks to articulate not only something of what God is but also something of how God sees reality and has revealed it to her in part, she offers a radically alternative vision of all created reality, including human existence. As we shall see in more detail in the next chapter, this results in two striking assertions. First, there is neither blame nor wrath in God (chapters 45–49). Second, and related to it, sin is "no deed" (chapter 11). In seeing God in everything (chapter 11) Julian also sees all things in God and therefore "in all this sin was not shown to me." Later, as she considers the paradox of how the experience of sin hinders her longing for God (chapter 27) she is taught that she could not see sin as she contemplated the Passion because "it has no kind of substance, no share in being, nor can it be recognized except by the pain caused by it." What is critical is that in her anthropology, Julian teaches that the essence of human nature is not "sinful." Sin is the cause both of human pain and of the Passion and yet "sin is necessary" (in Middle English, "behovely"). In Julian's thinking around the question of what sin means it is somehow a providential dimension of our contingent incompleteness and fallibility. Counter-intuitively, while sin often blinds us it also at times enables us to experience more deeply God's essential nature as love.

As we shall explore in the next chapter, God does not "see" human sin but only the ultimate bliss that will be ours. In God's vision this is the truth of human existence. Thus Julian, in her vision of God's eye-view, cannot see sin even though she knows its impact on human life and experience. This does not deny that human beings sin. However, it is to say that the centrality of sin in human experience is not reproduced on the level of God's essential relationship with humanity. Julian expresses this in terms of a paradox at the end of chapter 34: "When I saw that God does everything which is done, I did not see sin, and then I saw that all is well. But when God did show me about sin, then he said: All will be well."

The two assertions are based on God's "great endless love" (chapter 45). "God is that goodness which cannot be angry, for God is nothing but goodness" (chapter 46). However, as we have seen, the parable of a Lord and a Servant makes clear (chapter 51) that it all depends on a difference in ways of seeing. The point is that God looks on human beings and their failings with unending love and compassion and not with blame.

The fallen servant in the parable then sees neither his loving lord who remains nearby "nor does he truly see what he himself is in the sight of his loving lord." We do not see ourselves truly. Indeed, the next chapter (chapter 52) clearly states that "God sees one way and man sees another way." Essentially God can only see humanity in the light of his Son. "When Adam fell, God's Son fell [into Mary's womb]; because of the true union which was made in heaven, God's Son could not be separated from Adam, for by Adam I understand all mankind" (chapter 51). Julian finally understands the parable when she is granted an insight into how God sees humankind.

From this standpoint, the story of Adam's Fall and of Christ's "fall" into Mary's womb (the Incarnation) are inextricably linked; they are even somehow a single event. The moment of Adam's Fall becomes the moment of salvation as well. The parable is an exposition both of how God always views humankind and also of salvation history from God's viewpoint. God looks upon us as we are in Christ and sees us both in our original blessing and final integrity: healed, sinless, and glorified. In chapter 10 this unbroken connection between our creation and our redemption is related to the unchanging nature of God's love. "And he who created man for love, by the same love wanted to restore man to the same blessedness and to even more." In the light of eternity we are ever in union with God and always have been. "And for the great endless love that God has for all mankind, he makes no distinction in love between the blessed soul of Christ and the least soul that will be saved" (chapter 54).

The whole purpose of God's grace is not simply to overcome the fall but to "bring fair nature back again to the blessed place from which it came, which is God, with more nobility and honour by the powerful operation of grace" (chapter 63). In general, Julian's teaching about human nature is inseparable from her understanding of the fall and of redemption as she "saw" this in the vision of Christ on the cross and eventually came to understand it in the parable of a Lord and a Servant.

Substance and Sensuality

Julian's most extensive exposition of human identity appears in the chapters immediately following the parable of a Lord and a Servant. Indeed, her analysis of human nature is related directly to her prolonged attempts to understand the parable. As already noted, Julian's theology of human nature is complex and binary but it is not dualistic. We therefore need to understand what Julian means by her describing two dimensions of the "soul" or of human identity. These are entitled "substance" and "sensuality" and are elucidated especially in chapters 53–59. Julian is clear that these dimensions mutually support each other.

> Let either of them take help from the other, until we have grown into full stature as creative nature brings about; and then in the foundation of creative nature with the operation of mercy, the Holy Spirit by grace breathes into us gifts leading to endless life.
> *(Chapter 55)*

These two dimensions of human identity are not easy to define because the words have a number of connotations. What needs to be underlined is that they certainly do not mean "spirit" or soul versus "matter" or body.

The concepts of substance and sensuality bear some, but not total, resemblance to Augustine's concept of the higher and lower parts of the soul, understanding "soul" to mean the depths of human identity.[6]

Julian does not actually consider human embodiment in any systematic or extensive way. However, again it needs to be emphasized that she is free from any statements that devalue or demean the body. Indeed, as we have already noted, in chapter 6 Julian graphically illustrates how God is involved in even the lowliest of bodily functions, defecation. The important point is that Julian uses this involvement as an image of God's overall care for and service of humanity.

> A man walks upright, and the food in his body is shut in as if in a well-made purse. When the time of his necessity comes, the purse is opened and then shut again, in most seemly fashion. And it is God who does this, as it is shown when he says that he comes down to us in our humblest needs. For he does not despise what he has made, nor does he disdain to serve us in the simplest natural functions of our body, for love of the soul which he created in his own likeness.

Most fundamentally, the notion of "substance" refers to the core or essence of our humanity that is by its nature and creation for ever united to God. It is also the self that God persistently "sees." In chapter 53 Julian uses the image of "knitting" to describe the distinctive relationship between God and humanity. Human beings are "knit" to God in their making and God is "knit" to humanity by taking flesh.

> Therefore he wants us to know that the noblest thing which he ever made is mankind, and the fullest substance and the highest power is the blessed soul of Christ. And furthermore, he wants us to know that this beloved soul was preciously knitted to him in its making, by a knot so subtle and so mighty that it is united in God. In this uniting it is made endlessly holy. Furthermore, he wants us to know that all the souls which will be saved in heaven without end are knit in this knot, and united in this union, and made holy in this holiness

In the same chapter 53, Julian also writes of the "godly will." This will, "which never assented to sin nor ever will," is an aspect of what Julian calls our "substance." This echoes Augustine's anthropology. Julian also adopts Augustine's notion of the *imago Dei*. The human person, whether female or male, is created in the image of God-the-Trinity (chapter 10) and this is humanity's true nature: a sharing in the nature and substance of God. In chapter 10 Julian also notes that the human soul is an image of the Trinity. In her theological anthropology there is no hierarchy of male and female. Also, in Julian's exposition, the *imago Dei* within us does not imply that human existence is purely static. On the contrary, all humans have a dynamic tendency to return to God their origin. Thus substance "could never and should never be parted from him [God]." Chapter 54 develops the theme further. God dwells in our soul and our soul, while created, "dwells in God in substance, of which substance, through God, we are what we are." Julian then offers a radical understanding of substance.

> And I saw no difference between God and our substance, but, as it were, all God; and still my understanding accepted that our substance is in God, that is to say that God is God, and our substance is a creature in God.

Our soul is a created trinity, like the uncreated Trinity. "And so my understanding was led by God to see in him and to know, to understand and to recognize that our soul is a created trinity, like the uncreated blessed Trinity" (chapter 55).

There is a mutual indwelling between God and the essence or substance of human beings. "Greatly ought we to rejoice that God dwells in our soul; and more greatly ought we to rejoice that our soul dwells in God." God and the human soul are united and mutually indwell from the first moment each human soul is created.

Turning to the second dimension of Julian's exposition of human identity, "sensuality," this aspect of human nature is broadly speaking changeable (chapter 45). What is described as the lower part of the soul is united directly to the embodied dimension of human life in space and time. In a sense, sensuality expresses our incompleteness as human persons. As Julian puts it, "in our sensuality we are lacking" (chapter 57). However, this notion of "lacking" does not simply mean that we are faulty or flawed. Rather, it also suggests that we are incomplete in a more positive sense. We are unfinished beings and a "work in progress." As such we will ultimately be completed by God in heaven. In that sense, sensuality stands for the dimension of human existence that is necessarily a dynamic and evolutionary process. Importantly, Julian is clear that our sensuality is precious in God's eyes. Indeed, in and through Christ God dwells in our sensuality.

> I also saw that God is in our sensuality, for in the same instant and place in which our soul is made sensual, in that same instant and place exists the city of God, ordained for him without beginning.

He comes into this city and will never depart from it, for God is never out of the soul in which he will dwell blessedly without end.

(Chapter 55)

Sensuality may also be said to stand for the dimension of the human self that we perceive in our bodily, historical, context-specific lives. Neither image of "the self," whether substance or sensuality, is exclusively true. However, neither aspect is untrue. The paradox of human identity is somehow caught in the image of "the crown." We are God's crown. This is both a crown of thorns as Jesus Christ suffers for our sins (chapter 4) and also a crown of glory "which crown is the Father's joy, the Son's honour, the Holy Spirit's delight, and endless marvellous bliss to all who are in heaven" (chapter 51).

Yet we need to be careful. Substance and sensuality are not unequal or radically separated. "As regards our substance, it can rightly be called our soul, and as regards our sensuality, it can rightly be called our soul, and that is by the union [Middle English "oning"] which it has in God" (chapter 56). Our substance and sensuality are united through God's incarnation in human history. "And so in Christ our two natures are united." Also, "For the same time that God joined himself to our body in the maiden's womb, he took our soul, which is sensual, and in taking it, having enclosed us all in himself, he united it to our substance" (chapter 57). Thus sensual human life is gradually drawn up into the eternity of God.

In Julian's theological anthropology, her conception of human identity is fundamentally positive because it is grounded in her experience of God-as-love provoked by her dramatic visions of the sufferings of Christ on the cross. As Julian sees it, the cross is both a sign of our need for healing and also of our eternal and basic worth "in God's sight." In the end, Julian images our human nature as an "honourable city." Sensuality has dignity too. "That honourable city in which our Lord Jesus sits is our sensuality, in which he is enclosed; and our natural substance is enclosed in Jesus, with the blessed soul of Christ sitting in rest in the divinity" (chapter 56).

Julian and Apophatic Anthropology

In the minds of many people, the rich imagery used by Julian of Norwich in her text precludes thinking of her in terms of apophatic theology. Yet, while on the face of it, Julian has an overall "positive" or kataphatic approach to theology, I would suggest that in the end she also has an apophatic or "negative" dimension. Most immediately this applies to her theology of God. Thus, while the final chapter 86 of the Long Text indicates yet again that "Our Lord's meaning is love," and only love, on another level, as the same chapter also underlines, Julian's book, while begun by God's gift of "seeing," is "not yet completed." Julian's own theological journey as well as her theological teaching is necessarily incomplete because her theological reflections take us to the boundaries of the knowable to touch upon what cannot be fully known. In her own words, there is always and necessarily "a marvellous great mystery hidden in God" (chapter 27). Her theology is at the same time one of "seeing" (or knowing) truly in a new way and also of apophatic unknowing at the deepest level. This "negative" or apophatic dimension of Julian's theology does not concern only her approach to the reality of God. Precisely because human beings are created in the image of God and are forever united with God in their substance, this apophatic dimension to theology also applies to our inability to grasp the full depths of our human identity.

Julian's apophatic approach to human identity is hinted at in several places and in a number of different ways. For example, in the parable of a Lord and a Servant (chapter 51), the fallen and injured servant in the ditch cannot see himself truly precisely because he cannot see his lord who looks on him with pity rather than blame. Also, as we have noted earlier, in chapter 56 the true knowledge of our own soul (our fundamental identity) is dependent on having knowledge of God, because our identity is "in God." "And therefore if we want to have knowledge of our soul, and communion and discourse with it, we must seek in our Lord God in whom it is enclosed" (chapter 56).

Equally, when "oned" with God, I cease to be – or, rather, discover myself not to be – a "self" apart from God in the sense of an individualized and free-standing self. Julian echoes Augustine in seeing our deepest self, symbolized as the "heart" in Augustine and our "substance" in Julian, as the true "I am." This is where I am at one with God. In our highest powers, our "substance," we become by grace a "self" that cannot be distinguished from God except that we are created and God is not created (chapter 54).

> Our soul is made to be God's dwelling place, and the dwelling place of the soul is God, who is not made. It shows deep understanding to see and know inwardly that God, who is our maker, dwells in our soul, and deeper understanding to see and know that our soul, which is made, dwells in God's being; through this essential being – God – we are what we are.

In essence, in her quest to understand human nature, Julian is not given conclusive knowledge-as-fact but persistently senses a "surplus of meaning" to which she needs to return again and again. "So I saw him [God] and sought him, and I had him and I lacked him; and this is and should be our ordinary undertaking in this life, as I see it" (chapter 10). Even at the end of the Long Text (chapter 86) she is clear that "this book is begun by God's gift and his grace, but it is not yet performed, as I see it." This is both a reference to our incomplete understanding of our human nature and to an incomplete process of "becoming" (particularly in reference to the dimension of "sensuality") which will find completion only in heavenly joy.

Notes

1 This version is based on the modern translation of the Long Text by Edmund Colledge & James Walsh, in *Julian of Norwich: Showings*, Mahwah, NJ: Paulist Press, 1978, p 183. However, there is an unfortunate misprint which has not been corrected since the text's original publication in 1978. This misprint omits the answer to Julian's query. I have therefore inserted the answer as it appears in the Short Text, chapter iv, in *Showings*, p 130. This corresponds accurately to the Middle English text.

2 See Nicholas Watson & Jacqueline Jenkins, eds., *The Writings of Julian of Norwich*, University Park, PA: Pennsylvania State University Press, 2006, p 138, notes on Chapter 5; also Bernard McGinn, *The Varieties of Vernacular Mysticism: 1350–1550*, New York: Crossroad, 2012, Chapter 12 "Julian of Norwich: 'Love is oure lordes mening'," p 434 & note 53.

3 See Kerrie Hide, *Gifted Origins to Graced Fulfillment: The Soteriology of Julian of Norwich*, Collegeville, MN: The Liturgical Press, 2001, p 66.

4 See Colledge & Walsh, *Showings*, p 197. The chapter overall suggests a spatial image. Thus, "By which vision I saw that he is present in all things." Also, "For he is at the centre of everything."

5 See R.A. Markus, *The End of Ancient Christianity*, Cambridge: Cambridge University Press, 1998, p 78.

6 See, for example Grace Jantzen, *Julian of Norwich*, 2nd edition, London: SPCK, 2000, pp 137–149 and Joan M. Nuth, *Wisdom's Daughter: The Theology of Julian of Norwich*, New York: Crossroad, 1991, pp 104–116.

Chapter 6

Sin and Salvation

The themes of human sinfulness and of salvation are strongly present throughout Julian of Norwich's Long Text and are crucial to the development of her theological insight and teaching. In the context of her troubled times, Julian was gradually, and with considerable doubts and difficulties, led away from a conventional understanding of human sinfulness and of God's reaction to it. Eventually, albeit cautiously, Julian teaches a radically different understanding of sin and of the process of salvation.

In the context of the social and religious realities of Julian's times, the recurrence of the plague known as the Black Death reinforced a widespread emphasis in fourteenth-century England on the plague as God's punishment for sin. Such an approach is illustrated, for example, in William Langland's famous vernacular poem "Piers Plowman." In general, people feared eternal punishment by a God who was conceived essentially as a great lord and an intimidating judge of human failure and this perspective was reinforced by popular preaching. Religious catechesis in Julian's time was predominantly focussed upon the themes of sin and salvation. In terms of humanity's relationship with God, fear of God's wrath was a determining factor. An emphasis on God's love and God's mercy (except in the narrow sense of a merciful forgiveness of repentant sinners who confessed to a priest as God's representative) was relatively uncommon. Given that background, it is understandable that Julian had a persistent, deep, and personal struggle, which she describes in her writings. This concerned the apparent contradiction between the conventional teaching of "holy Church" about sin and the very different understanding that Julian believed God had shown her through the medium of her mystical revelations.[1]

Julian of Norwich: "In God's Sight" – Her Theology in Context, First Edition. Philip Sheldrake.
© 2019 John Wiley & Sons Ltd. Published 2019 by John Wiley & Sons Ltd.

Julian's Understanding of Sin

In summary, without doubt Julian inherited a thoroughly conventional medieval approach to human sinfulness. This was based on an understanding of human nature as fundamentally "fallen," flawed, and sinful. However, the example or parable of a Lord and a Servant (chapter 51), once Julian had come to understand it, became the foundation of her revised and positive theology of the meaning of sin and the process of salvation. Indeed, her growing understanding of this parable as a result of further interior teaching some 20 years after her nearly mortal illness and visionary experiences basically forced Julian to reconsider her inherited interpretation of human sinfulness in relation to how God actually sees things.

In practice, Julian never defines or describes the conventional concept of "original sin." In this concept, the fundamental identity of human beings is defined as an inherently sinful nature based on the "Fall" of Adam and Eve, the first humans and parents of all subsequent humanity. In contrast to this conventional understanding, for Julian human beings do not appear to be unavoidably contaminated as a result of an inherently, and inherited, depraved nature. For example in chapter 47 Julian is clear that human nature in this life is necessarily changeable but the result is that we fall into sin through naiveté and ignorance rather than because of evil or malice.

> I understand in this way. Man is changeable in this life, and falls into sin through naivete and ignorance. He is weak and foolish in himself and also his will is overpowered in the time when he is assailed and in sorrow and woe. And the cause is blindness because he does not see God.

Importantly, our human weakness is caused by blindness because we do not consistently have a sight of God. Julian is even more explicit about this in chapter 63.

> Here we may see that truly it belongs to our nature to hate sin and truly it belongs to us by grace to hate sin, for nature is all good and fair in itself and grace was sent out to save nature and destroy sin, and bring fair nature back again to the blessed place from which it came, which is God, with more nobility and honour by the powerful operation of grace. For it will be seen before God by all his saints in joy without end that nature has been tried in the fire of tribulation, and that no lack or defect is found in it.

Julian is clear that our human nature is not to be defined as fundamentally flawed. It "is all good and fair in itself." Sin is unclean, "more vile and painful than hell" but this is because it is unnatural and "in opposition to our fair nature."

Because sin is unnatural and comes to us against our will (chapter 82) we must not allow ourselves to become too depressed or sorrowful.

> But here our courteous Lord revealed the moaning and the mourn-ing of our soul, with this meaning: I know well that you wish to live for my love, joyfully and gladly suffering all the penance which may come to you; but since you do not live without sin, you are depressed and sorrowful, and if you could live without sin, you would suffer for my love all the woe which might come to you, and it is true. But do not be too much aggrieved by the sin which comes to you against your will.

This is a very different spiritual dynamic from attempts in the popular preaching of Julian's time to provoke guilt and to suggest that our human sufferings, including the plague, are God's punishment for our inherent sinfulness, evil tendencies, and resulting sinful actions.

Julian confronts the paradox of sin early in her text. In chapter 11 her vision of God in a "pointe" leads her to understand that God is present in all things and that God does everything that is done. This awareness produced "a softe drede," that is, awe rather than fear. Julian is therefore provoked to ask "what is sin?" For, if God does everything that exists, it is nevertheless obvious that God does not "do" sin. This leaves Julian with the conundrum of what exactly sin is. Julian's immediate conclusion is to state that sin is "no deed." That is, sin is not a positive "something" but a negative absence or privation. This understanding is reinforced by Julian's statement that "in all this sin was not shown to me."

> I was compelled to admit that everything which is done is well done for our Lord God does everything. For at this time the work of creatures was not revealed, but the work of our Lord God in creatures; for he is at the centre of everything, and he does every-thing. And I was certain that he does no sin; and here I was certain that sin is no deed, for in all this sin was not shown to me.

However, this question continues to haunt the remainder of the Long Text, returning particularly sharply in chapter 27.

The Importance of Chapter 27

In chapter 27, Julian returns to her fundamental deep longing for God. She comes to see that the only thing that gets in the way of this desire for God is sin. This leads her to speculate that if there had been no sin this problem would not have arisen. So why was sin not prevented by God from the very beginning of human creation? If it had been prevented everything would have been well.

> And after this our Lord brought to my mind the longing that I had for him before, and I saw that nothing hindered me but sin, and I saw that this is true of us all in general, and it seemed to me that if there had been no sin, we should all have been pure and as like our Lord as he created us.

As I have already stated briefly, here I do not believe that Julian was in the strict sense addressing the philosophical question of theodicy. Classical theodicy focuses on how the existence of an all-powerful and benevolent God is logically consistent with the existence of evil. In her text Julian records her questioning of God through which she is led to understand the nature of "sin" very differently. Behind her question in chapter 27 lies an assumption by Julian that the "wellness" of creation depends on the absence of sin. The sense that there is only one answer to this problem, that she could see it and was troubled by it, is then described as "lacking discretion." That is, her instinctive understanding was unwise or a failure of good judgment. Julian then experiences an answer from Jesus. First of all, she is told that "Sinne is behovely." What does the Middle English word "behovely" mean? The Colledge and Walsh modern translation uses the phrase "sin is necessary."

> But Jesus, who in this vision informed me about everything needful to me, answered with these words and said: Sin is necessary, but all will be well, and all will be well, and every kind of thing will be well.

However, the word "necessary" may seem to imply ontological necessity. This would raise theological and philosophical difficulties. However, "necessary" is also not the only possible translation of the Middle English word. In practice, "necessary" reflects the Latin word *necessarium* as it appears in the hymn of proclamation *Exultet* sung at the Easter Vigil Liturgy, as Julian would have known it. The relevant phrase from the hymn is *O certe necessarium Adae peccatum*: literally "Oh truly necessary sin of Adam." Some alternative modern English words for the Middle

English "behovely" would be that sin is "opportune," "suitable," or "advantageous." These would echo the sentiment of the following verse from the *Exultet*, that is, "Oh happy fault," *O felix culpa*, that earned for humanity such a great redeemer. In other words, although human sin is a fault and a failure it nevertheless paradoxically offers an opportunity that would not otherwise be there. Sin is therefore to be understood as a means to an end. And the "end" or purpose of the human capacity to sin is that God is able to show us love as the meaning of everything in even greater depth and force than if sin had never existed.

In addition, Julian notes once again that she did not see sin. It can only be recognized by the pain it causes both to the one who sins and to those who are sinned against. Sin has "no maner of substance, ne no part of being." In other words, sin has no ontological reality. It is an absence or a lack of something, especially of love and light. This is followed by the promise that "alle shalle be wele."

> But I did not see sin, for I believe that it has no kind of substance, no share of being, nor can it be recognized except by the pain caused by it.... And because of the tender love which our good Lord has for all who will be saved, he comforts readily and sweetly, meaning this: It is true that sin is the cause of all this pain, but all will be well, and every kind of thing will be well.

Sometimes the Middle English "shalle" is straight-forwardly translated as "will" in modern English. All will be well. That is, everything is going to be well in some undefined future. However, the word "shalle" can be distinguished from the word "will" and has more force than "will" because it implies necessity. That is, "shalle" suggests that it will *necessarily* be the case that God makes everything well. Julian expresses these sentiments once again in chapter 34.

> When I saw that God does everything which is done, I did not see sin, and then I saw that all is well. But when God did show me about sin, then he said: All will be well.

Spiritual Pain, Repentance, and the Forgiveness of Sins

Occasionally, throughout her text Julian expresses a more subjective experience of the impact of sinful fragility in her life. She first touches upon the experience of "woe" in chapter 1. This is linked to "the heaviness and weariness of our mortal life." However, she is clear that "the experience of woe comes as a temptation." Julian refers to this in relation to the Seventh Revelation which is her chapter 15. Julian found it astonishing that God-as-Trinity should fill her with joy (chapter 4). It was a marvel that God should be so "homely" with a sinful creature – that is, familiar or intimate. Julian assumed that this was a comfort offered to her before being "tempted by devils."

Experiences in this life of "supreme spiritual delight," which offer "everlasting surety, powerfully secured without any painful fear," are necessarily momentary. Soon "I was changed, and abandoned to myself, oppressed and weary of my life." Guilt and pain are an inherent part of our contingent existence. Chapter 38 of Julian's Long Text suggests that "there is indeed a corresponding pain for every sin" although Julian goes on to suggest that this will be matched by joys in heaven that reward our victories over sin. In the isolation caused by our failings (chapter 40), "when we see ourselves so foul, then we believe that God may be angry with us because of our sins." However, then God shows the divine presence to the soul, "welcoming it as a friend, as if it had been in pain and in prison" and referring to the soul as "My dear darling."

Julian occasionally refers to the spiritual practice of auricular confession to a priest. However, this is not expressed essentially in terms of guilt, judgment, and the giving of a penance to the penitent by way of punishment. Rather Julian describes confession in terms of healing and liberation from the pain of guilt. In chapter 39 sin is characterized as "the sharpest scourge with which any chosen soul can be struck." This can "break" a person. However, contrition may take hold of a person "by the inspiration of the Holy Spirit" and lead to the healing of wounds, the revival of the soul and the restoration of life. God "leads him to confession, willing to reveal his sins, nakedly and truthfully, with great sorrow and great shame that he has so befouled God's fair image." By "God's fair image" Julian means that the person has damaged himself (an image of God) rather than simply demeaned God. The person then "accepts the penance for every sin imposed by his confessor, for this is established in Holy Church by the teaching of the Holy Spirit." There is another reference to confession in chapter 66 when Julian describes a visit by "a man of religion" during her mortal illness. She is then, in her own words, "imprudent" when she describes something of her visionary experiences of the figure of the bleeding Christ. The visiting cleric clearly took her seriously and Julian felt ashamed. She then refers to wanting to make her confession "but I could not tell it to any priest."

How God Sees Sin

Most importantly of all, Julian is faced with the question of how God actually sees sin. In summary, the theme of chapter 51, the vitally important parable of a Lord and a Servant, is to suggest that God does not "see" sin in the way that human beings do. God only sees the bliss that will ultimately be ours. In God's "sight" eternal bliss is the ultimate truth for humankind. Thus, Julian in being offered a temporary and partial "sight" of reality from God's point of view also cannot "see" sin. As opposed to much medieval theology, Julian has a significant problem with the notion of God's anger, God's desire to punish sin, God desiring retribution, or God needing restitution. Julian does not deny sinfulness but refuses to attribute any anger to God.

As we have seen in Chapter 3, the parable of a Lord and a Servant clarifies a number of things. First, there is a teleological connection between Adam (who is understood by Julian to represent all of humanity) and Christ. That is to say, "in God's sight" the Fall of humanity and the redemption brought about by Christ through the Incarnation and Passion are a single "moment." Second, sin is certainly a deviation from our original creation. However, it involves a separation from a loving God rather than a conflict with a God who desires to punish us. Thus, Julian is led to see that the story of the Fall is not so much a wilful act of rebellion against God as a blindness and a sense of separation from God based on misadventure. The servant is said to be "injured in his powers"; that is, he is prevented from knowing that his "Godly will" that irrevocably unites him permanently to God is still preserved intact. The parable also focuses on God's promise of restoration rather than on punishment. The image of the servant trying to do the Lord's will but falling into a ditch and remaining trapped there points to "sin" as self-imprisonment rather than malice. Sin is its own punishment. Therefore sin is weakness rather than a cause of guilt. Our existential sin is a result of ignorance rather than the inevitable consequence of an inherently depraved nature. Even our conception of God as angry judge is a form of blindness. As a result, God looks on sinners, of which the servant is an image, with pity not with blame and as a healer rather than as a judge.

In chapter 78, Julian indicates that God wishes us to know four vital things about sin and about God's reaction to it. The foundation is that God only shows us our sin "by the light of his mercy" rather than in all its horribleness. First, God is the foundation from whom we have our ongoing life and being. Second, God protects us strongly and mercifully while we are in our sin. Third, God protects us courteously and helps us to know that we are going astray. Finally, God steadfastly waits for us and "does not change his demeanour." In the Middle English this is "changeth no chere." This refers back to chapter 51 where God's "chere" or demeanour refers to "rewth and pitte", that is, to compassion and pity. With this knowledge of four vital things "we may see our sin, profitably, without despair."

God's Mercy

Julian frequently refers to God's mercy. When she does this, what does she mean by "mercy"? The word is often understood mainly, even exclusively, as the gracious forgiveness of debt or of the faults and offenses of humanity. In human terms, the word "mercy" can also imply clemency or forbearance by those with power for those without power – the underclass who are at the mercy of powerful people or of impersonal forces. Such a viewpoint was frequently projected onto God.

However, even the *Oxford Dictionary* definition of mercy suggests something more. Mercy implies kind treatment, especially a disposition to forgive or to show compassion rather than the opposite. If mercy is linked to compassion – literally "to suffer with" (imaged in the life and death of Jesus Christ) – it embraces sympathy, fellow feeling, and, not least, an inclination to offer help to those in need.

From a Christian perspective, the foundation of our understanding of mercy is that it is an attribute of God and includes compassion. Human mercy is founded upon God's mercy, and is inspired by God. There is a realization that the human self, and all that it can do and give, does not have purely autonomous, individual, and self-focused "rights." There is an inherent solidarity in human existence in which both those who give and those who receive share the same foundation – that is, God's fullness. Mercy also, therefore, involves compassion towards those who do not have an obvious claim to our kindness and from whom no recompense is expected.

In her chapters 47 and 48 Julian tells how she was led to reinterpret God's mercy. She notes in chapter 47 that "by the teaching [of the Church] which I had before" God's mercy refers to how God remits the natural reaction of anger at human sins. This would make mercy a welcome experience for people "whose intention and desire is to love" because for such spiritually inclined people the anger of God "would be harder than any other pain." Julian then notes that at no point did this kind of mercy appear in her revelations.

Julian proceeds to diagnose the everyday human condition that forms the background to her reinterpretation of God's mercy. Recalling Julian's concept of "sensuality" as a dimension of human identity, we are changeable in this life. We fall into sin through ignorance. We are weak and can easily be assailed by sorrow and woe. Behind this lies a blindness that results from not seeing God consistently. In contrast, Julian gratefully acknowledges that in her revelatory experience she "saw" and "felt" in ways that "were great and plentiful" compared to "our common feeling in this life." She had a sight of God that drew her towards rejoicing and hope even though she knew that such experience could not persist. Yet she had hope in God's endless love and that "I should be protected by his mercy and brought to bliss."

Chapter 48 then outlines the true nature of God's mercy as Julian experienced it and believed that she was mandated to teach all her fellow Christians. The Holy Spirit is "endless life dwelling in our soul" who protects us, gives us peace, brings us ease, and reconciles us to God. "And this is the mercy and the way on which our good Lord constantly leads us." Julian goes on to state that the foundation of God's mercy is love and "the operation of mercy is our protection in love." Indeed, this was revealed to Julian in such a way that she could not see any other aspect of mercy "than as if it were all love in love." Anger and wrath do not belong to God, so that the notion of mercy as the remission of God's wrath is overturned in what Julian was shown. Indeed, she firmly asserts that wrath is a purely human emotion and "is nothing else but a perversity and an opposition to peace and love."

Interestingly, in chapter 48 Julian goes on to make an early reference to motherhood. She states that "mercy is a compassionate property, which belongs to motherhood in tender love." In the context of this chapter, motherhood is implicitly but not explicitly related to God. Julian concludes chapter 48 by listing the "works" of God's mercy as protecting, enduring, vivifying, and healing. In addition grace-filled mercy raises, rewards, and endlessly exceeds what human performance deserves. In this, mercy is associated closely with God's plenty, generosity, and "his wonderful courtesy."

In the chapters on either side of the parable of a Lord and a Servant, Julian continues to address the tension she experiences. In chapter 50 she lays her fundamental problem before God. As fallible humans "we sin grievously all day and are very blameworthy." Indeed, "We are often dead by the judgment of men on earth." Yet, to her astonishment, Julian has been led to understand that God shows no sign of blame. Indeed in the sight of God "the soul which will be saved was never dead and never will be." The effective dynamic of human existence is that "in this mortal life mercy and forgiveness are the path which always leads us to grace." Confronted with this paradox as a result of her interior insights, Julian cries out to God to be taught and told all she needs to know to resolve this conflict. The following chapter 51 and its parable is the medium for God to answer Julian. In chapter 52, as we have already seen, Julian asserts that God sees things one way and we see things in another way. Concretely, we "see" our falling and sinning and the harm that comes from these. Yet this becomes the medium for us also to "know the everlasting love which he [God] has for us, and his plentiful mercy."

Finally, at certain points in her elucidation of the two dimensions of human identity, substance, and sensuality (chapters 53–59), Julian seems to link the notion of "mercy" specifically to sensuality. That is to say that God's mercy operates most overtly in the context of our contingent existence which is incomplete and always "on the way" towards a full congruence with our "substance" – the dimension of human identity that is irrevocably united with God from our first creation. Thus, "Our sensuality is founded in nature, in mercy and in grace" (chapter 55). In chapter 56 "The profits of our tribulation" that we inevitably experience in our contingent sensual existence are obtained through God's mercy in the power of Christ's Passion. This brings our sensuality "up into the substance." God is the "substance" (the core) of human nature and from this "spring mercy and grace." "For in nature we have our life and our being, and in mercy and grace [active in our sensuality] we have our increase and our fulfilment." God's "mercy" not only involves kindness and compassion but also a process of drawing us into God's fullness.

Julian's Theology of Salvation

Julian's soteriology, her theology of human salvation, significantly undercuts classical "satisfaction" models of redemption. In the time of Julian of Norwich, the most influential satisfaction theory was that of Anselm, the eleventh-century philosopher, theologian, and Archbishop of Canterbury, in his work *Cur Deus Homo*. This spoke of human sin in terms of undermining the honor that was due to God. The death of Christ was interpreted as making "satisfaction" for this. It mends what has been broken by human sin. As the ultimate act of obedience, Christ's death reverses human disobedience and restores honor to God. Christ's selfless suffering for humankind pays honor to the Father and therefore makes up for the honor that human beings have generally failed to pay to God. In that sense Christ's suffering and death substitutes for the debt of honor that humans have failed to give God. This is not the same theology as later and much darker penal substitution theories which saw Christ's death as a process of taking upon himself the brutal punishment meted out by God that was otherwise due to all sinful humanity.[2] In chapter 12, Julian describes the powerful image of the bleeding body of Christ that she experienced in her visions. However, this suffering, the result of "vicious blows delivered all over the lovely body," is not presented as Jesus taking on God's brutal punishment that was otherwise due to us. Rather it becomes an image of washing and of the sacred drink in the sacrament of the Eucharist.

> Then it came into my mind that God has created bountiful waters on the earth for our use and our bodily comfort, out of the tender love he has for us. But it is more pleasing to him that we accept for our total cure his blessed blood to wash us of our sins, for there is no drink that is made which it pleases him so well to give us.

Counter-intuitively, in her chapter 22, Julian has Jesus "our good Lord" ask her if *she* is well satisfied. "Arte thou well apaide that I suffered for thee?" When Julian responds positively she hears Jesus Christ say "If thou arte apaide, I am apaide." This reverses conventional satisfaction theology. Here God-in-Christ is satisfied if humans are satisfied. Julian's schema of salvation is not that divine justice is satisfied and salvation secured by an atonement performed by Jesus suffering in our place on the cross. Rather, human need is satisfied and thus humanity becomes Christ's joy.

In the parable of a Lord and a Servant in chapter 51, Jesus takes upon himself all our blame. However, in context this is not the classic "satisfaction" theory but refers to our own self-blame, the unproductive sense of guilt and worthlessness which makes us feel separated from God. Jesus redeems or heals our blinded sight and false perceptions that make us unaware of God's irreversible love.

As we also saw in Chapter 3, the parable of a Lord and a Servant acts as an answer to Julian's background problem of how to relate her conventional understanding of human sin to her inner awareness of God's irreversible love for humanity. In chapter 45 of her text she is clear that the teaching of the Church was that human beings as sinners sometimes deserve God's anger. Yet her visionary experience showed her that there was neither blame nor anger in God. The parable may well have been part of Julian's original mystical experience even though it needed further inward instruction over many years before Julian came to understand it properly and to accept what it expressed. This understanding made it clear in Julian's theological reflections that, unlike the theology of Anselm, God neither was angry with humanity nor felt dishonored by human failings. This insight underpins Julian's theology of salvation (or redemption) as an act of compassionate healing on the part of God. Adam's sin "was the greatest harm ever done or ever to be done until the end of the world" (chapter 29). However, Julian was also taught that "the glorious atonement" was more pleasing to God than sin is harmful. Indeed, as we have already seen, Julian's fundamental inner insight, or "revelation," leads her to a deep realization of the fundamental nature of God as love rather than as judge. The impact on her is therefore not fear but joy. "And in the same revelation, suddenly the Trinity filled my heart full of the greatest joy" (chapter 4). Also God desires that "we have true delight with him in our salvation, and in it he wants us to be greatly comforted and strengthened" (chapter 23).

Again, as we have already seen, Julian's fundamentally positive theology of human nature is an important partner to her theology of sin and salvation. The image of God as our "clothing" in her chapters 5 and 6 underlines God's intimacy with us. As we have seen, this contrasts with the language of the Book of Genesis, chapter 3, where the emphasis is on Adam and Eve's nakedness as an image of humanity's loss of innocence. For Julian, the essence of her theological anthropology is that humankind is not inherently sinful. As God sees things, sin is "no deed" (chapter 11) and has no substance or "being" even though sin hinders our longing for God (chapter 27). That is, sin is an absence of good rather than a concrete and evil "something." While Julian in her life experience is well aware of human frailty and failings, when she is briefly shown reality as God sees it she could not see sin. While sin is the cause of human pain, Julian is led to understand that it is somehow "appropriate" because our frailty and failings lead us providentially into a deeper awareness of God as love.

In terms of salvation, God's "sight" is of humanity's ultimate bliss as the truth of human existence. So, when God does touch upon the question of sin God carefully affirms that ultimately all will be well (chapter 34). Equally, when God brings to mind Julian's capacity to sin (chapter 37), she was fearful. However, God responds with the words "I protect you very safely." God also leads Julian to the insight that this applies not just to her but to "all my fellow Christians."

The chapter ends with an anticipation of the detailed discussion of the binary nature of human identity as both substance and sensuality (chapters 45–53). Here Julian simply states that part of the nature of "the soul" is a Godly will that never assents to sin. In the following chapter 38, God shows Julian something equally startling. This is the paradox that "sin will be no shame but honour." This seems to go beyond a common notion that those who are in heaven may well remember their sins but would not be shamed by them. However, Julian is led to see that sin is "wurshipe to man" – that is, honor.

In terms of her theology of salvation, Julian records that she was constantly shown "a great marvel," that God cannot be said to forgive "because he cannot be angry (chapter 49)."

> For it was a great marvel, constantly shown to the soul in all the revelations, and the soul was contemplating with great diligence that our Lord God cannot in his own judgment forgive, because he cannot be angry – that would be impossible....
>
> For I saw most truly that where our Lord appears, peace is received and wrath has no place; for I saw no kind of wrath in God, neither briefly nor for long; for truly, as I see it, if God could be angry for any time, we should neither have life nor place nor being; for as truly as we have our being from the endless power of God and from his endless wisdom and from his endless goodness, just as truly we have our preservation in the endless power of God and in his endless wisdom and in his endless goodness. For though we

may feel in ourselves anger, contention and strife, still we are all mercifully enclosed in God's mildness and in his meekness, in his benignity and in his accessibility.

While human beings cannot easily forgive themselves but are subject to angry self-judgment (see the end of chapter 48), God's only characteristic is mercy (that is, compassion) rooted in God's unchangeable love of humanity. In chapter 49 Julian also returns to the image of God's "friendship" with human beings expressed in her vision of heaven in chapter 14. Thus, "It is the most impossible thing which could be that God might be angry, for anger and friendship are two contraries."

Julian and Universalism

Over the years, the question has regularly been asked about whether Julian is fundamentally a universalist. In other words, does Julian believe that everyone will ultimately be redeemed and eternally "oned" with God? If this is so then, in an obvious literal sense, "all will be well, and every kind of thing will be well." Opinions about this question have differed because Julian's own perspective is both complex and ambiguous.

In recent years, the scholarly consensus is broadly that there are clear hints of universalism in Julian. However, the consensus is also that Julian is deliberately ambiguous. This is partly because universal salvation does not easily correspond with her sense of the damage caused by human sinfulness. Equally, Julian does not wish to set up a conflict between what she believes she has been led to understand through her revelations or inner teaching and the "common teaching of holy Church."[3]

During the early Christian centuries there had been theological speculation about the possibility of universal salvation, or what was called *apokatastasis*. A number of commentators have suggested that such major theologians as Origen, Clement of Alexandria, and Gregory of Nyssa addressed the restoration of all creation and the reconciliation to God of sinful humanity as a whole at the end of time through the medium of God's overwhelming love and mercy. However, without going into the complexities of the related debates, there are a number of interpretations of each of these writers that make it uncertain what their views were about the possibility of universal salvation.

It seems that there was further theological speculation about universalism during the Middle Ages. For example, in the ninth century there was a carefully argued defense of universalism by the Irish philosopher and theologian John Scotus Eriugena in his work *Periphyseon*.[4] Later, during the fourteenth century, apart from Julian of Norwich, the German

Dominican mystical theologian Johannes Tauler and the Flemish theologian Jan van Ruysbroeck (or John Ruusbroec) are also sometimes cited as possible universalists. However, conventional Church teaching, at least in the Western Church, affirmed clearly that hell existed, that the devil was certainly damned, and that eternal damnation was always a theoretical possibility for unrepentant human beings. This was deemed to be necessarily the case in the context of human free will. However, apart from the devil, the Church never officially defined whether anyone was actually in hell.

In their 1978 scholarly edition of Julian's texts, Colledge and Walsh note that the final "great deed" which Julian was told God would perform and which would make all things well cannot be contemplated by humans until it is done. Meanwhile, as Colledge and Walsh put it, there is definitely "a contrary which reasoning cannot resolve." That is, there seems to be a conflict between Church teaching and Julian's vision. In chapter 33 Julian writes that she did request a sight of purgatory and hell but that this was not given to her.

> And yet in this I desired, so far as I dared, that I might have had some sight of hell and purgatory.... But for all that I could wish, I could see nothing at all of this except what has already been said in the fifth revelation, where I saw that the devil is reproved by God and endlessly condemned.

Julian also recalls that in all her visions of Christ's Passion she did not see any of "the damned" except for the devil.

In reference to the devil, in the Fifth Revelation (chapter 13) Julian saw that the devil is overcome by Christ's Passion, is shamed and scorned by God, and despised "as nothing" as a result of which Julian "laughed greatly."

> Also I saw our Lord scorn his malice and despise him as nothing, and he wants us to do so. Because of this sight I laughed greatly, and that made those around me to laugh as well; and their laughter was pleasing to me. I thought that I wished that all my fellow Christians had seen what I saw. Then they would all have laughed with me....

According to Colledge and Walsh, the most important thing is that Julian is not explicitly drawn away from any article of Church teaching. The latter affirmed that eternal damnation was always a possibility. As chapter 33 asserts, "I saw that the devil is reproved by God and endlessly condemned." Julian also understood that "every creature who is of the devil's condition in this life and so dies is no more mentioned before God and all his saints than is the devil." However, it can never be definitively asserted that anyone is actually "of the devil's condition" when they die. Equally, as we shall see, the meaning of the phrase "no more mentioned" is ambiguous. In summary, what Colledge and Walsh underline is that basically Julian is not shown a conclusive answer to her question about sin and salvation.[5]

In their more recent scholarly edition, Watson and Jenkins refer to chapter 9 of the Long Text where Julian makes the first of many references to "those who will be saved" and suggest that "the saved" are an unknowable body. Equally, Julian says nothing about anyone else. In fact the phrase "that shalle be saved" is used some twenty-five times in the Long Text to qualify Julian's teaching. Watson and Jenkins suggest that there is a kind of universalizing logic to chapter 9 but that the phrase "those who will be saved" appears to be Julian's way of cautiously balancing out that apparent logic. In Julian's Thirteenth Revelation (chapters 27–40) she explicitly confronts ideas of universal salvation. "Alle shalle be wele" dominates the insights of the Revelation. However, as Watkins and Jenkins note, chapter 27 uses the phrase "to alle that shalle be saved" to qualify what would otherwise appear to be overt universalism. Like Colledge and Walsh, they also note that chapter 32 suggests that God's final "great deed," which "will make well all which is not well," cannot be resolved until the last day. This is partly because Julian and all human creatures are incapable of understanding it now and partly because the logic of such a great deed is that it is a conclusion to everything and necessarily lies beyond the end of time.

Chapter 32 also outlines the traditional categories of "the damned": the fallen angels who are now devils and those who "die out of the faith of Holy Church" whether they are pagans or baptized people who nevertheless lived unchristian lives. Further (and more controversially) in chapter 33, Julian indicates that she had been taught that the Jews who put Jesus to death "were eternally accursed and condemned, except those who had been converted by grace." I have already noted in Chapter 1 that the city of Norwich had a particularly unpleasant relationship with the Jewish community. Overall, as she indicates in chapter 32, Julian struggled with God's message that everything will be well given "that one article of our faith is that many creatures will be damned."

It is worth noting that both Watson and Jenkins and Barry Windeatt, in what is the most recent scholarly edition of Julian, suggest that she apparently writes of two distinct "deeds" in chapters 32 and 36.[6] Watson and Jenkins suggest that this second deed relates to Julian's comment in chapter 35 that once sin has ceased to "harass righteous souls" everything "will be brought into righteousness and stand fast there forever." This second mysterious deed has a more limited compass than the first deed which embraces both unbelievers and those who have led an un-Christian life. Unlike the first deed which is entirely eschatological, beyond time and this present world, the second deed appears to be begun here, will be known by each person when they die, and is aimed primarily at "all his lovers on earth." Its purpose seems to be to redeem God's lovers from the fear that they are inextricably trapped in their status as sinners. The aim of the deed is to offer joy and to "make us rejoice in him and in all his works." However, as both Watson and Jenkins and Barry Windeatt note, later in the chapter this second deed also seems to expand beyond "his lovers" to include the more mysterious "all who will be saved." Fundamentally, Colledge and Walsh, Watkins and Jenkins, and Windeatt all agree that Julian's position on universalism, and on who is to be saved, is highly ambiguous because it is unresolved in her own mind.

More critically, Julian's God is not some fierce judge who saves or damns but one who acts out of love to make all things well. Equally, the heart of her anthropology is that human beings are created with their "being" in God. Their destiny is to return to God and to be delivered from the non-being of sin. In his study of Julian's theology, Denys Turner suggests that sin offers a false narrative which sets the story of sinful human beings and the "story" of God in a relationship of mutual exclusion. As the parable of a Lord and a Servant makes clear, human failure and falling, like the servant in the ditch, is its own hell. The fallen, injured servant cannot see the Lord looking at him nor can he "see" himself as God sees him. He can only feel his failure and experience his woundedness. As Turner puts it, we tend to create a negative reality out of the unreal. However, to do that is to replace God as creator and lover with God as a judgmental tyrant.[7]

However, the late Grace Jantzen, a philosopher of religion, in her study of Julian points out that the logic of human free will is that we must remain free to identify with the "nothingness" of sin even though it goes against our true selfhood in God. Interestingly Jantzen relates the "nothingness" of sin in the present life to the possibility of ultimate nothingness when we die. In that sense, hell would seem to be not a state of eternal punishment but rather an option for literal self-annihilation. However, Jantzen interprets Julian as implicitly affirming that there is the hope that in practice this possibility will not be actualized in anyone.[8] The possibility of falling into nothingness or oblivion is also mentioned speculatively by Joan Nuth in her study of Julian's theology. This is in reference to the comment in Julian's chapter 33 that every creature who dies "in the devil's condition" is "no more mentioned" before God. Not being "mentioned" may refer to being overlooked as irrelevant or it may imply falling into nothingness rather than enduring eternal punishment.[9] Nuth feels that Julian's ambiguous and careful approach to the question of salvation strongly suggests that the "all" that will ultimately be well includes every "particular" human being. Therefore, on balance, Nuth suggests that Julian's underlying position is that it is much more likely that everyone will be saved than that some will be damned.

In her chapter 45 Julian contrasts God's higher judgment with our lower judgment in "our changeable sensuality." Logically, this lower judgment is not confined to individuals. It necessarily applies also to the contingent nature of what the institutional Church teaches. The higher judgment is full of hidden mysteries. Thus, there may be a further salvific act by God at the end of time whereby all will be saved. However, God does not wish Julian to speculate and so she does not do so.[10] Overall, what is critical is that, in the light of the parable of a Lord and a Servant, human damnation or annihilation, if true, would be our perverse choice rather than the result of God's wrath or desire to punish.

Conclusion

Throughout her Long Text Julian struggles with the experience of sin in her own life and in the wider world, the damage and pain it causes, and the sense that it separates her from God and goes against her deepest longing. Yet, in her sixteen revelations Julian is shown a radically different vision of the meaning of sin and God's reaction to it. This leads to a profound inner struggle which runs as a continuous thread throughout her text. In the end, God does not "see" sin but only the ultimate bliss that will be ours. In God's vision this is the truth of human existence. Thus Julian, in her revelation of God's perspective, cannot see sin even though she knows its impact on human life and experience. This does not deny that human beings sin. However, it is to say that the centrality of sin in human experience is not reproduced on the level of God's essential relationship with humanity. Julian expresses this in terms of a paradox at the end of chapter 34: "When I saw that God does everything which is done, I did not see sin, and then I saw that all is well. But when God did show me about sin, then he said: All will be well."

Julian's questioning was clearly never totally eradicated. Doubtless this is one reason why at the start of her final chapter 86 she states clearly that while what she writes "is begun by God's gift and his grace," it remains incomplete or, as she puts it, "it is not yet performed." Yet Julian also concludes her text with the striking affirmation of God's love as the meaning of everything.

> And from the time that it was revealed I desired many time to know in what was our Lord's meaning. And fifteen years after and more, I was answered in spiritual understanding, and it was said:

What, do you wish to know your Lord's meaning in this thing? Know it well, love was his meaning. Who reveals it to you? Love. What did he reveal to you? Love. Why does he reveal it to you? For love. Remain in this, and you will know more of the same. But you will never know different, without end.

Notes

1 On the Black Death as God's punishment for our essentially sinful lives, see for example, Caroline Walker Bynum, *Holy Feast and Holy Fast: The Religious Significance of Food to Medieval Women*, Berkeley, CA: University of California Press, 1987, pp 208–218; also Richard Kieckhefer, *Unquiet Souls: Fourteenth Century Saints and their Religious Milieu*, Chicago, IL: University of Chicago Press, 1984, pp 1–3.

2 See *Cur Deus Homo*, in S.N. Deane, ed., *Saint Anselm: Basic Writings*, 2nd edition, LaSalle, IL: Open Court Publishing, 1962.

3 For example, see Edmund Colledge & James Walsh, eds., *A Book of Showings to the Anchoress Julian of Norwich*, Toronto: Pontifical Institute of Mediaeval Studies, 1978, Part One, pp 105–106; also Nicholas Watson & Jacqueline Jenkins, eds., *The Writings of Julian of Norwich*, University Park, PA: The Pennsylvania State University Press, 2006, p 154 and notes to Long Text Chapters 27 and 32; also Kerrie Hide, *Gifted Origins to Graced Fulfillment: The Soteriology of Julian of Norwich*, Collegeville, MN: The Liturgical Press, 2001, pp 184–190; also Denys Turner, *Julian of Norwich, Theologian*, New Haven, CT: Yale University Press, 2011, Chapter 4, pp 103–109; also Grace Jantzen, *Julian of Norwich*, 2nd edition, London: SPCK, 2000, pp 178–179; and Joan M. Nuth, *Wisdom's Daughter: The Theology of Julian of Norwich*, New York: Crossroad, 1991, pp 18–19 & 162–169.

4 See John the Scot (Johannes Scotus Eriugena), *Periphyseon on the Division of Nature*, Eugene, OR: Wipf & Stock, 2011. There are helpful comments in the Introduction by Jean A. Potter, pp xxxiii–xl. I am grateful to Bernard McGinn for drawing my attention to Eriugena's defense of universalism.

5 See Edmund Colledge & James Walsh, eds., *A Book of Showings to the Anchoress Julian of Norwich*, Toronto: Pontifical Institute of Mediaeval Studies, 1978, Part One, pp 105–106.

6 See Barry Windeatt, ed., *Julian of Norwich: Revelations of Divine Love*, Oxford: Oxford University Pres, 2016.

7 See Turner, p 105.

8 See Jantzen, pp 178–179.

9 See Nuth, p 164.

10 Nuth, p 165.

Chapter 7

Prayer: A Journey of Desire

A final important theme in this study of Julian of Norwich's theology is her rich teaching on prayer and more broadly on the spiritual journey. As I indicated in the Introduction, there are theological implications to the way Julian approaches the subject of prayer-as-relationship.

A fundamental question is how she defines the nature of prayer and then, more generally, deals with the practice of prayer. Prayer is the main focus of chapters 41–43 of the Long Text which form the beginning of what is commonly known as the Fourteenth Revelation. In addition, the subject of prayer is treated somewhat differently in the equivalent section of the Short Text and is briefly touched upon in other parts of the Long Text.

In their scholarly edition of Julian's two texts, Colledge and Walsh suggest that there is a notable contrast between her treatment of prayer in the Short Text and in the Long Text. Thus, in chapter xix of the Short Text, under the category of "prayer" she includes a range of approaches. These include vocal prayer (such as the Pater Noster, Ave Maria, and Credo) and petitionary prayer focussed on the well-being of her "evenchristen." Colledge and Walsh then compare this with Julian's approach in her Long Text where they consider that she is less concerned with her own experiences and practices of prayer than with God's intention.[1] However, other Julian scholars such as Ritamary Bradley feel that this contrast between the two texts is too sharply drawn.[2]

What immediately occurs to the many contemporary readers of Julian's Long Text is that she does not focus on prayer merely as a spiritual practice or discuss specific methods of prayer. Rather, for Julian the notion of "prayer" expresses something far deeper and more extensive. Prayer is a relationship rather than a set of practices. Indeed, "prayer" is the word that Julian uses to describe our life-long relationship with God and God's relationship with us. This relationship may at times be revelatory. It is also, as we shall see, associated with our persistent longing and desire

Julian of Norwich: "In God's Sight" – Her Theology in Context, First Edition. Philip Sheldrake. © 2019 John Wiley & Sons Ltd. Published 2019 by John Wiley & Sons Ltd.

which matches God's desire for us. At the heart of this relationship is an assurance, and regular moments of reassurance, that we are irrevocably embraced by love.

Thus, in her Long Text, chapter 24, in the context of her vision of Jesus' wounded side, with "his blessed heart split in two" and his blood "shed for love," Julian is reassured by the words "see how I love you." Thus, prayer becomes a continual revelation of endless love:

> How could it now be that you would pray to me for anything pleasing to me which I would not very gladly grant to you? For my delight is in your holiness and in your endless joy and bliss in me.

The nature of prayer-as-relationship is also an experience of healing, not least the healing of our flawed self-understanding. In chapter 40 "our courteous Lord" not only shows "supreme friendship" by protecting us tenderly even in our sinfulness. When we are moved to prayer because "we see ourselves so foul" and "believe that God may be angry with us because of our sins," then "our courteous Lord" shows himself to the human soul "welcoming it as a friend…saying: My dear darling, I am glad that you have come to me in all your woe. I have always been with you, and now you see me loving, and we are made one in bliss."

Finally, this relationship, in which we long for and seek God through the medium of prayer, is never an experience of being consistently united with God in this present life. "So I saw him and sought him, and I had him and lacked him; and this is and should be our ordinary undertaking in this life, as I see it" (chapter 10).

The Foundations of Prayer

At the heart of Julian's teaching about prayer-as-relationship is the powerful image of longing and desire. "Desire" is the dynamic that drives our life-long relationship with God. In her chapter 40 Julian expresses something similar to the famous words of *The Cloud of Unknowing*, chapter 2: "Now you have to stand in desire all your life long."[3] Because we cannot be completely at peace while we are here in this present life "therefore it is fitting for us to live always in sweet prayer and in loving longing with our Lord Jesus."

This notion of a desire for God appears early in Julian's Long Text. "God, of your goodness give me yourself, for you are enough for me" (chapter 5). The immediate context of this request by Julian appears at first sight to be a critique of the human tendency to give too much attention to contingent reality ("something small, no bigger than a hazelnut") rather than focusing primarily on God. However, at a deeper level the chapter shows how Julian is led to understand two positive realities. First, in her vision of the bleeding head of Christ in the Passion, she is shown "a spiritual sight" of God's intimate love. God, as revealed in the suffering Christ, is "everything which is good and comforting for our help." God not only wishes to be known but seeks to be our rest and that we become "substantially united to him." Thus, second, God desires that we "have him who is everything." This is the basis for what Julian refers to as "the loving yearning of the soul" in response to God's own desire to fill us, restore us, and preserve us.

While Julian's main teachings about prayer-as-relationship, as revealed to her by God, appear in chapters 41–43 there is an important prelude in chapter 40. Here, as we have already seen, Julian suggests that initially we may be moved to prayer out of contrition because "we may see ourselves so foul" because of our sins. Julian indicates that initially she shared in this human experience. However, God welcomed Julian with the words "my dear darling." You may, like Julian, come to God "in all your woe" but we are all led on from this to repose in love, assurance, and the promise of bliss. Because we cannot experience completely everything good "whilst we are here," we are bound "to live always in sweet prayer and in loving longing with our Lord Jesus." Then our Lord Jesus revealed to Julian his own "spiritual thirst," or longing, to bring us to the fullness of joy.

It was after this that, according to chapter 41, "our Lord revealed about prayer." This begins the main teachings that Julian wishes to pass on to all her fellow Christians. At the outset, Julian sets out two fundamental characteristics (or "conditions") of prayer "in our lords mening", that is, from God's viewpoint. The first is "rightfulle prayer," or the spirit of prayer, properly understood as Julian outlines later in the chapter. The second is "seker trust," prayer as an expression of confident or certain trust in God. After these two important foundations, Julian proceeds with her teaching as she believed it had been revealed to her by God.

In the remainder of chapter 41, Julian first identifies with the common human experience that we sometimes feel nothing in prayer. In her words, we feel as barren and dry after prayer as we did before. We think that this is the result of our unworthiness. However, Julian goes on to say that God clearly revealed to her that our Lord is the "grounde of thy beseking" – that is, the cause of our entering into prayer. It is important to be clear that "beseke" is not just a word for prayer or specifically for petition or beseeching. It also implies the sense of "to seek," or "to search for." God desires this relationship. God then makes us desire it and so we seek it. Thus, as God reveals to Julian, if our Lord is the foundation of prayer how could we not have what we pray for? Everything that God "maketh us to beseke" (to seek) is God's own desire for us from all eternity. In summary, God is the ground or foundation of our prayer-as-relationship.

Such "beseking" or seeking is an enduring aspect of our relationship with God in prayer. Our Lord assures Julian that he accepts our prayer and "sends it up above" where it becomes part of the divine treasure house (no doubt echoing the Gospel of Matthew 6, 20) "where it will never perish." Our eternal bliss is guaranteed. By implication, this is true even when we feel nothing in prayer. God instructs Julian to pray wholeheartedly ("interly") even if there is "no savour." Stick with it, trust, and believe that our Lord is in our prayer. In fact, the best prayer is in weakness, presumably because it implies greater trust. The assurance that our Lord accepts our prayer implies that our relationship with God is direct and intimate rather than with a distant lordly God and therefore necessarily via intermediaries.

If "our work in prayer and in good living" is actively understood to be "by his help and his grace" it will be "with discretion" – that is, with discernment. The implication is that prayer-as-relationship should be moderate and balanced rather than excessive, oppressive, or over-exuberant.

Chapter 41 ends with Julian teaching that "thanksgiving also belongs to our prayer." This is another aspect of "rightful" prayer and is also based on God moving us interiorly. Again, thanksgiving in prayer is not merely a practice but is an attitude expressing, in another form, our fundamental trust in God's care and God's power. "And so the power of our Lord's word enters the soul and enlivens the heart and it begins by his grace faithful exercise, and makes the soul to pray most blessedly, and truly to rejoice in our Lord." This is what true thanksgiving means.

Julian begins her second section on prayer, chapter 42, with the thought that our Lord wants us to have "true understanding" in and through our relationship of prayer. This thought acts as a reminder of, and further underlines, three crucial things that she had taught in the previous chapter. First, our prayer originates in God. Our Lord says "First, it is my will [desire]." God is the "ground" of our prayer. The second crucial thing concerns how our prayer is "performed." This performance is not a matter of how prayer is practiced but implies that our "wille," our wish or desire, comes from God. So we need to bring our wishes or desires into conscious alignment with God's wish or desire. The use of "wille" may well echo the phrase "Thy will be done" in the Our Father prayer but in the context of Julian "wille" is not an authoritarian image but the wish and desire of a loving God. Finally, we need to understand the purpose of prayer-as-relationship and where that relationship leads. We are to be "oned and like to our lorde in althing." That is, we are being led to the point of being united with, in union with, and wholly identified with our Lord. Again, this is not authoritarian but is a "loving lesson" based on God's desire "to help us."

God's will and desire is that our prayer (and our trust in God) "be both alike large." That is, it should be generous and possibly ambitious rather than cautious or uncertain. Our trust in God should be as wide as our prayer as a whole. Otherwise we do not pay full honour to our Lord. To pay honour is to realise, live within, and respond to God's desire. Otherwise "we tary and paine ourselfe" – that is, we impede and trouble ourselves. This is because we do not fully understand that God is the "ground" – that is, the source and guarantee – of our prayer. If we really and truly grasped that prayer comes from God's action and love we would trust that all our deep desire is a gift of God. We desire it because God desires it in us and for us and therefore we will receive it.

However, there is sometimes a problem. On occasions we feel that we have prayed long and hard yet we do not have our desire. Julian teaches that we must not get too depressed by this experience. The meaning must be that "either we are waiting for a better occasion, or more grace, or a better gift." Behind all this is God's desire that we truly have an understanding of how God is and how God works. "He is being." That is, God is fundamental reality. We are "to take our place and our dwelling in this foundation." Implicitly Julian is teaching her fellow Christians that we are to make complete trust in God the foundation of our life.

God wishes us to grasp three crucial things. The first is "our noble and excellent making." The second is "our precious and lovable redemption." The third reflects the rather anthropocentric medieval understanding of the created order that everything God has created that is "inferior to us" is nevertheless protected for love of us. God reassures Julian that all this was done "before your prayer" – that is, it is not dependent on our prayers. We should contemplate this with thanksgiving and also pray for "the deed which is now being done." That is, God guides us to his glory in this life and also brings us to his bliss. Thus God has done everything already. God wants us to see this and therefore not to be doubting or depressed. In terms of our relationship of prayer, God desires that we pray for, and live within, everything God has ordained even though this is beyond our understanding in this life.

Julian describes prayer as "a right understanding" of the fullness of joy which is to come. This approach to prayer is fundamentally relational rather than instrumental. True longing and trust are the two foundations of prayer-as-relationship as Julian is shown by God and as she teaches her fellow Christians. The "failing of our blisse" to which we are destined implies a partial seeing but also incompleteness. Therefore we are led to long and to desire even more. "In these two werkings" – that is our actions of longing and of trust – are our duty. So we are to work diligently on both. Yet we are always aware that what we do is really nothing. While this is true, we are nevertheless to do what we can and to trust that "everything which is lacking in us we shall find in him" (that is, in God). For, as Julian reminds us, God says "I am the foundation of your beseeching." "And so in these blessed words with the revelation I saw a complete overcoming of all our weakness and all our doubting fears." Here Julian ends this part of her teaching on prayer.

Contemplation and Union

Julian begins the third part of her focused teaching on prayer in chapter 43 with the comment that "prayer oneth the soule to God"; that is, "prayer unites the soul to God." This reflects the two basic aspects of human existence. On the one hand we are "often unlike him [God] in condition" – that is, in our contingent existence – because of sin. We are still on a transformative journey towards final union. Yet we are always like God "in nature" and in "substance restored by grace." In that sense we are already united or "oned" with God, and always have been from our first creation.

The action of human prayer is a witness to the fact that in its deepest identity the human soul wills as God wills. Prayer "eases conscience" and leads us to a firm trust. Because God beholds us in love and "wants to make us partners in his good will and work," God moves us to pray for what God already wishes to do. In response to our prayer and "good desire," which comes to us as a gift, God will give us "endless mede" (eternal reward). All this is shown in words that echo chapter 41: "And thou besekest it!" God shows great pleasure as if God is beholden to us for our good deeds. However, in fact God is the one who "does" them.

God wishes us to entreat "mightily" (that is, vehemently), wisely, and "wilfully" (that is, sincerely) that God should do what God wants done. In this process of prayer-as-relationship, "the soule…is acorded with God" (that is, harmonized and made at one with God's desire). When God "shows himself to our soul we have what we desire." Thus, the desire or longing that according to chapter 42 generates prayer now disappears and the remainder of chapter 43 focuses on silent contemplation. Rather than asking God for more "all our intention and all our powers are wholly directed to contemplating him."

Julian describes contemplation, "beholding" in Middle English, as "a high and unperceivable prayer," a sublime and imperceptible prayer. The whole reason for prayer is said to be so that we can "be united into the vision and contemplation of him." The more "the soul" sees of God, the more it desires God. When we do not "see" God, we then feel the need to pray. Also when tempted and troubled and left in "unrest," we need to pray to make ourselves "suppul and buxom to God": compliant and obedient. However, we cannot make God "suppul" or compliant to us. For God is changeless in love of humanity. When, by special grace rather than by the activity of prayer, we "plainly beholde him," seeing no other reality or "medes" (necessity), we necessarily follow God. God's abundant goodness satisfies all the powers of our soul ("all our mightes"). God's continual working is done so "divinely" that it transcends all that we can think or imagine. Then, all we can do is contemplate, enjoying God and with a great desire to be "oned" with God. In our "meke, continual prayer" we are drawn more and more into union with God in the midst of this life "by many secret touchings of sweet spiritual sights and feelings" to the degree that we can bear it. However, this "presence" to God is never more than intermittent. Until we die we shall always continue to long and to desire.

> And so we shall by his sweet grace in our own meek continual prayer come into him now in this life by many secret touchings of sweet spiritual sights and feelings measured out to us as our simplicity may bear it. And this is done and will be done by the grace of the Holy Spirit, until the day that we die, still longing for love.

In a clearly eschatological reference Julian states that after "the day that we die" we shall transcend the limitations of what we can bear in this life. "For so can no man see God and live afterwards, that is to say in this mortal life." However, there are moments even here when God may choose to show the divine self. In such contemplation God gives the person "more than its own strength." In this sense, a contemplative immediacy of presence to God is a gift rather than the result of prolonged spiritual practice or of any particular method of prayer. God "measures the revelation according to his own will, and it is profitable for that time."

The Spiritual Senses

Julian concludes her chapter 43 with an apparent reference to what are classically known as the "spiritual senses."

> And then we shall all come into our Lord, knowing ourselves clearly and wholly possessing God and we shall all be endlessly hidden in God, truly seeing and wholly feeling, and hearing him spiritually and delectably smelling him and sweetly tasting him.

As far as I can detect, among the scholarly editions of Julian's texts only Colledge and Walsh make an explicit reference to Julian's apparent awareness of the historic notion of the "spiritual senses."[4] However, in his recent full scholarly edition of Julian's texts, Barry Windeatt does note that this reference to all five senses in one place is exceptional in her text.[5] Julian refers to "truly seeing," "wholly feeling," "hearing him [God] spiritually," "delectably smelling him," and "sweetly tasting him."

The notion of the spiritual senses originates with the early Christian theologian Origen of Alexandria (*c.*185–*c.*254 CE), especially in his inter-pretation of the *Song of Songs* in the Hebrew bible as the highpoint of the mystical life. This was further developed in the writings of another patristic theologian, Gregory of Nyssa (*c.*335–*c.*395 CE). The notion of spiritual senses also had a significant influence on the Western mystical tradition, especially on the Cistercian Bernard of Clairvaux and on the Franciscan theologian Bonaventure, not least in his *Itinerarium mentis ad Deum*. Fundamentally, our outer material lives operate through five physical senses. The inner, spiritual dimension of a person also has five spiritual senses which echo the physical senses. In a way the notion of "spiritual senses" underlines an integration of the sensory or bodily with the spiritual dimension of human experience. Such a sensory frame-work for contemplation effectively counteracts any tendency towards a purely intellectualist approach to the notion of contemplative awareness of, or "oneing" with, God.[6]

Origen understood the spiritual senses not only as an expression of spiritual sensitivity but also as the basis for our ability to discern between good and evil. They are a gift of God's grace. However, interestingly, while Origen suggests that not everyone has these inner spiritual senses because they are hindered by sin, Julian's language is more inclusive. She states that "we shall all come into our Lord" and her apparent reference to the spiritual senses seems to apply to all her "evenchristen."

Prayer and the Spiritual Life

For orthodox medieval Christians such as Julian, an important dimen-sion of a life of prayer, or of prayer-as-life, was participation in the Church's public worship and reception of the sacraments. As I have already discussed in Chapter 1, on balance I believe that it is unlikely that Julian had previously been a monastic nun before entering the anchorhold attached to St Julian's Church in Norwich. For example, in the context of Julian's participation in public worship it is striking that there is no men-tion of, or echoes of, the liturgy of the Divine Office which is so central to monastic life. It is also interesting that on the two occasions in her chap-ters 4 and 8 when Julian uses a Latin phrase, *Benedicite dominus*, it seems to echo a phrase sung in the monastic Office of Prime and the greeting of one monastic person to another. However, the phrase as used by Julian is grammatically incorrect. This seems unlikely if she had been a former nun.

In fact, there are relatively few references to public worship or the sacraments in Julian's texts although those that do appear are thoroughly conventional.[7] In both the Short Text, chapters i and ii and the Long Text, chapter 2, Julian refers to the three graces or gifts that she had asked for before her illness and revelatory experiences. The second of these was a severe bodily sickness "so that I might in it receive all the rites which Holy Church has to give me (Long Text, chapter 2)." In the medieval Church this refers to what were known as the Last Rites: personal Confession and Absolution, the Viaticum or reception of Communion, and Extreme Unction which was the anointing of the sick person with blessed oil. In her Long Text, chapter 57, Julian writes of the classical seven sacraments in relation to the gift of faith. "Also in our faith come the seven sacraments, one following another in the order God has ordained them in for us." Finally, in chapter 60 in her treatment of the theme of Jesus as Mother, Julian refers specifically to the Eucharist and more generally to "the life of the sacraments."

> The mother can give her child to suck of her milk, but our precious Mother Jesus can feed us with himself, and does, most courteously and most tenderly, with the blessed sacrament, which is the precious food of true life; and with all the sweet sacraments he sustains us most mercifully and graciously.... I am he whom Holy Church preaches and teaches to you. That is to say: All the health and the life of the sacraments, all the power and the grace of my word, all the goodness which is ordained in Holy Church for you, I am he.
>
> *(Chapter 60)*

In terms of Julian's approach to the progress of a spiritual life, a number of commentators have already noted that she broke with a common approach to this in other medieval theological and spiritual writers. That is, Julian does not describe the spiritual journey in terms of distinct stages such as the classic three-fold way (*triplex via*).[8] In this tradition, spiritual transformation led people through the successive stages of "the way of purgation" or purification (beginners), followed by "the way of illumination" or contemplation (proficients), and ending with the "way of union" (the perfect). Other writers, such as Franciscans associated with the school of Bonaventure, posited that the three "ways" were dimensions of the spiritual path that might be experienced simultaneously rather than in a temporal sequence. If Julian does not adopt this way of portraying the spiritual life, nor does she describe the spiritual life in terms of a ladder of ascent away from the everyday material world to encounter God "above" – for example, as outlined by her contemporary Walter Hilton in his *The Scale* (or *Ladder*) *of Perfection.* The nearest Julian comes to a sense of rising above the everyday is her affirmation in chapter 5 that while the littleness of "everything which is made" is created, loved, and preserved by God nevertheless "our hearts and souls are not in perfect ease" if we rest in this littleness rather than in God "who is everything."

While Julian does not portray a detailed spiritual itinerary her teaching is that nevertheless prayer is a journey, but a journey from God to God as we have already noted. Julian has clear teachings about the spiritual journey. In her Second Revelation, chapter 10, it is clear that our "sight" or "beholding" of God is inevitably always partial. "By grace we see something of him" and this provokes a desire for more. "And when by grace we see something of him, then we are moved by the same grace to seek with great desire to see him for our greater joy." This incompleteness of our "beholding" of God in this life is expressed by Julian in the same chapter as "so I saw him and sought him, and I had him and lacked him." As Julian asserts, this is inevitably how things are "in this life."

Prayer and Spiritual Practices

I have already noted that Julian teaches nothing directly about methods of personal prayer and meditation. However, what she writes does offer indirect evidence of, or references to, prayer-as-practice. For example, in her chapter 6, Julian notes that alongside her fundamental understanding that we need to "adhere to the goodness of God" what she refers to as "our habits of prayer" were brought to her mind. In particular Julian writes of our use of "intermediaries" – for example, conventional devotion to "his holy Passion" (the cross), to "the sweet mother who bore him" (the Virgin Mary), or to "the help that we have from particular saints." At first, Julian seems to suggest that it is better if we pray simply and directly to God rather than employ all these intermediaries because "this is too little." Yet, she goes on to say that such intermediaries are good because they have been provided by God to help us precisely as expressions of the love and goodness of God. At the same time Julian underlines that when seeking God through intermediaries we must nevertheless understand clearly that it is God who is the goodness of everything. Thus, "the highest form of prayer is to the goodness of God, which comes down to us to our humblest needs." Later in the same chapter, as already noted, Julian illustrates this point that God's providence is present in "our humblest needs" by referring to the process of defecation.[9]

Vocal Prayer

However, as I have already noted, in reference to devotional prayer it is noticeable that when Julian turns to her main teaching on prayer in the Long Text, chapter 41, she omits the references in the equivalent part of the Short Text, chapter xix, to conventional vocal prayer such as reciting the Our Father, the Hail Mary, and the Creed "with such devotion as God will give us."[10] In both the Short Text, chapter xxiii and the Long Text, chapters 69 and 70 there seem to be further references to such vocal prayer. Here, Julian mentions her sense of being visited by the devil on her sick bed. "I fixed my eyes on the same cross in which I had seen comfort before, and I occupied my tongue in speaking of Christ's Passion and in repeating the faith of Holy Church" (Short Text, chapter xxiii). Also "And our good Lord God gave me grace to trust greatly in him, and to comfort my soul by speaking words aloud" (Long Text, chapter 69) and "I set my eyes on the same cross in which I had seen comfort before, my tongue to speaking of Christ's Passion and repeating the faith of Holy Church" (Long Text, chapter 70). Here vocal prayer seems to mean reciting the Creed and also possibly intercessory prayer.

Ejaculatory Prayer

Although Julian does not actively teach the practice of ejaculatory prayer there are numerous examples in the Long Text of her own use of such ejaculations. These are spontaneous short phrases which express strong sentiments such as wonder, gratitude, thanksgiving, or praise of God. As in the case of Julian, these may be spoken out loud. Her usual form of words was to bless God. As already noted, according to manuscript evidence, Julian's ejaculations in chapters 4 and 8 were spoken in Latin. "And I said: Blessed be the Lord! This I said with a reverent intention and in a loud voice..." (chapter 4). Such phrases may be repeated and become a form of continuous prayer as Julian suggests when she had the initial vision of the bleeding head of Jesus. "I could not stop saying these words: Blessed be the Lord!" (chapter 8). As we have seen, one of the three main elements of prayer-as-relationship in Julian is thanksgiving. "And some-times the soul is so full of this that it breaks out in words and says: Good Lord, great thanks, blessed may you be" (chapter 41). In some cases, Julian's ejaculations were spoken in the context of a wider conversation with God or with her vision of Jesus on the cross. "Then our good Lord put a question to me: Are you well satisfied that I suffered for you? I said: Yes, good Lord, all my thanks to you; yes, good Lord, blessed may you be" (chapter 22). Finally, Julian suggests that such ejaculations will be the expression of gratitude common to everyone when "we are all brought up above" into the presence of God where the mystery of reality will finally be revealed.

> We shall all say with one voice: Lord, blessed may you be, because it is so, it is well; and now we see truly that everything is done as it was ordained by you before anything was made.
>
> *(Chapter 85)*

In this sense, Julian's texts reveal that her relationship with God regularly embraced the practice of prayer-as-conversation. This conversation was not one-sided but mutual. In other words, Julian's spiritual experiences were not simply ones of "hearing" or interiorly experiencing God or Jesus on the cross addressing her or offering some important insight and teaching. Often what Julian experienced was in the form of a question or series of questions from God that required responses from her. A good example is the Eleventh Revelation in chapter 25. Here Jesus on the cross asks Julian whether she wishes to see "my blessed mother;" that is, "our Lady St Mary." "Do you wish to see her? I answered and said: Yes, good Lord, great thanks, yes, good Lord, if it be your will." Equally, however, Julian feels free to question God. The whole of chapter 50 is an anguished question addressed to God about the clash between the fact that Julian knows that "we sin grievously all day and are very blameworthy" and yet that "I saw our Lord God showing no more blame to us than if we were as pure and as holy as the angels are in heaven." The chapter ends with Julian crying out with all her might: "Ah, Lord Jesus, king of bliss, how shall I be comforted, who will tell me and teach me what I need to know, if I cannot at this time see it in you?" As I discussed in Chapter 3, the answer God gives to Julian's anguished questioning is contained in the *exemplum* of a Lord and a Servant.

Penitential Practices

How does Julian deal with penance and asceticism, two other common features of medieval spiritual practice alongside prayer? We have already explored in Chapter 5 Julian's understanding of human identity. Here it is important to underline yet again that Julian does not have a negative view of the body. Julian's chapter 6, in its image of God's providence manifested in the image of the body as a purse and in the process of defecation, graphically underlines the positive role of the human body against traditional images of the body as base, sinful, and "carnal." Julian is silent about leading a life of chastity versus an active sexual life nor does she overtly advocate fasting, bodily mortification, or acts of self-denial. Although Julian makes references to penance as an attitude of repentance, there are no references to extensive penitential practices. For example, in chapter 39, penance is mentioned in reference to making confession to a priest, revealing one's sins, and accepting whatever "penance" the confessor imposes. This was most usually reciting additional prayers or undertaking an act of almsgiving and charity.

Fundamentally, Julian bypasses the question of penitential activity. She lacks the purgative attitude of some of her contemporary visionaries. Her attitude is not typified by self-loathing or a desire for humiliation. Indeed, in chapter 77, she notes: "As to the penance which one takes upon oneself, that was not revealed to me; that is to say, it was not revealed to me specifically." What was revealed to her was "that we ought meekly and patiently to bear and suffer the penance which God himself gives us, with recollection of his blessed Passion." In remembering the Passion we "suffer with him as his friends did who saw it." This is not a question of adopting artificial penitential practices. Also, fundamentally, Julian was taught that "this life is penance" and "your life is profitable penance" but that the result should not be depression but a sense that "our Lord is with us, protecting us and leading us into the fullness of joy." An important dimension of everyday life as penitential is related to our perpetual longing and desire which remains unfulfilled until we are led to a final union with God (chapter 56). Importantly, God is here with us in our life-as-penance.

> For it is the greatest glory to him of anything which we can do that we live gladly and happily for love of him in our penance. For he regards us so tenderly that he sees all our life here to be penance; for the substantial and natural longing in us for him is a lasting penance in us, and he makes this penance in us, and mercifully he helps us to bear it.
>
> *(Chapter 81)*

This approach contrasts strongly with a common intensification of penitential piety during the fourteenth century in response to the bleak experiences of such things as the Black Death. As already noted, this was commonly portrayed in sermons as God's punishment for our essentially sinful lives.[11] There is no sense of this in Julian's teachings.

Julian and Visualizations

More controversially, it has been suggested by several commentators on Julian that her "sight" of the crucified Jesus, including the bleeding of his head, may not simply be a question of an unprovoked, ecstatic experiences in isolation. There may also be affinities with a medieval practice of "visualizations" during meditation. It has been suggested that in Julian's case her vivid, almost photographic portrayal of the details of Jesus Christ's bleeding head and the drying of his body may have been influenced by the rich religious artistic culture of Norwich and, more broadly, by the important school of medieval East Anglian art.[12] However, as I will describe in more detail in a moment, Julian's visualizations may also relate to the growing practice, not least among lay people, of meditating imaginatively on scenes from the gospel, especially the Passion. This is not to deny that such forms of visual meditation, whether inspired by art or by scripture, did not or could not lead the person praying on to a spiritual level beyond mere formulae or a self-conscious meditative process.

To reflect specifically on Passion meditation, as Grace Jantzen notes in her chapter on Julian's prayers there was shift in late medieval devotion from a focus on the image of Christ in majesty to God sending the Son to identify with humankind. In contrast to the kingship of the glorified Christ, the growing emphasis on the humanity of Jesus Christ was especially related to his suffering for us. In parallel to this there was a growth of affectivity in meditation which was particularly related to the increasing laicization of spirituality.[13] Taken together, a growing practice of focusing meditation on the suffering of Jesus sought to enable the one praying to come to identify with this suffering. This echoes Julian's description of her three youthful desires "by the gift of God" (Long Text, chapter 2) expressed in prayer. All of these, in different ways, reflect a wish to identify with the suffering Jesus. First there was Julian's desire for a "bodily sight" so that she could share in a deeper knowledge of the Passion in parallel with our Lady and "all his true lovers." Then there was a bodily sickness. While Julian does not explicitly relate this desire for a deadly sickness to Jesus's suffering her words "if it be your will that I have it" may echo Jesus's prayer to the Father in the Garden of Gethsemane as expressed in the Gospel of Matthew 26, 39: "My Father, if it is possible, let this cup pass from me; yet not what I want but what you want." Equally the desire for this to happen when she was 30 years old may not be incidental. Given Julian's overall desire to identify with the humanity of Jesus Christ this could relate to the statement in the Gospel of Luke (3, 23) that Jesus's ministry began when "he was about thirty years old." Finally, there was a desire to receive what she refers to as explicitly "three wounds" in her life: true contrition, loving compassion, and longing for God.

In the growing medieval tradition of meditating on Christ's life, including the Passion, people were encouraged to enter imaginatively into gospel scenes as people who were present and active, perhaps as themselves or by identifying with one of the people in the scripture narrative. To relive the gospel scene in this way was not simply a question of artificially re-enacting precisely what the gospel scene portrayed. Rather, instead it might well be an experience of being drawn spiritually into a uniquely personal narrative and dynamic. In the case of Julian, what she "sees" in relation to Christ's Passion is very selective. It is not chronological nor does it embrace all the events and elements in the scriptural narrative. Her concentrated focus is personal which is very much in the tradition of visual meditation.

Barry Windeatt suggests that this approach to visual meditation was regarded as especially appropriate for beginners in meditation, and especially for women. He draws attention to the *Horologium Sapientiae* of the fourteenth-century Rhineland Dominican Henry Suso, part of which was available in translation in England. Suso suggested that frequently visualizing the Passion moves the ignorant to becoming learned and eventually makes spiritual amateurs into teachers.[14] Suso's remarks underline that imaginative or visual meditation on the gospels was not a purely emotional or devotional exercise. It points towards an experience of spiritual deepening and transformation. It was not necessarily the case that visual meditation was essentially for beginners. However, it was certainly a way in which an increasingly spiritually minded laity was able to draw upon the longer monastic tradition of scriptural meditation known as *lectio divina*.

The origins of the tradition of *lectio* lie in early Egyptian desert monasticism where famous fifth-century collections of "sayings" from monastic teachers (known as the *Apophthegmata Patrum*) frequently mention meditating or ruminating upon scripture. The practice was later systematized in a twelfth-century treatise, *Ladder of the Monks*, by the Carthusian monk Guigo II. This framework was described in terms of four "stages": *lectio* (reading and quietly pronouncing a scripture text), *meditatio* (memorizing, repetition of words or phrases or other ways of digesting the scripture so that it was retained in the heart), *oratio* (literally "prayer" but understood as a desire-filled offering of oneself to God), and finally *contemplatio*. In later approaches, such as that of Guigo II, *contemplatio* designated an elevated spiritual state or immediacy of presence to God. In this context, the use of visualization or imagination was linked to *meditatio*, the second element of *lectio*. Interestingly, as we have already seen, in Julian's text the overall process of "prayer" leads from a foundation of longing to beseeching (both asking and seeking) and then to "beholding."[15]

This form of imaginative gospel meditation (or "contemplation" in the language of Ignatius Loyola) became particularly well known via the sixteenth-century Ignatian *Spiritual Exercises* which ensured its survival in spiritual practices up to the contemporary era. However, it is important to note that Ignatius Loyola derived this meditative practice from earlier medieval sources including the *Meditationes vitae Christi* by an anonymous thirteenth-century Franciscan, known as pseudo-Bonaventure. This text was known in Julian's England. Indeed, the Passion section of this work was available in a fourteenth-century Middle English translation known as *The Privity of the Passion*. The person meditating was advised to "pay attention…carefully to every point [of the Passion scene] as if you were there bodily." Similar recommendations were made by Aelred of Rievaulx in his twelfth-century text for women anchoresses, *De Institutione Inclusarum*. It may well be that Julian's "bodily sights" of the Passion owe something to this meditative tradition. The fact that Julian does not narrate the whole story of Christ's Passion but focuses on particular moments corresponds to the meditative tradition which advises the one praying to stay where they were obtaining spiritual fruit rather than to feel bound to follow through the whole scriptural narrative. In the words of the Jesuit scholar Javier Melloni, this form of meditation, by making one "present," ideally means that the person praying ceases to be a spectator and becomes, spiritually speaking, an "actor." Through this, there is a deepening of "interior knowledge" and perhaps of contemplative "beholding."[16] Importantly, the scholar of medieval English Denise Nowakowski Baker, who supports the possibility that Julian had been influenced by this meditative tradition as well as by the East Anglian school of art, is clear that this does not exclude the potential authenticity of Julian's visionary experience.[17]

Conclusion

Julian's prayers led her to reflect on the meaning of her spiritual experiences and that starting point moved her onward to construct a complete theology. Indeed, as Denys Turner rightly notes, there is no valid distinction between Julian as theologian and Julian as teacher about the spiritual life.[18] The love of God manifested in her vision of the wounded Christ becomes the basis for Julian's theology of the salvation of humanity. In this Julian finds a response to her struggles to grasp the meaning of sin and why it was allowed. Human brokenness is met by God's love so that the "wounds" of human beings become a means to achieving a maturity of joy beyond simplistic and ignorant innocence. Julian's early desire for three wounds – contrition, loving compassion, and longing – become the means of a progressive spiritual maturity. In the first wound, contrition, Julian is led to abandon the self, to turn away from focusing on herself to focusing on God as the center from which all her actions should flow. In the second wound, loving compassion, Julian is led to identify with the suffering Christ and to share in his compassion for all people. Again, in this spiritual process, Julian turns away from self-preoccupation to focus her care on the others, her "evenchristen," for whom she writes her text and for whom she believes her teachings are intended. Finally, in the third wound, longing, she finds a single-mindedness that drives her onwards to seek God's presence and also to desire to communicate to others her radical message of God's unshakable love.

Notes

1 See Edmund Colledge & James Walsh, eds., *A Book of Showings to the Anchoress Julian of Norwich*, Toronto: Pontifical Institute of Mediaeval Studies, 1978, Part One, p 116.

2 See Ritamary Bradley, *Julian's Way: A Practical Commentary on Julian of Norwich*, London: Harper Collins, 1992, "Julian at Prayer," p 27 with Ritamary Bradley's additional references to other scholars.

3 See James Walsh, ed., *The Cloud of Unknowing*, Classics of Western Spirituality series, New York: Paulist Press, 1981.

4 See Colledge & Walsh, *A Book of Showings*, Part One, Introduction, pp 119 & 120.

5 See the scholarly edition of Barry Windeatt, ed., *Julian of Norwich: Revelations of Divine Love*, Oxford: Oxford University Press, 2016, pp 241–242, note to Chapter 43, line 38.

6 On the origin of the notion of spiritual senses, especially in Origen, see Andrew Louth, *The Origins of the Christian Mystical Tradition: From Plato to Denys*, Oxford: Clarendon Press, 1992 edition, especially pp 67–70 & 93–94. For a general summary of the notion of "spiritual senses" see Philip Sheldrake "Senses, spiritual," in Philip Sheldrake, ed., *The New SCM Dictionary of Christian Spirituality*, London: SCM Press, 2005 (in the USA, *The New Westminster Dictionary of Christian Spirituality*, Louisville, KY: Westminster John Knox Press, 2005).

7 For some reflections on Julian's possible references to the liturgy, see Annie Sutherland, "Julian of Norwich and the Liturgy," in Liz Herbert McAvoy, ed., *A Companion to Julian of Norwich*, Rochester, NY: Boydell & Brewer, 2008, pp 88–98.

8 For example, Bernard McGinn, *The Varieties of Vernacular Mysticism 1350–1550*, New York: Herder & Herder/Crossroad, 2012, Chapter 12 "Julian of Norwich: 'Love is oure lords mening,'" p 470.

9 On prayer and intermediaries, see McGinn, *The Varieties of Vernacular Mysticism 1350–1550*, p 466.

10 On this point, see Barry Windeatt, "Julian's Second Thoughts: The Long Text Tradition," Chapter 8, pp 101–115, especially p 111, in McAvoy, ed., *A Companion to Julian of Norwich*.

11 See, for example, Caroline Walker Bynum, *Holy Feast and Holy Fast: The Religious Significance of Food to Medieval Women*, Berkeley, CA: University of California Press, 1987, pp 208–218; also Richard Kieckhefer, *Unquiet Souls: Fourteenth Century Saints and their Religious Milieu*, Chicago, IL: University of Chicago Press, 1984, pp 1–3.

12 See P. Lasko & N.J. Morgan, eds., *Medieval Art in East Anglia 1300–1530*, London: Thames & Hudson, 1974. Also see references in Denise Nowakowski Baker, *Julian of Norwich's Showings: From Vision to Book*, Princeton, NJ: Princeton University Press, 1994, pp 40–44 and in Barry Windeatt, ed., *Julian of Norwich: Revelations of Divine Love*, Oxford World Classics, Oxford: Oxford University Press, 2015, p xxii.

13 See Grace Jantzen, *Julian of Norwich*, 2nd edition, London: SPCK, 2000, Chapter 4 "Julian's Prayers." Also for shifts in medieval spirituality, not least a growing focus on the humanity of Jesus Christ, see Philip Sheldrake, *Spirituality: A Brief History*, 2nd edition, Oxford: Wiley-Blackwell, 2013, Chapter 4 "Spirituality in the City 1150–1450," especially pp 83–84.

14 See Windeatt, ed., *Julian of Norwich: Revelations of Divine Love*, Oxford World Classics, p xvii.

15 On the tradition of *lectio divina*, and its systematization in the Middle Ages, see Philip Sheldrake, *Spirituality: A Brief History*, 2nd edition, Oxford: Wiley-Blackwell, 2013, pp 42, 62, & 66–67. For a modern translation of Guigo's *Ladder of Monks*, see E. Colledge & J. Walsh, eds., *Guigo II: The Ladder of Monks & Twelve Meditations*, New York: Doubleday Images Books, 1978.

16 See Javier Melloni, *The Exercises of St Ignatius Loyola in the Western Tradition*, English translation, Leominster: Gracewing, 2000, p 20–34.

17 See Denise Nowakowski Baker, *Julian of Norwich's Showings: From Vision to Book*, Princeton, NJ: Princeton University Press, 1994, pp 40–51.

18 See Denys Turner, *Julian of Norwich, Theologian*, New Haven, CT: Yale University Press, 2011, pp 135–136.

Conclusion

According to Julian's own description in the final chapter 86 of *A Revelation of Love*, or the Long Text, the heart of her teaching was that God's "meaning" was love.

> And from the time that it was revealed, I desired many times to know in what was our Lord's meaning. And fifteen years after and more, I was answered in spiritual understanding, and it was said: What, do you wish to know your Lord's meaning in this thing? Know it well, love was his meaning. Who reveals it to you? Love. What did he reveal to you? Love. Why does he reveal it to you? For love. Remain in this, and you will know more of the same. But you will never know different, without end.

This affirmation is the climax and conclusion of Julian's text and the teaching she believes she has been mandated to pass on to her "evenchristen." However, the affirmation of love is more than simply the conclusion. It also provides the overall interpretative key to Julian's text. In that sense God's "meaning" is the heart of God's revelation to Julian and this is reflected throughout her teaching.

In this Conclusion to my study of Julian's theology, it is important to emphasize two things. First, echoing my comments in the Introduction, what I have tried to do is to outline as faithfully as I can Julian's own theological vision and teaching within its historical context. I have not sought to use Julian's text as a starting point for my own theological speculations provoked by reading her. Second, I also want to underline that even though I have studied and taught Julian's writings for over 30 years I discover something new each time I read her. Sometimes this is an aspect of her thought that I had previously overlooked and at other times I understand certain familiar things in a new way. For this reason

Julian of Norwich: "In God's Sight" – Her Theology in Context, First Edition. Philip Sheldrake.
© 2019 John Wiley & Sons Ltd. Published 2019 by John Wiley & Sons Ltd.

my study of Julian's theology is necessarily provisional and, echoing Julian's statement in her final chapter 86, is begun but is not finally completed.

Once again, it is important to ask what kind of text Julian actually wrote. In terms of Julian's own approach to her writings, neither the Short Text nor the Long Text is simply a work of devotion, a record or spiritual diary of her mystical experiences. On the other hand, in particular reference to the Long Text, this is not an abstract theological treatise. As we have seen, it is undoubtedly a work of theology in three ways. It is mystical theology in the sense that its reflections are based on an immediacy of presence to God and on an inward experience of God as opposed to being an attempt to systematically analyze and define the nature of God. It is also a work of vernacular theology in the sense of being a response to the growing interest in religious ideas and desire for spiritual teaching among an increasingly literate fourteenth-century laity. Julian explicitly aims her writing at "mine evenchristen" or "my fellow Christians" rather than at a more limited audience of clerics, monastics, or theological teachers. Finally, and arising from this, Julian's text has an explicitly pastoral purpose. In that sense it is an exercise in practical-pastoral theology because Julian believed that she had been granted an important message about the nature of God, about how we are to understand material creation and human nature, and about how God relates in practice to the human condition with all its weaknesses and flaws. This pastoral vision was undoubtedly deeply challenging in the context of Julian's times but Julian also saw it as urgent and potentially transformative.

There is an intimate interconnection between Julian's own personal struggles and what she came to teach. Julian regularly asks how her inherited and traditional beliefs, as taught by "Holy Church," fit with her interior revelations and the insights and knowledge that these brought to her. This tension must have been particularly sharp at a time when the hierarchical and clerical institution often appeared to be anything but holy! Julian is consistently honest about these struggles throughout her reflections in the context of her desire to communicate a pastoral message to her fellow Christians.

For Julian, part of her attempt to be faithful was to call Christians back to their fundamental ideals. "Holy Church," as "mine evenchristen," was the whole Christian community rather than merely an often dysfunctional institution and hierarchy. One striking example is Julian's teaching on the centrality and inclusivity of Christian love. This must have been a challenging – and, arguably, intentional – message in the context of war, social unrest, the fear of heresy, the Great Schism in the Western Church, and multiple examples of mutual condemnation and rejection. Thus, in her Short Text, chapter vi (also expressed more briefly in the Long Text, chapter 9) Julian affirms with hints of universalism:

> It is in this unity of love that the life consists of all men who will be saved. For God is everything that is good and God has made everything that is made and God loves everything that he has made, and if any man or woman withdraws his love from any of his fellow Christians, he does not love at all, because he has not love towards all. And so in such times he is in danger, because he is not at peace; and anyone who has general love for his fellow Christians has love towards everything which is. For in mankind which will be saved is comprehended all, that is, all that is made and the maker of all; for God is in man and so in man is all. And he who thus generally loves all his fellow Christians loves all, and he who loves thus is safe.

Through the medium of her writings it is possible to see how carefully Julian attempted to hold together the personal, the theological, and the pastoral dimensions. Julian was no longer a passive "victim" of her context and its difficult social and religious circumstances. Through her writings, Julian became an active agent, seeking to transform people's attitudes and consequently change their lives. We have no idea about how well the specifics of her pastoral message were received in her own times although the various bequests to Julian as well as Margery Kempe's description of her visit to Julian suggest that overall she was highly respected as a spiritual guide.

Julian's Eschatology

Beyond Julian's key theological themes of God, creation, human nature, sin and salvation, and prayer, there is also a deep message of hope. This should not be reduced to a simplistic embrace of the immediately comforting words "all will be well." The more extended phrase, "all will be well, and all will be well, and every kind of thing will be well" appears in chapter 27 in relation to the existence of sin. The phrase follows God's assertion that sin is "behovely" (or opportune). As we have already seen, scholarly opinion is that the Middle English phrase "alle shalle be wele" implies more than a future-orientated "everything will be made well sometime later." "Shalle" also implies necessity. Part of the eschatological vision presented to Julian is that God *necessarily* redeems everything. This is not a matter of straightforward comfort because the notion of "all will [or shall] be well" is also complex and deeply challenging. God's final completion is a mystery that is hidden from us. However, as Julian affirms in her chapter 85 towards the end of the revelations, when "we are all brought up above" we shall no longer say that if only things had been different back on earth then it would have been well. Rather "we shall all say with one voice: Lord, blessed may you be, because it is so, it is well; and now we see truly that everything is done as it was ordained by you before anything was made."

Another dimension of Julian's eschatological vision is also that she was informed about two great deeds that God will do but which we are not shown in our present lives because we could not fully comprehend them. In that sense, as I noted in Chapter 5, there is an apophatic, incomplete, and open-ended quality to Julian's overall theology. This applies also to her eschatological vision of ultimate reality that goes beyond the conventional imagery of heaven and hell.

The first deed appears in chapter 32 and is broadly based. It is a deed which "the blessed Trinity" will carry out "on the last day." It was ordained by God "from without beginning" and is known only to God because it is beyond our human capacity to grasp. However, through this broadly based deed God will make "everything well which is not well." However, Julian notes that this deed of making everything well, apparently without exception, appears to conflict with "the faith of Holy Church." This faith conventionally asserts that "many creatures will be damned" – the fallen angels (now devils), pagans, and those Christians who "die out of God's love" because they have led unchristian lives and have not repented. By implication this deed will be at the end of time.

In contrast, the second deed appears in chapter 36 and is more personally orientated. As Julian puts it, "it will be honourable and wonderful and plentiful, and it will be done with respect to me." However, by "me" Julian is clear that this also applies to "all his lovers on earth," "men in general," or "all who will be saved." This second deed will be "begun here" and we will all see it "with wonderful joy" when "we come to heaven." From the way Julian talks about this second deed, it appears to bridge the gap between an experience of individual salvation and the ultimate act by God of making all things well at the end of time. In Julian's words, "it will go on operating until the last day" even though its honor and bliss "will last in heaven before God and all his saints eternally."

The Journey of Perpetual Departure

As we have already seen, Julian notes at the start of her final chapter 86 that "this book is begun by God's gift and his grace, but it is not yet performed, as I see it." By their very nature the revelations received by Julian have an open-ended quality. The twentieth-century Welsh priest-poet

R.S. Thomas was fascinated by the inconclusive and elusive quality of the mystical path as a way of unknowing. His poem "Journeys" expresses the theme of life as a perpetual experience of departure.

> The deception of platforms
> where the arrivals and the departures
> coincide. And the smiles
> on the faces of those welcoming
>
> and bidding farewell are
> to conceal the knowledge
> that destinations are the familiarities
> from which the traveller must set out.[1]

Like so many other mystical writers, Julian of Norwich is frequently interpreted in terms of her assurance of the abiding presence and compassion of God in her soul and in the inner depths of her fellow, "even" Christians. However, Julian is also strongly aware of what I refer to as "perpetual departure" within the Christian mystical tradition. This is one aspect of apophatic theology, not least in Julian. The Lord, Christ, whose permanent dwelling, according to the parable of a Lord and a Servant, is in the heart of the human soul is also the one who travels ever onwards in perpetual pilgrimage. The Christian disciple is not left in a comfortable and comforting *stasis* but is drawn to follow after Christ in perpetual dissatisfaction with what is less than everything and in pursuit of what Julian refers to as an indescribable "bliss in heaven."

> Our good Lord revealed himself in his creature in various ways, both in heaven and on earth; but I saw him take no place except in man's soul. He revealed himself on earth in the sweet Incarnation and his blessed Passion, and he showed himself in other ways on earth, where I said that I saw God in an instant of time [a poynte]; and he showed himself in another way on earth, as if it were on pilgrimage, that is to say that he is here with us, leading us, and will be until he has brought us all to his bliss in heaven.
>
> *(Chapter 81)*

Note

1 R.S. Thomas, "Journeys," in *Mass for Hard Times*, Newcastle upon Tyne: Bloodaxe Books 1992, p 28.

Appendix

The Fate of Julian's Texts

There are various theories about why the three surviving Long Text manuscripts differ from each other and what degree of authority should be accorded to each. This is linked to the overall fate of Julian's texts after her lifetime. What can we surmise about this? The evidence about both the circulation and the readership of Julian's texts during the first two centuries of their life is extremely limited and ambiguous. The so-called Long Text presents particular difficulties.[1]

Extracts

The only likely medieval manuscript associated with the Long Text consists of a limited number of short extracts in what is known as Westminster Cathedral Treasury Manuscript 4. This florilegium appears to date from the middle of the fifteenth century. The extracts appear in a different order from the full Long Text and are written in very neutral English. As a result, it is not clear whether medieval readers had access to Julian's full text or how closely any available text reproduced what Julian actually wrote.

Full Texts

The earliest full manuscripts of the Long Text date from either the late sixteenth century or from the first part of the seventeenth century. It seems probable that at some point before this, perhaps during the Henrician Reformation and dissolution of the monasteries, a copy or copies of the Long Text were in the hands of Benedictine nuns who then went into exile. Thus, the so-called Paris manuscript (Bibliothèque National Fonds Anglais Ms 40, designated by Julian scholars as P) was

Julian of Norwich: "In God's Sight" – Her Theology in Context, First Edition. Philip Sheldrake.
© 2019 John Wiley & Sons Ltd. Published 2019 by John Wiley & Sons Ltd.

held by the English convent at Cambrai. The Sloane 1 manuscript (BL Sloane Ms 2499) is much plainer and there are some differences in content from P. This manuscript may have been produced by the Benedictine nun Clementina Carey of Cambrai who was responsible for founding a daughter house in Paris. The third full manuscript, known as Sloane 2 (BL Sloane Ms 3705), is probably a copy of Sloane 1 and dates from later in the seventeenth century. The first printed edition of the Long Text was published in 1670 by an English Benedictine monk at Douai, Serenus Cressy (or de Cressy). He had fled England as an Anglican priest during the Civil War and subsequently converted to Roman Catholicism. Cressy based his edition on the Paris manuscript and this was reprinted several times during the nineteenth century and again in 1902, with a fascinating Preface by the famous Anglo-Irish Jesuit George Tyrell who was shortly afterwards condemned for the supposed heresy of Modernism.

Differences between Manuscripts

There are debates about how and why the Paris and Sloane versions of the Long Text came to differ. It could be that the differences simply reflect Julian's various re-workings of the text. However, this is not the consensus among scholars, not least because the differences involve language as well as content. A more likely reason for the differences is the impact of different scribes and textual compilers between the time of Julian's own version of the Long Text and its reappearance in seventeenth-century France.

There are a range of hypotheses. The scholar Marion Glasscoe argues that the Paris manuscript (P) is a modernization. For this reason she chooses Sloane 1 as the basis for her edition of the Long Text.[2] However, Sloane 2 also sometimes modernizes Sloane 1 although overall they are the same and Sloane 2 is basically a copy. There are also some possible dialect variations. It has been suggested that Sloane 1 derives from Norfolk while Paris sporadically employs Northern words. However, other commentators note the same sporadic use of Northern words in Sloane! In their scholarly edition, Colledge and Walsh point out that there were Northern women among the Benedictine nuns at Cambrai where Sloane was copied and they therefore suggest that the Northern elements do not reflect Julian but were introduced by the manuscript scribes.

Another suggestion is that Sloane 1 imitates an earlier exemplar (now lost) in Northern dialect which, if true, suggests that either Julian herself or an anonymous amanuensis was originally from Northern England.

Without forming a judgment about this hypothesis, it is worth noting that the use of an amanuensis was not unusual even among the educated, literate upper classes. This text may have remained standard until English adopted a more Southern form as the norm. For example, Watson and Jenkins in their recent scholarly edition of Julian's texts argue (page 11) that the Paris manuscript was not in the original dialect of the Long Text. Rather it represents a version of the text in the East Midlands dialect that had become standard English by around 1420 for any works being copied for wider circulation. This standardization of English in the fifteenth century offers an alternative explanation of the Paris manuscript against the notion that it was simply a later seventeenth-century modernization of the earlier and "purer" language used by the Sloane manuscript.

It is important to remember that the mid-fifteenth-century Westminster Cathedral extracts from the Long Text is also post-standardization. Therefore its failure to mimic the Northernisms of Sloane does not automatically undermine the notion that Sloane's Northernisms either preserve Julian's own dialect or preserve the dialect of an anonymous amanuensis. The fact that the single surviving Amherst manuscript of the Short Text also employs numerous Northern dialect words may reinforce the idea that Julian was a Northerner who moved to Norwich but equally it may reinforce the possibility that Julian employed a Northern amanuensis who wrote down both the Short Text and the Long Text in her or his native dialect.

My own view is that, on balance, there is no convincing reason to depart from the long-standing perception that Julian was a woman of Norwich rather than a woman from the North.

A final question concerns content. Which of the Sloane or Paris manuscripts is more authentically Julian in its content? The point is that Paris contains both phrases and whole passages that are not present in either Sloane 1 or Sloane 2. Some of these simply gloss certain words but others actually clarify important ideas. So, the question is whether material was left out of the Sloane manuscript or was added to the Paris manuscript? Any response to this is necessarily inconclusive. However, a growing consensus is that Sloane carelessly omits material rather than that Paris adds material.

As a result of this growing consensus, it seems probable that Paris is the earliest surviving manuscript of the Long Text, possibly dating from the late sixteenth century. Nowadays it is also widely agreed by scholars to be the most complete version of what Julian actually wrote. However, while Paris mimics medieval script it also modernizes the language in relation to the Middle English of Julian's own time. As already noted, it has been "translated" into the standard English that derived from the dialect of the East Midlands.

In comparison, Sloane 1 appears to be a slightly later seventeenth-century manuscript. However, whoever created it from a previous text seems to have preserved the Middle English of East Anglia. This would bring it closer to Julian's own times. However, the main problem with Sloane 1 (and with Sloane 2 which essentially copies it) is that, as already mentioned, it seems to have made careless slips and omissions during the copying process.

Notes

1 For a useful summary of the Long Text manuscript tradition, see Elisabeth Dutton, "The Seventeenth-Century Manuscript Tradition and the influence of Augustine Baker," in Liz Herbert McAvoy, ed., *A Companion to Julian of Norwich*, Cambridge: D.S. Brewer, 2008, pp 127–138.
2 Marion Glasscoe, ed., *Julian of Norwich: A Revelation of Love*, Exeter: Exeter University Press, 1976.

Select Bibliography

Julian's Texts: Scholarly Editions

Colledge, E. and Walsh, J. (eds.), *A Book of Showings to the Anchoress Julian of Norwich*. Toronto: Pontifical Institute of Mediaeval Studies, 1978.

Glasscoe, M. (ed.), *A Revelation of Love*. Exeter: University of Exeter Press, 1993.

Watson, N. and Jenkins, J. (eds.), *The Writings of Julian of Norwich*. University Park, PA: The Pennsylvania State University Press, 2006.

Windeatt, B. (ed.), *Julian of Norwich: Revelations of Divine Love*. Oxford: Oxford University Press, 2016.

Julian's Texts: Modern Translations

Colledge, E. and Walsh, J. (eds.), *Julian of Norwich – Showings*. Mahwah, NJ: Paulist Press, 1978.

Spearing, E. (ed.), *Julian of Norwich: Revelations of Divine Love*. London: Penguin Books, 1998.

Windeatt, B. (ed.), *Julian of Norwich: Revelations of Divine Love*. Oxford World's Classics, Oxford: Oxford University Press, 2015.

Further Reading

Abbott, C., *Julian of Norwich: Autobiography and Theology*. Cambridge: D.S. Brewer, 1999.

Allen, R.S. (ed.), *Richard Rolle – The English Writings*. Mahwah, NJ: Paulist Press, 1989.

Anselm of Canterbury, *Cur Deus Homo*, in S.N. Deane, ed., *Saint Anselm: Basic Writings*, 2nd edition. LaSalle, IL: Open Court Publishing, 2nd edition 1962.

Julian of Norwich: "In God's Sight" – Her Theology in Context, First Edition. Philip Sheldrake.
© 2019 John Wiley & Sons Ltd. Published 2019 by John Wiley & Sons Ltd.

Baker, D.N., *Julian of Norwich's Showings: From Vision to Book*. Princeton, NJ: Princeton University Press, 1994.

Barratt, A., "Lordship, Service and Worship in Julian of Norwich," in E.A. James, ed., *The Medieval Mystical Tradition in England*. Exeter Symposium VII, Cambridge: D.S. Brewer, 2004, pp 177–188.

Bauerschmidt, F.C., *Julian of Norwich and the Mystical Body Politic of Christ*. Notre Dame: University of Notre Dame Press, 1999.

Beer, F., *Women and Mystical Experience in the Middle Ages*. Woodbridge: Boydell & Brewer, 1992.

Beer, F., *Julian of Norwich: Revelations; Motherhood of God*. Cambridge: D.S. Brewer, 1998.

Bennett, J.M. and Karras, R.M. (eds.), *Oxford Handbook of Women and Gender in Medieval Europe*. Oxford: Oxford University Press, 2010.

Bradley, R., *Julian's Way: A Practical Commentary on Julian of Norwich*. London: Harper Collins, 1992.

Bynum, C.W., *Jesus as Mother: Studies in the Spirituality of the High Middle Ages*. Berkeley, CA: University of California Press, 1982.

Bynum, C.W., *Holy Feast and Holy Fast: The Religious Significance of Food to Medieval Women*, Berkeley, CA: University of California Press, 1987.

Bynum, C.W., *Fragmentation and Redemption: Essays on Gender and the Human Body in Medieval Religion*. New York: Zone Books, 1992.

Clark, J.P.H. and Dorward, R. (eds.), *Walter Hilton – The Scale of Perfection*. Mahwah, NJ: Paulist Press, 1991.

Clark, M. (ed.), *An Aquinas Reader: Selections from the Writings of Thomas Aquinas*. New York: Fordham University Press, 2008.

Colledge, E. and Walsh, J. (eds.), *Guigo II: The Ladder of Monks & Twelve Meditations*. New York: Doubleday Image Books, 1978.

Davies, B., *The Thought of Thomas Aquinas*. Oxford: Oxford University Press, 1993.

De Certeau, M., "'Mystique' au XVIIe siècle: Le probleme du language mystique," in *L'Homme Devant Dieu: Mélanges offerts au Père Henri du Lubac*. Paris: Aubier, 1964.

De Certeau, M., *The Mystic Fable*, volume 1. Chicago, IL: University of Chicago Press, 1992 & volume 2, 2015.

De Certeau, M., "Mystic Speech," in *Heterologies: Discourse on the Other*. Minneapolis, MN: University of Minnesota Press, 1995.

De Certeau, M., *The Mystic Fable*, volume 2. Chicago, IL: University of Chicago Press, 2015.

Dreyer, E., "The Trinitarian Theology of Julian of Norwich," in *Studies in Spirituality* 4, 1994, pp 79–93.

Dupré, L., "Spiritual life in a secular age," in *Daedalus* III, 1982, pp 21–31.

Durka, G., *Praying with Julian of Norwich*. Winona, MN: St Mary's Press, 1989.

Furlong, M. (ed.), *The Wisdom of Julian of Norwich*. Grand Rapids, MI: W.B. Eerdmanns, 1996.

Furness, J., *Love is His Meaning: Meditations on Julian of Norwich*. Essex: McCrimmons, 1993.

Gadamer, H.-G., *Truth and Method*, English translation. London: Sheed & Ward, 1988.

Haight, R., *The Experience and Language of Grace*. New York: Paulist Press, 1979.

Harris, G., *Shaping the Nation: England 1360–1461*. Oxford: Clarendon Press, 2005.

Heimmel, J.P., *"God is Our Mother": Julian of Norwich and The Medieval Image of Christian Feminine Divinity*. Salzburg: Instituut für Anglistik und Amerikanistik, 1982.

Hide, K., *Gifted Origins to Graced Fulfillment: The Soteriology of Julian of Norwich*. Collegeville, MN: The Liturgical Press, 2001.

Horrox, R. and Ormrod, W.M., *A Social History of England 1200–1500*. Cambridge: Cambridge University Press, 2006.

Innes-Parker, C., "Subversion and Conformity in Julian's *Revelation*: Authority, Vision and the Motherhood of God," in *Mystics Quarterly* XXIII/2, March 1997, pp 7–35.

Jantzen, G., *Power, Gender and Christian Mysticism*. Cambridge: Cambridge University Press, 1995.

Jantzen, G., *Julian of Norwich*, 2nd edition. London: SPCK, 2000.

John-Julian, *The Complete Julian of Norwich*. Brewster, MA: Paraclete Press, 2009.

Jones, E.A., "Anchoritic Aspects of Julian of Norwich," in McAvoy, L.H. (ed.), *A Companion to Julian of Norwich*. Cambridge: D.S. Brewer, 2008, pp 75–87.

Kieckhefer, R., *Unquiet Souls: Fourteenth Century Saints and their Religious Milieu*. Chicago, IL: University of Chicago Press, 1984.

Knowles, D. and Neville Hadcock, R., *Medieval Religious Houses, England & Wales*. Harlow: Longman, 1971.

Lamm, J., "Revelation as Exposure in Julian of Norwich's *Showings*," in *Spiritus: A Journal of Christian Spirituality* 5/1, 2005, pp 54–78.

Lasko, P. and Morgan, N.J. (eds.), *Medieval Art in East Anglia 1300–1530*. London: Thames & Hudson, 1974.

Leclercq, J., *The Love of Learning and the Desire for God: A Study of Monastic Culture*, 3rd edition. New York: Fordham University Press, 1982.

Leech, K. and Ward, B., *Julian Reconsidered*. Oxford: SLG Press, 1988.

Le Goff, J., *The Medieval Imagination*. Chicago, IL: University of Chicago Press, 1988.

Le Goff, J., *Medieval Civilisation*. Oxford: Basil Blackwell, 1990.

Lerner, R., *The Heresy of the Free Spirit in the Later Middle Ages*, Berkeley, CA: University of California Press, 1972.

Llewelyn, R., *Circles of Silence: Explorations in Prayer with Julian of Norwich*. London: Darton, Longman & Todd, 2002.

Louth, A., *The Origins of the Christian Mystical Tradition: From Plato to Denys*. Oxford: Clarendon Press, 1992.

Luibheid, C. and Rorem, O. (eds.), *Pseudo-Dionysius: The Complete Works*. Classics of Western Spirituality, Mahwah, NJ: Paulist Press, 1987.

Markus, R.A., *The End of Ancient Christianity*. Cambridge: Cambridge University Press, 1998.

Mate, M., *Women in Medieval English Society*. Cambridge: Cambridge University Press, 2001.

McAvoy, L.H. (ed.), *A Companion to Julian of Norwich*. Cambridge: D.S. Brewer, 2008.

McGinn, B., *The Foundations of Mysticism: Origins to the Fifth Century*. London SCM Press 1992, Appendix.

McGinn, B., *The Varieties of Vernacular Mysticism: 1350–1550*. New York: Crossroad, 2012, Chapter 12, "Julian of Norwich: 'Love is oure lordes mening'".

McGinn, B., "The future of past spiritual experiences," in *Spiritus: A Journal of Christian Spirituality* 15/1, 2015, pp 1–17.

Melloni, J., *The Exercises of St Ignatius Loyola in the Western Tradition*, English translation. Leominster: Gracewing, 2000.

Merton, T., *Mystics and Zen Masters*. New York: The Noonday Press, Reprinted 1993.

Mursell, G., *English Spirituality: From Earliest Times to 1700*. London: SPCK/Louisville, KY: Westminster John Knox Press, 2001.

Myers, A.E., *England in the Late Middle Ages*. London: Penguin Books, 1981.

Newman, B., "Eliot's Affirmative Way: Julian of Norwich, Charles Williams and Little Gidding," in *Modern Philology* 108/3, 2011, pp 427–461.

Nuth, J.M., *Wisdom's Daughter: The Theology of Julian of Norwich*. New York: Crossroad, 1991.

Nuth, J.M., *God's Lovers in an Age of Anxiety: The Medieval English Mystics*. London: Darton, Longman & Todd/Maryknoll, NY: Orbis Books, 2001.

Ormrod, W.M., *Political Life in Medieval England 1300–1450*. London: Macmillan, 1995.

Palliser, M.A., *Christ Our Mother of Mercy: Divine Mercy and Compassion in the Theology of the Showings of Julian of Norwich*. Berlin: de Gruyter, 1992.

Pastoureau, M. and Cruse, M.I., *Blue: The History of a Color*. Princeton, NJ: Princeton University Press, 2001.

Pelphrey, B., *Love was His Meaning: The Theology and Mysticism of Julian of Norwich*. Salzburg: Institute für Anglistik und Amerikanistik, 1982.

Pelphrey, B., *Christ our Mother: Julian of Norwich*. Wilmington, DE: Michael Glazier, 1989.

Pepler, C., *The English Religious Heritage*. London: Blackfriars, 1958.

Petroff, E.A. (ed.), *Medieval Women's Visionary Literature*. Oxford: Oxford University Press, 1986.

Phillips, K., "Femininities and the Gentry in Late Medieval East Anglia: Ways of Being," in McAvoy, L.H. (ed.), *A Companion to Julian of Norwich*. Cambridge: D.S. Brewer, 2008, pp 19–31.

Raitt, J., ed., *Christian Spirituality: High Middle Ages and Reformation*, London: Routledge & Kegan Paul/New York: Crossroads Publishing, 1987.

Rawcliffe, C. and Wilson, R. (eds.), *Medieval Norwich*. London: Hambledon (Palgrave Macmillan), 2004.

Ricoeur, P., *Interpretation Theory: Discourse and the Surplus of Meaning*, English translation. Fort Worth, TX: TCU Press, 1976.

Rolf, V.M., *Julian's Gospel: Illuminating the Life and Revelations of Julian of Norwich*. Maryknoll, NY: Orbis Books, 2013.

Rubin, M., *The Hollow Crown: A History of Britain in the Late Middle Ages*, London: Penguin Books, 2005.

Ruud, J., "Nature and Grace in Julian of Norwich," in *Mystics Quarterly* XIX/2, 1993, pp 71–81.

Salih, S. and Baker, D.N. (eds.), *Julian of Norwich's Legacy: Medieval Mysticism and Post-Medieval Reception*. New York: Palgrave Macmillan, 2009.

Salih, S., "Julian's Afterlives," in McAvoy, L.H. (ed.), *A Companion to Julian of Norwich*. Cambridge: D.S. Brewer, 2008, pp 208–218.

Savage, A. and Watson, N. (eds.), *Anchoritic Spirituality: Ancrene Wisse and Associated Works*. Mahwah, NJ: Paulist Press, 1991.

Sheldrake, P., *Spirituality and History: Questions of Interpretation and Method*, Revised edition. London: SPCK/Maryknoll, NY: Orbis Books, 1995.

Sheldrake, P., *Spirituality and Theology: Christian Living and the Doctrine of God*. London: Darton, Longman & Todd, 1998/Maryknoll, NY: Orbis Books 1999.

Sheldrake, P., "Spiritual Senses," in Sheldrake, P. (ed.), *The New SCM Dictionary of Christian Spirituality*. London: SCM Press, 2005/*The New Westminster Dictionary of Christian Spirituality*. Louisville, KY: Westminster John Knox Press, 2005.

Sheldrake, P., *Explorations in Spirituality: History, Theology and Social Practice*. Mahwah, NJ: Paulist Press, 2010.

Sheldrake, P., *Spirituality: A Brief History*, 2nd revised edition. Oxford: Wiley-Blackwell, 2013.

Sheldrake, P., "Two Ways of Seeing: The Challenge of Julian of Norwich's Parable of a Lord and a Servant," in *Spiritus: A Journal of Christian Spirituality* 17/1, 2017, pp 1–18.

Soskice, J.M., *The Kindness of God: Metaphor, Gender, and Religious Language*. Oxford: Oxford University Press, 2008.

Sutherland, A., "Julian of Norwich and the Liturgy," in McAvoy, L.H. (ed.), *A Companion to Julian of Norwich*. Cambridge: D.S. Brewer, 2008, pp 88–98.

Tanner, N., *The Church in Late Medieval Norwich 1370–1532*. Toronto: Pontifical Institute of Mediaeval Studies: Studies & Texts 66, 1984.

Turner, D., *Julian of Norwich, Theologian*. New Haven, CT: Yale University Press, 2011.

Walsh, J. (ed.), *The Cloud of Unknowing*. Mahwah, NJ: Paulist Press, 1981.

Walsh, J. (ed.), *The Pursuit of Wisdom and Other Works*. Mahwah, NJ: Paulist Press, 1988.

Watson, N., "The Composition of Julian of Norwich's Revelations of Love," in *Speculum* 68, 1993, pp 637–683.

Williams, R., *Holy Living: The Christian Tradition for Today*. New York: Bloomsbury Continuum, 2017.

Windeatt, B. (ed.), *The Book of Margery Kempe*. London: Penguin Classics, 1985.

Windeatt, B., "Julian's Second Thoughts: The Long Text Tradition," in McAvoy, L.H. (ed.), *A Companion to Julian of Norwich*. Cambridge: D.S. Brewer, 2008, pp 101–115.

Index

Julian of Norwich: "In God's Sight" – Her Theology in Context, First Edition. Philip Sheldrake.
© 2019 John Wiley & Sons Ltd. Published 2019 by John Wiley & Sons Ltd.